Gods of Management

Professor Charles Handy was born the son of an archdeacon in the Church of Ireland. His education was based on the philosophy and history of Ancient Greece and Rome. When he left University, he went to work for an oil company in Malaysia and later was an economist in the City of London. All this provided a useful background to the study of organisations with which he then became concerned at the London Graduate School of Business Studies, first as Senior Tutor, then as Professor. He is now Warden of St George's House in Windsor Castle where he lives with his wife Elizabeth and two children.

Charles Handy

Gods of Management

How they work, and why they will fail

Pan Books London and Sydney

First published 1978 by Souvenir Press Ltd
This edition published 1979 by Pan Books Ltd.
Cavaye Place, London SW10 9PG
© Charles Handy 1978
ISBN 0 330 25832 X
Printed in Great Britain by
Richard Clay (The Chaucer Press) Ltd, Bungay, Suffolk

ACKNOWLEDGEMENTS

To all those who contributed to my thinking I am deeply grateful. If I have not acknowledged them in the text, it only means that they have entered my thought processes in some subliminal fashion. I live by the constant interchange of thought and ideas, in teaching, argument, private discussion or exchange of letters. I am grateful to all those colleagues, students and friends who have, often unwittingly contributed to my thinking.

Few, if any, of my ideas can be original. The notion of using Greek Gods to symbolise cultures has been around for some time. Nietzsche used it, and so did Ruth Benedict. I was first introduced to it by Roger Harrison one sunny morning in the hills of Maine. I am grateful to him for this and many other ideas.

The idea was first developed by me in a Chapter in 'Understanding Organisations' (Penguin 1976) where the theoretical underpinnings of the idea are also presented.

I would also like to thank the following for permission to quote from their work:
Punch Publications Limited
Harford Thomas
James Seymour
Derek Sheane
Irving Borwick
James Robertson

I am particularly grateful to Terry Hamaton who has enlivened the text with his perceptive illustrations, and to my publishers for their constant stimulus and encouragement.

CONTENTS

Sad Symbol of Our Time

Chapter 1

THE ORGANISED SOCIETY AND ITS DILEMMAS

Sir Christopher Wren asked that his work be his only memorial. To anyone looking across the Thames at the time of his death towards the Cathedral of St Pauls and the other lovely churches which Wren built in London's centre, the sky-line of those days was indeed an impressive memorial to a great architect. It was a memorial not only to him but to the values of his age, for the changing skylines of our cities are perhaps the most telling commentaries on a changing society. The Egyptians built great houses for their dead. Rome had its fine arches and columns for her conquering Emperors. In the Renaissance the towns of Europe were dominated by their great Cathedrals, houses for their God, soon to be replaced in splendour by houses for their nobles and their monarchs. The Victorians in England built museums, galleries, theatres—houses for possessions and entertainment. Today the view that Wren saw is greatly changed. New shapes break the sky-line, the houses not of gods but of organisations—the symbols of our *organised society*.

We may sometimes disapprove aesthetically of the new skylines, but we have long taken it for granted that the organisations which they house are a necessary and useful part of our societies. After all, 90 per cent of those who work do so in a formal organisation, although they may prefer to think of it as the firm, the bank, the hospital, the school or just 'the office'. To be 'organised' is good, 'disorganised' bad, and the benefits of organisation have indeed been dramatic in the past hundred years. In the 'organised societies' famine, pestilence, and penury are words of the past. Our children now are expected to live to maturity and to have food and shelter for the rest of their lives. The great mass of our people have the new freedom of private money and the choice of how to spend it, even if neither the money nor the choice is always as great as they would wish. Scarcity, one might say, is a solved problem in the organised societies. It is only the problems of more effective and equitable distribution which are left us – the problems of abundance not of scarcity. We have much to thank organisations for, for it is in large part our organisations and their managers that have harnessed our advancing technologies to our service. Today, in the organised societies, the luxuries of our parents are the toys of our children. The necessities of life which our parents laboured for are demanded by us as of right, whether we labour or not. Compare the organised societies with those of the developing world, if you need any proof of the benefits of organisation, of harnessed technology and its management.

If anyone in the Britain of 1977 feels disposed to argue that scarcity is far from being a solved problem in *his* society, he should remember that these matters are always comparative, and he might ponder the following figures which were computed for the *Readers Digest* in 1977. They compare conditions in The Silver Jubilee Year in Britain with those of 1952, 25 years before, when the Queen came to the throne.

In 1952 the small family car cost the equivalent of $62\frac{1}{2}$ weeks' work by the average industrial worker. In 1977 it needed only $32\frac{1}{2}$ weeks.

Barcelona by scheduled flight from London cost $4\frac{3}{4}$ weeks' work in 1952, only $1\frac{1}{2}$ in 1977.

22 minutes work now earns enough to buy a dozen eggs compared with 57 minutes in 1952, 23 minutes earns a pound of butter instead of 32 minutes, 8 minutes work a pint of milk instead of 11 minutes, and 11 minutes a packet of cornflakes instead of $17\frac{1}{2}$ minutes.

Even a bottle of Scotch now costs only $2\frac{3}{4}$ hours work against $7\frac{1}{4}$ in 1952.

Scarcity is always comparative. We are richer than we think.

Yet we should never take the organisations of work for granted. In unintended ways they have always sent out tentacles into the lives of all of us. For example, in the nineteenth century factory production pulled work out of the home into the factory. It made goods cheaper, to be sure, but it also created an empty space in the lives of those left at home, giving to many women days without purpose, lives full of non-productive chores and boredom. The women's liberation movement can be seen as a long-delayed reaction to the creation of the factory organisation. Today the effects of our organisations and their need to specialise have hit our homes and communities. In the pursuit of efficiency, organisations tend to specialise, so work, learning, recreation, fighting, politicking, worshipping all now take place in different institutional settings, often separated by miles in distance and by days in time. The home for many has become the motel, a place for sleeping and occasional meals. An individual belongs to a range of different communities, each built around a different activity, and each interacting only seldom with the others. The idea of the rounded individual – farmer in spring, soldier in summer, churchwarden in autumn, handyman, teacher, stalwart of the local hostelry, all of his parts played out within the same community – has gone from us, because of our pursuit of organisation efficiency. Have we lost or have we gained? The figures for Gross Domestic Product look clear enough. Unfortunately those for Gross Domestic Happiness are harder to establish. Are our organisations, then, always worth the money we pay for them? The cost to the consumer of a box of bananas in the U.S. in 1972 was $5.35. The price paid to the grower was 70c. In between was the cost of organisation.

There is a notorious new landmark in London's panorama, called 'Centre Point'. It is a tall and some would say handsome skyscraper, built for offices ten years ago. You can stand in the street today and see right through it to the sky the other side, because only one floor of it has ever been occupied. Maybe this empty house for organisations is a symbol for the future? Are the costs of organisations beginning to outweigh their benefits? Are the organisational towers entering their last decade? Has the time come for the skyline to change once more?

Some there be who would destroy these organisational towers of our society altogether, and have us return to the self sufficient communities of earlier days, to an un-organised society. Some others would destroy these towers only to replace them with others of another ideology. I too believe that the towers must go. But I hope that they will be replaced by other structures, housing new gods for new principles. This book is written in that hope. It is a book about our organisations – their present state and their likely future. It is addressed to those who work in, and particularly those who manage, those organisations. For to them, for once, the opportunity is clear to influence their own destiny.

The manager, despised by many as the mercenary, the hired hack of an organisation's owners, may, can, must, come into his own as the missionary of a new age, an age still built upon organisations, but organisations with a difference.

But before we can plan for a new age, we must understand our own, for it is out of the tensions of the present that the future can be born. Our present society as I see it, faces three great problems or dilemmas. The problems differ only in the urgency with which they press upon us, for they span between them the next two decades of our history in the Western World. The first problem is with us now. The second is round the corner, although it is a corner we have already nearly turned. And the third, perhaps the most important and interesting of all, is still a decade or two away – at least in the sense that it may be twenty years from now before we can no longer ignore it. But by then, of course, it may be too late to do anything except react.

The First Dilemma: Slack, the Thermometer of Incompetence

The most immediately pressing problem of the organised society is the growing incompetence of a great many of our organisations. The spread of perceived incompetence is eroding the credibility of the organised society. If an organisation cannot even be competent how can it justify its existence? It is a capitalist tradition that incompetence is punished by death of the organisation, and that competence is ensured by the survival of the fittest. But this tradition is of course a myth, applying only to those small, often unseen, companies in the private sectors of industry and commerce. It is seldom true of the larger, more visible companies who cannot be allowed to die, and it is never true of the non-competing institutions of health, education, welfare or public service whose incompetence can only be felt, not proven, and therefore not punished.

The thermometer of unpunished incompetence is *organisational slack*. Any cushion that makes life easier for an organisation is its slack. More time, more materials more latitude in quality, greater margins in bookings, spare labour, spare capacity. Comfort is tempting, and some cushioning is necessary to cope with the peaks and troughs of an uneven flow of work. But comfort unrestrained becomes overdue deliveries, unanswered queries and complaints, depleted stocks, over-booking and underbooking, poor quality and shoddy workmanship. The surplus manpower turns into serried layers of people watching people. The spare capacity becomes outdated assets or surplus inventory. The results for those outside are inconvenience, frustration and unnecessary costs, the irritant sores of an organised society in distress. For slack is the slow cancer of the organised society which, unchecked, can kill.

In the past we assumed that the lure of profit and the discipline of competition would check the disease. But profit turned out to sit well with slack as long as competition was quiescent. Since some monopolies appeared to be in everyone's best interest, governments themselves tried to regulate them. But this has seemed only to feed the slack, building further bureaucracy into the overheads and rewarding the increased costs with increased prices.

I want to argue that it is impractical to consider a return to a pure competitive state for the organised society – although some moves might be made in this direction, which I shall discuss in dealing with the second and third dilemmas. Competence in the present world would, I believe, have to be a matter of deliberate organisational self-discipline, rather than of trial and error in a competitive jungle, or conformity to a government regulation. And this is where management comes in. Incompetence results, as often as not, from using the wrong management principles ('cultures' I shall call them). If you are using the 'Culture' you are comfortable with instead of the one appropriate to the organisation, incompetence is cushioned. It is up to those who run our institutions to exercise some 'cultural' self-discipline, and this they must do because it is right, not because it pays. We need a theory of 'cultural propriety', a theory which is explained in the first part of this book.

The Second Dilemma: The Rise of Individualism

Relieving the pressure problems of obvious incompetence will, however, only uncover a deeper dilemma in the organised society. It is becoming clear that organisations which are managed for maximum efficiency come into conflict with other human needs, the needs of the individual for self-expression and autonomy in everyday life.

It was Rousseau who said that people who are too well off are apt to become unmanageable. Let us amend Rousseau a little and say that our ways of managing will at least have to change when people work more from choice than necessity, and one result of improved efficiency will be more choice and less necessity. We shall have to look for our new models to those organisations which have had already to adapt to working with people who enjoy a *protected individualism*. By these

I mean our professional partnerships, universities and voluntary associations – organisations of consent and contract. These organisational models are not always noted for their efficiency. As *everyone* begins to demand a protected individualism in all spheres of work, whether it be justified by his talents or not, does this mean that some degree of efficiency will have to go? In this clash between efficiency and individualism we find our second dilemma.

The new ways of managing this individualism will fundamentally alter the shape of our organisations and the ways they function. To survive, the manager, be he mercenary or missionary, must adapt. The mercenary will see the growth of individualism as a threat: the missionary will glimpse a great opportunity to combine efficiency with human dignity. This is indeed a new opportunity never until now available because in times of scarcity the demands of efficiency are always preeminent. The challenge is one for the post-scarcity age, the age made possible by the efficiency of our organisations.

The Third Dilemma: The Organisation – Instrument or Community?

Looking further into the future, however, it seems likely that even radical changes in the ways we manage our organisations are not going to be enough. The whole relationship of organisation to society is going to be called into question.

Traditionally, organisations have been encouraged to regard themselves as the independent instruments of society. Efficiency, measured by cost-effectiveness, growth of profitability, has been the criterion of success. How they achieved it was up to the organisations. The traditional separation of powers, between owners, clients and workers, each having a separate relationship with the organisation, has meant that little difference exists in practice in the functioning of organisations whether the owners are the state or private individuals.

I shall argue that this instrumental view of the organisation has resulted in increased alienation in society, that it can even be counterproductive economically, and that it is a recipe for an over-organised society which cannot work.

Looking at possible scenarios I shall maintain that we would be wise to begin to think of the organisation not as an instrument but as a *community*: a community to which people belong and which belongs to them, whose outputs are measured in units broader than money, whose responsibilities are wider than economic success and whose methods and values mirror those of the wider democratic societies we claim to live in.

There are problems of course. Some of them we can foresee and prepare for. There are also implications for the ways in which we see almost every institution in our society, education, government, finance, even our transport systems. I can only hint at these implications, not produce a blueprint.

Prophecies, however, are neither helpful nor even very interesting if there are *no* clues to the action required. The message that links the three levels of dilemma is that there is an immediate need to change our view of the task of management and managers in the organised society. If organisations make up the fabric of our modern society, then those who design and weave that fabric become rather crucial people, and their methods and values of more than passing interest. 'Management' may of course in the future be felt to be an inappropriate term for decision making in the new society, with its implications of one man set above another, of manipulation, of orders and controls. But it is the word we use today for the governance of organisations, so it will do us as a starting point.

I used to think that management was a science based upon a set of rational laws. Problems arose simply because we had not as yet unravelled all the implications of those laws. I am convinced now that my view was altogether too simple. Management, as I have studied it in many situations and many countries, is not so much a science, more a way of life. It is

true that there are technical aids to management, but they are
to do mainly with the ordering of numbers and materials. It
is true that there are some propositions about the behaviour
of people and groups which seem to hold good over time and
across nations, and wise managers make use of these aids
and propositions. But some 80 per cent of what managers do
seems to be the outcome of a set of attitudes, values, beliefs,
assumptions about the way people do or should behave, should
be organised, motivated or co-ordinated, about the rights of
management and the tasks of organisations. There is not,
however, just one set of these beliefs, leading to one uniform
style of management. There are several, and one can see each
of them at work successfully in different situations.

I have come to see varying views of management as different
cults, and the organisations managed in those ways as different *cultures*. And I can best capture the flavour of each
management philosophy by identifying it with one of those
powerful figures in the imagination of our culture, the Gods
of Ancient Greece.

What, the reader may reasonably ask, have the gods of
Ancient Greece to do with management? Let me explain. The
Greeks used their Gods to symbolise certain values or attributes. Without taking them too seriously, they intuitively
identified with the god or gods that symbolised their preferred
values. Beautiful women might court Aphrodite, strong men
Hephaestus. In the same way I have chosen four gods (or to
be precise, three gods and one goddess) to symbolise the values,
attitudes and practices which go with what I see as the four
predominant philosophies of managing. Zeus, the head of the
gods, famed for his impulses and the power of his presence,
is one of them. Apollo, fond of rules and order, is another.
Athena is the goddess, protectress, as I see her, of problem
solvers. Dionysus, for me the supreme individualist, is the
fourth. Although classical scholars may shudder at the treatment of these ancient figures, I use them purely as allegorical
figures to demonstrate that the management of organisations
is more a set of values than a science, more a cult or a fashion

than a theory. But the Greeks had many Gods. Their individual popularity changed with the times. And so I argue, it must be with the managerial cults of the organised society. Our accustomed gods must give way to others as times change. In the past one hundred years we have already found managerial fashion changing radically. It is my thesis that the time has come for it to change again. New gods for new cities.

I found however, as the Greeks did, that the gods failed me at the end. Whilst the cults, symbolised by the gods, provided clear alternative models for behaviour with which I and, I hope others could identify, they did not provide any sort of political theory on which to base a whole system of organisation for the coming society. Once the instrumental view of organisations is called into question, *management is not enough* of an answer. Community is a concern for human beings not for gods. So the Greeks, in their political thinking, turned to the *Demos* (the people) and the idea of democracy was born. It is a word that time has corrupted and practice distorted but I can do no better than turn like the Greeks to the concept of 'the people' in my confrontation with the Third Dilemma. The reasons will, I hope, become clear. If I may now add some allegorical subtitles to the three problems of the organised society, they are:

1. GODS IN CONFUSION
2. THE APOLLONIAN CRISES
3. DEMOS EMERGING

I live and work in Britain and many of my experiences are inevitably based in that country. That, for my theme, may be no disadvantage. For Britain, by chance and not design, is possibly closer to an organisational revolution or evolution than any other country. I suspect, however, that the dilemmas of the organised society are or will be common to all the countries of what we know as the industrialised West. Perhaps as citizens of the oldest and most stable of the world's democracies, Britons are likely to be particularly conscious of the anti-democratic tendencies of the organised societies, and less appreciative of its main supposed virtue, efficiency. In consequence the counter-arguments to efficiency are likely to surface earlier in Britain than elsewhere.

In any case it is clear that roughly since 1890 the organised society in Britain has produced a level of economic growth below that of her neighbours, justifying an increasing disillusion with 'management' and 'organisations', and the now visible migration of managerial talent towards the continent of Europe. The discontent is manifest already.

One reason for this lack-lustre economic performance may well be that Britain's imperial success led her to confuse administration with management – in other words, in the management of the wealth-creating part of her organised society Britons have pursued the wrong managerial god. Mounting economic crisis has only recently forced them to attend to this error, the first dilemma.

The pursuit of efficiency has been further hampered by the fact that Britain has not in recent years been able to shield her citizens from the worst rigours of the organised society by the employment of 'guest-workers', temporary immigrants from other lands, in menial jobs. Britain's immigrants are all her citizens and do not intend to return to their original homes. This has given Britain an enforced early experience of a totally citizen work-force, an experience soon to be shared by other countries, and one which leads directly to the second of my dilemmas.

For these reasons Britain may well be the Western World's organisational laboratory. Other countries may be able to postpone confronting the second and third of my dilemmas for a while, and will no doubt profit from the organisational experiments that, in my view, will have to occur in Britain on a large scale. Ironically, the oldest industrialised society may once more find itself the pioneer, and become the first of the 'Fifth world' countries, by which I mean the 'post-industrial' societies. It is a role for which Britain's history has well prepared her, and to which she may rise with relish.

BRITAIN FIRST?

Derek Sheane has well expressed Britain's accidental opportunity:

'I have an endearing and persistent feeling that before the end of this century the United or un-United Kingdom, as the case may be, will emerge as the first geopolitical unit to evolve itself to a higher level of social and industrial conduct. This will be demonstrated by the fact that the Americans, Germans, Japanese and all other latter-day 'men of progress' will be coming over here paying large sums of money or other tributes to find out how we survived capitalism, socialism, marxism, bureaucracy, internationalism, parochialism, intellectuals, economic forecasting, debt, differentials, and even the Irish, the English, oil, moral decay, outmoded organisations and a loss of values.'

In fact in a small way experiments in evolving the re-organised society are already taking place all over the organised world.

On 1st April 1977 the Norwegians actually passed a *law* requiring every organisation to give every worker a meaningful job. The other Scandinavian countries have long tried to practise this principle. One of the most interesting examples of democracy at work occurs in newly-democratic Spain, at Mondragon. Co-operative organisations exist in all countries from Israel to Peru. Only in Jugoslavia, however, is there anything like a common national *ethic* of organisation and management.

The changes I am proposing will however not be without difficulty in realisation. They would be much easier to achieve in a closed economy, as Jugoslavia was, than in an open one. Only by an unusual combination of courage and wisdom by its managers and leaders will the open organised society be able to change its organisational skyline and maintain the living standards of its citizens. Efficiency and human dignity are uneasy bedfellows. This book is a plea for a marriage.

THE FIRST DILEMMA: GODS IN CONFUSION

The Theory of Cultural Propriety

The mixed-up management of our organisations produces organisational *slack*. Slack is, broadly speaking, waste, or the inefficient use of resources. It shows up in unnecessarily high prices, in wasted time, in poor quality, in late deliveries, in underused capacity, in boredom. The excessive slack in many of our organisations not only undermines the credibility of the organised society, it puts its very survival in some doubt.

Mixed-up management results from a confusion of managerial philosophies, or, as I would put it, from following the wrong managerial gods. There seem to be four of these gods, each lending his or her name to a particular managerial philosophy, style or cult. Organisations develop their own *cultures,* always some mixture of the basic cults. Few organisations are culturally pure, devoted to only one managerial god; and this blend of gods, as we shall see, is desirable. But does each organisation have the *right* mix of cults, and if so are they properly bonded together? If not, incompetence, inefficiency, and slack will be the inevitable outcomes. These endemic diseases of organisations do not usually result in the death of the organisation, but they infect it, and through it, the surrounding society.

Individuals as well as organisations have their preferred managerial gods. The organisational comfort of an individual is greatest when the individual's preferred god is also that of the organisation. But comfort, alas, is no guarantee of quality. Comfort can be the breeding-ground of slack for both individuals and organisations.

The following section attempts to unravel the idea of the 'cultural' approach to management. It is written for both mercenaries and missionaries. At one level it can be read as a purely practical diagnostic aid for consultants or top managers. At another it provides clues to the comfort or discomfort of the individual: a follower of Apollo for instance will seldom be at ease or at his best in a Zeus situation. At a third level it attempts to explain that slack need not be an endemic disease in an organised society. It is avoidable, and is avoided in effective organisations, if the management is culturally appropriate, blending the gods of management in the most suitable mix. Mixed management, not mixed up, is the underlying theme. Cultural Propriety.

The supporting evidence for the cultural approach to management has to come from the experience of the reader. If the ideas click with his experience then there is some likelihood that they are valid. To the reader without direct organisational experience these chapters would no doubt read like the description of snow to a native of Borneo! But most of us after all have some experience of institutions: schools, hospitals, clubs and even families are organisations. To help I have included some examples and illustrations from my own experience and from the studies of others in this field. They are illustrations rather than evidence, and are printed in italics to distinguish them from the main text.

Choose Your God

Chapter 2

THE FOUR GODS OF MANAGEMENT

Each of the four gods gives its name to a *cult* or philosophy of management and to an organisational culture. Each of these cultures has also got a formal, more technical, name, as well as a diagrammatic picture. The name, picture and the Greek God each carries its own overtones, and these overtones combine to build up the concept I am trying to convey. They also help to keep the ideas in one's memory.

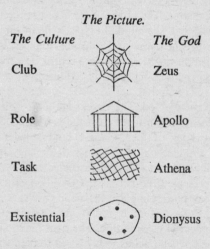

The Picture.

The Culture		*The God*
Club		Zeus
Role		Apollo
Task		Athena
Existential		Dionysus

These names and signs and Gods do not amount to definitions, for the cultures cannot be precisely defined, only recognised when you see them. If you know organisations at all the descriptions should be recognisable as you read on.

It is important to realise that each of the cultures, or ways

of running things, is *good*—for something. No culture, or mix
of cultures, is bad or wrong in itself, only inappropriate to its
circumstances. The fact that you do not like or approve of one
of them makes it unsuitable for you—not wrong or bad or inefficient in itself. This principle is the heart of the theory of
cultural propriety and I shall revert to it again and again.

The Club Culture (Zeus)

The picture is that of a Spider's Web. The organisation which
uses this culture will, like all other organisations probably have
divisions of work based on functions, or product. These are
the lines radiating out from the centre, like the lines of a
traditional organisation chart. But in this culture those are not
the lines that matter. The crucial lines here are the encircling
ones, the ones that surround the spider in the middle; for
these are the lines of power and influence, reducing in importance as they get more distant from the centre. The relationship
with the spider matters more in this culture than any formal
title or positive description.

Zeus is the patron God. The Greeks chose, or created, their
gods to represent certain features of the world as they saw it.
Zeus was the King of their Gods, who reigned on Mount
Olympus by thunderbolt (when crossed) or shower of gold
(when seducing). He was feared, respected and occasionally
loved. He represented the patriarchal tradition, irrational but
often benevolent power, impulsiveness and charisma.

Historically, this culture is found most frequently in the
small entrepreneurial organisation. The boat fanatic who finds
he can sell the boats he builds, gets his son to help with manufacturing, his nephew to sell them, his cousin to keep the accounts, is Zeus, and that is the way Zeus slowly builds his web.
But the culture also prevails in broking firms, in investment
banks, in many political groupings, in start-up situations of
all sorts and on the bridge of many a ship.

The club culture is an excellent one for *speed of decision.* Any situation where speed is vital will benefit from this style of management. Of course speed does not guarantee quality. *That* depends on the calibre of Zeus and of his inner circle – an incompetent, ageing or disinterested Zeus will quickly contaminate and slowly destroy his own web. *Selection* and *succession* are therefore rightly regarded as critical variables in these organisations, and much time and effort are given to them.

The culture achieves speed through an unusual form of communication – empathy. I watched the young executive of a small broking firm at work in the metal exchange one afternoon. He was making a series of rapid purchase and sale decisions of what seemed to me to be alarming magnitudes, with no calculators, formulae or resource to higher authority or expertise. 'How do you make these decisions', I asked, 'and what formal approval and authority do you need from your firm.' 'Oh,' he said, 'I make my own decisions, but I try always to double-guess what the old man would do.' 'And if you fail?' I asked. 'Curtains' he said 'for me'.

The club culture can be a cruel culture if your empathetic guess is wrong. But empathy needs no memos, committees or formal authorities. Club cultures indeed are very short on documentation. Zeus does not write, he speaks, eyeball to eyeball if possible, if not, then by telephone. Many a successful Zeus has been illiterate, if not always innumerate. Instead empathy depends on *affinity* and *trust.*

You cannot guess what the other man is thinking unless you think like him. There is little empathy between opposites. Your brother's son, your cricketing chum, your drinking companion are more likely to read your mind intuitively, and quickly, than the stranger off the street. Do not despise nepotism, it can be a good base for empathy. Yet empathy without trust is dangerous, for it can be used against you. Again it is more difficult to trust a stranger than someone whom you, or your friends have known long. Selection to club cultures is usually preceded by an introduction, and often confirmed by a meal. You know your friends at table.

These cultures, then, are clubs of like-minded people introduced by like-minded people, working on empathetic initiative with personal contact rather than formal liaison. They are tough clubs, because if empathy or trust is seen to be misplaced the man must go. Weak clubs will not survive because they will either have to inject other methods of communication (and so lose speed), or risk too many mistakes.

Club cultures are cheap cultures to run. Trust is cheaper than control procedures, and empathy costs no pence. Money is channelled to where it matters, to people and the promotion of personal contact: the telephone and travel bills of these cultures are very high, for Zeus will not write when he can talk. They are effective cultures in situations where speed is more important than correct detail, or the cost of a delay higher than the cost of a mistake (which can often be rectified by a subsequent deal). They are good cultures to work in—provided you belong to the club—because they value the individual, give him free rein and reward his efforts.

Club cultures make history, and Zeus figures are the managers most beloved of journalists. (Most organisations started as club cultures, and many have not changed when they should have, for speed of decision and the personal imprint of the leader usually become less important as the organisation reaches its first plateau of routine.) These cultures depend on networks of friendship, old-boys and comrades, and can appear therefore to be nepotistic closed shops, unpopular in these days of meritocracy and equal opportunity. They smack of paternalism and the cult of the individual, of personal ownership and personal power, the kinds of things that gave the industrial revolution a bad name. They are unfashionable cultures, and derided as examples of amateur management and relics of privilege. They should not be. Of course these methods of managing can be abused and often have been – an evil Zeus will do evil things – but these organisational squirearchies are very effective in the right situation, for trust based on personal contact is not a bad base for getting things done.

The Role Culture (Apollo)

When we think of an 'organisation' it is usually the *role* culture that we envisage. It is a culture which bases its approach around the definition of the role or the job to be done, not around personalities.

Apollo is its patron God, for Apollo was the god of order and rules. This culture assumes that man is rational and that everything can and should be analysed in a logical fashion. The task of an organisation can then be subdivided box by box until you have an organisational flow chart of work, with a system of prescribed roles (specified in things called 'job descriptions') and held together by a whole set of rules and procedures (call them manuals, budgets, information systems or what you will).

Its picture is a Greek Temple, for Greek Temples draw their strength and their beauty from the pillars. The pillars represent functions and divisions in a role organisation. The pillars are joined managerially only at the top, the pediment, where the heads of the functions and divisions join together to form the Board, Management Committee or President's office. The pillars are also linked by tension wires of rules and procedures. A typical career would involve joining one of the pillars and working up to the top with perhaps occasional sight-seeing visits to the other pillars ('to broaden one's base'). It is a picture of a bureaucracy if you like, but 'bureaucracy' has come to be a contaminated word and this culture has its merits.

The Apollo style is excellent when it can be assumed that tomorrow will be like yesterday. Yesterday can then be examined, pulled to pieces, and put together again in the form of improved rules and procedures for tomorrow. *Stability* and *predictability* are assumed and encouraged. And thank God for them. That the sun will rise tomorrow can be a most reassuring recollection in some of the bleak moments of the late night. Wherever, therefore, the assumptions of stability are valid, it makes sense to codify the operation so that it follows a set and predictable pattern. Individuals are, usually, indispensable to the operation of the pattern, although, as technology advances, more and more stability can be automated. Individuals in the role culture are, therefore, part of the machine, the interchangeable human parts of Henry Ford's dream. The *role*, the set of duties, is fixed. The individual is he, or she, who is slotted into it. That the individual has a name is irrelevant, a number would do as well. That he has a personality is downright inconvenient, because he might then be tempted to express his personality in his role and so alter the role. And that would throw the whole precise logic of the operation out of gear. In a role culture you do your job – neither more, nor less. Efficiency is getting the train in on time, not early, not late. Efficiency is meeting standard targets. Beat them and it must be assumed that the targets needed revising.

'An interchangeable human part'. It sounds deadening. 'The occupant of a role' sounds like a sort of organisational squatter. To many the pure role culture is a denial of humanity because of its insistence on conformity. But to others it is blessed release.

How pleasant it can be to know *exactly* what is required of one. How relaxing it sometimes is to be anonymous; how pleasurable not to have to exercise one's initiative, leaving all that creative energy for the home or the community or the sports field.

The Apollo culture is secure, psychologically and, usually, contractually. Apollo was a kind God in ancient Greece, the protector of children and sheep as well as of order. Once you join your Greek temple you can nearly always rely on staying there for life. After all, the temple assumes it will be there, may even have a twenty-year forecast of what it, and even you, will be doing. The temple will take over your work life for you, tell you what to do, where to go, what you can earn. It may even arrange your insurance for you, provide a house or a car, make cheap shopping available or legal advice. It can and will do some or all of these things because of its assumptions about the predictability of the future.

It is no accident, therefore, that life insurance companies are an almost pure example of role cultures. The notion of predictability is built into the whole ethos of their work. Monopolies, including the civil service, state industries and local government can reasonably assume predictability too, since there is no competition around to disturb their vision of the future. Organisations with a long history of continued success with one product or service or tradition can also be forgiven for thinking that things will continue as before. And if that is so, then the more you rationalise, codify, standardise, the more effective you will be. If you have the same set of menus for breakfast, lunch and supper every day the catering operation in your home will be greatly simplified, the costs of labour and materials will be reduced and the managerial energy required will be minimal. It may be boring, of course, but where food is not enjoyment but only the necessary fuel of life you will find Apollonian catering.

Apollo cultures are efficient when life is predictable. They hate the obverse – change. They will usually respond to a changing environment first by ignoring it, then by doing *more* of what they are already doing. Responses tend to be stylised in these cultures. When costs go up, raise the prices, or the fares. If sales are flagging, sell harder. If the backlog of administration is getting too big, work more overtime. Greek temples are built on firm ground. If the ground starts to shake, the pillars quiver and have to be bonded together. If they aren't, the pediment will fall. Translating the analogy, role cultures respond to drastic changes in the environment (changing consumer preferences, new technologies, new funding sources) by setting up a lot of cross-functional liaison groups in an attempt to hold the structure together. If these measures don't work the management falls, or the whole temple collapses in merger, bankruptcy or a consultants' re-organisation.

ZEUS OR APOLLO?

I once worked in a Greek Temple organisation. It was safe, predictable and promised a secure career. But at 28 it was boring. An acquaintance with whom I lamented my condition said 'why not come and join us, we are looking for an economist to do our project analysis'.

'Who is "us"?' I asked. 'An investment bank,' he replied, specialising in the developing countries'. 'But I'm not an economist,' I said. 'I read philosophy at University.'

'Ah! But it was the right University wasn't it?' he said, as if that made it all all right. 'Come and have lunch with the Board on Tuesday.'

I had lunch. We talked long about many things – politics, sport, the world. No one mentioned the job, or economics, or my previous experience. Next week they offered me the job of Economist, a new post. Two months later I joined them.

They gave me a fine office, a nice secretary and the Financial Times – and then left me alone. Nobody phoned, no memos, letters, nothing. After a week I went to see my friend.

'It's very nice to be here,' I began.

'Good to have you,' he replied.

'But . . .' I said.

'Well?'

'I wonder if I could see my job description, get an idea of my role and responsibilities, reporting relationships, and the general organisation structure.'

'What on earth are you jabbering about, old boy?' he said, looking startled and worried, 'we don't use those sort of words here – what's worrying you?'

'What am I meant to do?' I blurted out.

'Why, what the rest of us do,' he said, 'search out opportunities to use our resources, get on planes, go and meet people, find some hot news; you know the kind of thing we're interested in, get some more of it.'

I returned to my office alarmed for myself and for them.

But then I thought I saw it. They had wanted an economist because they were secretly very worried about this slap-dash way of doing things. Clearly some serious professional project appraisal was urgently needed. Luckily I had just happened to bring along with me from my previous organisation a set of procedures and tables for project appraisal. These could be readily adapted and then I could propose introducing a little more system and procedure into the current craziness.

In a week I was ready. The Chairman agreed that I should present my ideas to a meeting of the Board. They all listened very attentively and politely. At the end the Chairman thanked me for all the work I had put into it and then said

'I suppose a project would have to be very marginal indeed to justify all this analysis and procedure?'

'Well,' I said, 'it's obviously vital for marginal propositions, but you can't even know if it's marginal till you've done this kind of formal analysis.'

'Hmm. You see, we're probably wrong' (in the tone of voice Englishmen use when they know they're not), 'but in this Group we've always thought that we got success not by making better *decisions than our competitors on* marginal *propositions, but* quicker *decisions on* obvious *propositions.'*

I defended myself, but I knew at the time that he was right. They were brokers, trading in companies. Speed was vital. The accuracy of a decision only relative. They were Zeus. I was Apollo.

I never did get into their club. In the end I realised that I had a different cast of mind and left before they threw me out.

The Task Culture (Athena)

This culture takes a very different approach to management. Management is seen as being basically concerned with the continuous and successful solution of problems. First define the problem, then allocate to its solution the appropriate resources, give the resulting group of men, machines and money the go-ahead, and wait for the solution. Judge performance in terms of results, solved problems.

Its picture is a net, because it draws resources from various parts of the organisational system in order to focus them on a particular knot or problem. Power lies at the interstices of the net, not at the top, as in the Apollo culture, or at the centre, as in Zeus organisations. The organisation is a network of loosely-linked *commando units*, each unit being largely self-contained but with a specific responsibility within an overall strategy.

Its god is a young woman, Athena, the warrior goddess, patroness of Odysseus, that arch problem-solver, of craftsmen and of pioneering captains. The culture recognises only expertise as the base of power or influence. Age does not impress, nor length of service nor closeness of kin to the owner. To contribute to your group, talent is what is needed, and creativity, a fresh approach and new intuitions. It is a culture where youth flourishes and where creativity is at a premium. The youth, energy and creativity associated with Athena fit the task culture quite well.

It is a good culture to work in if you know your job. Since the group has a common purpose (the solution of a problem), there is a sense of enthusiasm and joint commitment with little of the private agenda conflicts that befoul the first two cultures. Leadership in a common-purpose group is seldom a hot issue, instead there is usually mutual respect, a minimum of procedural niceties, and a desire to help rather than exploit when others get into difficulties. It is a *purposeful commando*.

TASK CULTURES IN BLOOM

A friend, employed as an executive with a venerable and traditional British heavy engineering company, went on a working visit to one of the aerospace companies of Southern California, towards the end of the sixties when the space race was at its height and the US Defence Department was the world's largest customer, commissioning a long succession of solutions to high technology problems, often on a cost-plus basis.

Although he was not to know it, the aerospace companies of that time were the epitome of the successful task culture. Often as much as 30 percent of their managers had a Ph.D qualification. Their formal structures of organisation were of the matrix type. They worked in project groups which were continually being dismantled and re-assembled. They were at that time financially ebullient.

He returned to Britain with his eyes gleaming, 'It was extraordinary,' he said. 'In those companies not only did the sun shine all day outside, but the managers were young, intelligent, earning high salaries and having fun, and the organisation made money.

'In my company,' he said ruefully, 'we believed that these things were incompatible.'

That is the ideal. It works well, indeed excellently, when the product of the organisation is the *solution to a problem.* Consultancy companies, research and development departments, advertising agencies – after all an advertisement is a response to a client's expressed need – are all one-off problem-solving factories. But put a task culture into a repetitive situation and there will be trouble. Variety not predictability is the yeast of this kind of management. Ask Athenians to manufacture pencils and they will devise you the best (and most expensive?) pencil known, or disrupt the process, or depart.

Task cultures come expensive. They are staffed by experts who can demand their market price. They talk together a lot, and talking costs money. Problems are not always solved just right the first time, so there is the necessity for experimentation and the inevitability of errors. Errors cost money even if they are speedily corrected. Expensive task cultures, therefore, tend to flourish in times of expansion, when the products, technologies or services are new, or when there is some sort of cartel arrangement which provides a price floor. In times of expansion you can get away with high prices – there is more than enough cake to go round. Similarly, new technologies or new products create, for a time, a sort of monopoly situation which lasts until the technology settles down or competitors arrive. During this monopoly situation the costs or the task structure can be covered by higher charges and prices. In short, task cultures work well when one is venturing into new situations. Luckily it is in those situations that success is rewarded with the money to pay for it.

Come hard times however, or an end to venturing, or the need to make the solutions permanent or routine, and the task culture will be seen to be unduly expensive. These cultures are not for plateaux. Athena did not care for domesticity and the routine chores of housekeeping. So task cultures often have a short life. If they are too successful they get big and to pay their way take on a lot of routine or maintenance work – which require Apollonian cultures. Failure, however, is one problem they find it hard to solve (it is hard for a co-operative group to dismiss half of its members), and in hard times a Zeus will usually emerge to deal with the crisis. Or the members may just get older and want more routine, or more personal power.

ATHENA IN A STORM

In 1972 the advertising business in Europe was thriving. Advertising agencies competed strenuously, but on quality and service, not on price, which was still fixed at a standard percentage of the cost (effectively a cost-plus system). The agencies were full of well paid creative talent, usually young.

I was asked to look at the management process of one agency. It was a model task culture. The whole place was a network of temporary project groups (called 'accounts'), pull-

ing in the individual resources from the specialist functions. Most people worked on three or more accounts. Strict standards were applied to the end products (the advertisements), but control and systemisation of the means were minimal. How and when the groups worked was left to them. The allocation of personnel to groups was virtually the only managerial task retained in the centre. Salaries were high, but based on expertise, as recognised by the market-place (there was a lot of mobility between agencies). There was very little formal hierarchy, but an informal class system based on renown, not closely associated with age. Money was not a crucial factor, it was always there. Success was measured by public approval, which meant new clients clamouring at the door. The place resembled a luxurious art school, where everyone seemed to be earning vast sums for indulging in his or her hobby. 'Management' was in fact not a word that was used or a concept that was wanted.

Two years later and world recession, inflation and tightened company budgets knocked the bottom out of the advertising market, whilst hitting the agencies' most vulnerable cost factor – the salaries of their people, their human assets. Agencies began to compete on price. Companies demanded better and quicker service for reduced expenditure. Costs had to be controlled since the business could no longer operate on a cost-plus basis in an expanding market.

Budgets, computer print-outs of individual expenses, management committees, redundancy, reductions in office space, a freeze on salaries, lowered mobility, the beginnings of staff unionisation – the symptoms of 1974 were numerous. Revisiting the agency the task culture was gone. 'Accounts' were administered. *Procedures abounded. People talked about 'the management', and indeed the top personnel had changed, to bring in a more managerially-minded group who talked of profit margins and cost-effectiveness and systems. Errors could not be afforded, were controlled for and eliminated – but so were the experiments that accompanied them. Conformity and predictability had begun to flavour the advertisements. They no*

*longer made bad ads, but some thought they no longer made
great ones either.*

*Suddenly it was just like another business. The art school
had become an ad-factory. The task culture was now a role
culture with a few Zeus figures at the top.*

*Necessary? Perhaps. Sad? Certainly. Task cultures don't easily
weather storms.*

The Existential Culture (Dionysus)

Dionysus, God of Wine and Song, presides over this culture
because he if anyone represents the existential ideology among
the Gods. Existentialism starts from the assumption that the
world is *not* some part of a higher purpose; we are not simply
instruments of some God. Instead, although the fact that we
exist at all is an accident, if anyone is responsible for us and
our world it is ourselves. We are in charge of our own destinies. This is not a recipe for self-indulgent selfishness, for
Kant's categorical imperative applies, that whatever we ordain
or wish for ourselves must be equally applicable to the rest
of mankind. Wine and orgies won't work unless someone
makes the wine, and that someone must potentially include us.

The organisational implications of existential thinking are
great. In all the other three cultures the individual is subordinate to the organisation: the style of the relationship may vary,
but the individual is there to help the organisation achieve its
purpose, and is paid in one way or another by the organisation
for doing that. In this fourth existential culture the organisation
exists to help the individual achieve his purpose.

How might this be? Well, think of doctors: four of them,
each an individual with his own speciality, but who agree to
share an office, a telephone, a secretary and to form a partnership association. Or think of architects, or barristers in their
chambers, or a co-operative of artists. Theirs is a commune
culture, existing for its participants. Its picture is a cluster

of individual stars, loosely gathered in a circle. But the picture will remain essentially unchanged if a star or two departs. The stars are not mutually interdependent.

The existential culture is excellent, therefore, where it is the talent or skill of the individual which is the crucial asset of the organisation.

This is the culture preferred of professionals. They can preserve their own identity and their own freedom, feeling owned by no man. And yet they can be part of an organisation, with the colleagues, the support and the added flexibility and even bargaining power that association brings.

Dionysians recognise no 'boss', although they may accept co-ordination for their own long-term convenience. Management in their organisations is a chore, something that has to happen like housekeeping. And like a housekeeper, a manager has small renown: an administrator amongst the prima donnas is bottom of the status lists.

Dionysian cultures are splendid places to work in. I have worked in one myself – a University. Professionals usually have job security, agreed fee scales, allocated territories or spheres of influence, guarantees of independence. This is marvellous for them. But not for those who have to lead or organise or manage such people.

For there are no sanctions that can be used on them. Dismissal, money, perks or punishment are all outside the jurisdiction of the leader. Even promotion or selection decisions are made, as a rule, by groups of equals. Professionals do not willingly receive orders, fill in forms or compromise on their own plans. Every teacher likes to be the uninterrupted king in his own classroom, just as every doctor is god of his consulting room. You enter by invitation only, criticise on request, command by consent. For these are the organisations of consent, where the manager governs with the consent of the governed, and not with the delegated authority of the owners. It may be democracy, but it is very difficult, and exhausting, to deal with.

One would not expect to find many such organisations
around, certainly not in the business or industrial scene, where
organisations by their charters have objectives that outlive and
outgrow their employees. Indeed the Dionysian culture is something which causes shudders in any more usual organisation or
manager – precisely because of the lack of mandated control.
Where you can manage only by consent, every individual has
the right of veto so that any co-ordinated effort becomes a
matter of endless negotiation. Only where every individual
can do his own thing, and could in fact operate without the
organisation at all, is there less problem. Antique hyper-
markets where individual dealers ply their trades independently although under one roof, a marketing
co-operative for independent growers or craftsmen, can usually·
be managed (they would not use the word) without too
much difficulty. There would be a few conflicting objectives,
few needs to compromise individual desires for a common
good.

Organisations, however, put the common good before the
individual need and so they tend to try to translate Dionysians
into Athenians, the existential into the task culture. They are
of course right, as judged by their own interests, to try to do
so. Individuals, however, like the notions of individuality and
personal professionalism which reside in the Dionysian idea.
There is a growing band of 'new professionals' – individuals
who define themselves according to their trade, not just doctors
and lawyers, but now also the 'systems analyst', 'research
scientist', 'public relations adviser', 'consultant'. These individuals see themselves as independent professionals who have
temporarily loaned their talents to an organisation. They are
often young, usually talented and can command an open-
market salary and reputation. They behave as Dionysians,
and as long as they are talented they can get away with it, for
the organisation needs them enough to manage them on the
terms of their consent. Increasingly, therefore, the specialist
groups and any research or development activities are acquiring an existential flavour.

Wherever individual talent is at a premium the Dionysian flavour is probably necessary, and organisations do well to recognise it and accommodate it. But the cult of Dionysus is growing and is no longer related to individual talent. We would all like the benefits of existentialism without its responsibilities and risks. Existentialism on the shop-floor is a new phenomenon. We shall return to it in the second part of this book.

FAMILY CULTURES

Have families changed their cultures?

Once upon a time the paterfamilias ruled as Zeus over his table. He was master and all knew it. They did as he commanded when he commanded.

Then Apollo became the fashion. To each his duties and his status. The men made the money, women the food, children the beds.

Democracy brought Athena into the family. Not duties but tasks, projects and small group activities became the feature. 'Why don't you both . . .?' or 'shall we . . .?'

And now Dionysus? A temporary liaison of individuals. If individual interests start to diverge the liaison cannot be enforced. Joint activities (e.g. holidays) cannot be assumed or imposed, only negotiated.

Do organisations follow a similar sort of cultural inevitability? If so, where are we on the route?

Which Are You?

You will probably not identify yourself completely with any of the four gods. Most people, the Greeks included, are too complex to do that, and pay homage to more than one philosophy. Similarly your organisation will probably include aspects of all four cultures.

Do my classifications apply to your experience? Only you can judge that for yourself, but in some recent research on

US Corporations, Michael Maccoby* produced his own four classes of organisational characters:

The Jungle Fighter.
His goal is power. He experiences life and work as a jungle, where winners destroy the losers. There are two sub-types, the lion and the fox, different in the way they walk their jungles.

The Company Man.
His sense of identity is based on being part of the powerful protective company. He is concerned with the human side of the company, his interest is in the feelings of the people around him but he also has a commitment to maintain the organisation's integrity.

The Gamesman.
The gamesman is the new man. His main interest is in a challenging competitive activity. He enjoys new ideas, new techniques, fresh approaches. He is a team player, playing for the corporation.

The Craftsman.
His interest is in the *process* of making something, in doing a craftsmanlike job. Many scientists in organisations fall into this category. They want to do their own thing rather than to master or manage the system.

The resemblance to the four Greek gods is unmistakable.
There is, too, some historical significance in the order in which I have placed the gods. Most organisations originated as club cultures, almost squirearchies built around the personality of the founder, the owner or the patriarch. These are the traditional tribes – the first form of organisation, I suppose, informal, intuitive and personal. This form of Zeus

* *The Gamesman: The New Corporate Leaders*, Secker and Warburg, 1978.

management lasted for a long, long time. Take even the railways of England, built in the early nineteenth century, incredible examples not only of engineering but of co-ordinated manual effort in which over 200,000 men were at one time working with pick and shovel – even their organisation was based on sub-contracting to gangs of navvies working for a Zeus figure. It was the introduction of the factory that changed things, with the idea that work could be broken down into its component parts rather than multiplied out, so that instead of having 100 gangs working on 100 different engines you divided up the bits of the engine. This change in the technology of work required rules and procedures – the role culture. The role culture produced enormous cost reductions when linked to the new self-powered technology of steam, and then electricity. It turned out, however, to be a very expensive culture for one-off jobs and to be slow at reacting to the unexpected.

The committee of experts, on the other hand, had always been around. But it was not until the pace of change hotted up that it began to be a widely-used basis for management, called the project team or task force. As so often, it was probably the innovative pressures of war that fostered the task culture as a method of organisation.

And now, today, the increased specialisation of technology is beginning to make Dionysians of us all. The idea that armies, for instance, will soon be just groups of scientists is not such a remote possibility.

If you examine the history of most organisations, you will find that they have progressed through the club (Zeus) culture to the role (Apollo) culture, to which they have subsequently added the task (Athenian) and existential (Dionysian) cultures as they have needed to change and develop. By now most organisations of any size are some mix of all four.

Organisations however need to do more than merely equip themselves with a mix of cultures and their attendant gods. The cultures must first be internally consistent within themselves, for Apollonian assumptions of order and rationality will not produce results in the task culture (Athenian) part of the organisation, or vice versa. Second, of course, you need the right culture for the right job: a club (Zeus) culture for the accounts department would nearly always be inefficient. These are the two most common causes of mixed-up management, and we shall go on to examine them. Meantime the Dinner Party Game may enliven the occasional boring evening.

THE DINNER PARTY GAME

Try this rudimentary form of cultural diagnosis when at your next party. Ask your neighbour what he does for a living.

If he replies 'I work for X', naming an individual whom you are supposed to have heard of, he will turn out to be in a Zeus culture.

If he says 'I work with Y Co. or organisation,' going on perhaps to define his job title, he will be in an Apollonian role culture.

If he puts his title first and then his organisation as for example 'I am in marketing, with W. Co.' then he probably sees his part of the organisation, and himself, as a task culture. If he just says 'I am a barrister', or 'I paint', he is a Dionysian.

The Mix of Differences

Why should these very different gods be required in the same organisation? Well, looked at one way, life is just a set of jobs to be done. Organisations are just larger sets of jobs to be done. These jobs seem to fall into three types:

STEADY – STATE
DEVELOPMENT
ASTERISK

Let me explain.

STEADY – STATE describes those jobs which are programmable because they are predictable. They can be handled by systems and routines, by rules and procedures. In a typical organisation they might actually account for 80 per cent of the quantity of work to be done.

DEVELOPMENT jobs are those which attempt to deal with new situations or problems. In many cases the result may be a new system or routine, which ensures that the next time the event occurs it will not be a problem, merely an incident in the steady-state. These are the jobs which ensure, if they are well done, that the organisation adapts. In many organisations the groups responsible for them will include the word 'Development' in their title (as in Product Development or Systems Development).

Not all problems are development jobs however. Some are what I can best describe as ASTERISK situations. Asterisk situations are the exceptions, the occasions where the rule-book has failed, the emergencies where instinct, and speed, are likely to be better than logical analysis or creative problem-solving. These situations have to be resolved by personal intervention.

Each of these job-types has its matching symbol and its god. The wrong god matched to the wrong job causes mixed-up management and its consequence, inefficiency.

The Steady-state is a square ☐ , and Apollo of the role culture is its god.

Development activities require a creative cell and Athena is their Goddess, with her problem-solving capacity.

Asterisk situations are represented, naturally, by an asterisk *, and here Zeus and Dionysus share the honours (a liaison which has caused some confusion).

'Management' happens when these activities are linked

together in an appropriate fashion and given some common purpose or direction. Symbolically –

The 'manager' therefore has to embrace within himself all four cultures. He has to be able to emulate each god in the appropriate circumstances. If you want an explanation for the lure of management, this is it – the simultaneous call of four gods. And if managers look weary, well they might after this quadruple culture shock – cultural schizophrenia.

Most people can't do it, of course. Most people revert, particularly when tired or stressed, to their favourite culture. So organisations, which are made up of managers and managees after all, tend to get culture-bound. When individuals or organisations get culture-bound they start to define jobs to fit their cultural inclinations. Zeus characters will see development problems as asterisk situations calling for their personal intervention. Apollonians will make everything fit into the rulebook, even if that is obviously the most complicated way of doing it. Athenians love creation. They are prone to inventing fine solutions to unnecessary problems (the 'Concorde' phenomenon), or to devising answers which, though immaculate, are hugely expensive to implement. To be adequate is not a challenge to Athenians, only to Apollonians. Mixed-up management.

ZEUS IN THE CARPET WAREHOUSE

My wife has in her time worked as an interior designer and decorator. She used then to complain that the problems of management did not require the complex and elaborate

*theories of management academics for their solution. 'Com-
monsense', she said, 'and the ability to read and write'. 'Consider', she would say 'the carpet problems that I have. Last
week I ordered a red carpet to be sent on Tuesday to King-
ston. Instead they sent a blue carpet on Thursday to Richmond.
No great problem for me,' she added 'I got on to Fred up in
the warehouse, cursed him and chatted him up. "That's all
right Luv," he assured me, "Bill will get the van out, pick up
the blue carpet, bring it back here and get your red carpet to
your customer by this afternoon".' And so they did. They
always get it right the second time. But the cost to them must
be tremendous. Efficiency just means getting it right the first
time.'*

*She was right, of course. But getting it right the first time
would mean a system of checks and controls, matching orders
to delivery chits to lorry schedules to calendar dates. All very
straightforward but involving bits of paper and files and
checks. Boring stuff, at least for Fred who has been running
the warehouse for 30 years and likes to keep everything in his
own head. That way he can spend his day giving orders, dealing with questions, settling disputes, placating angry customers
and allocating drivers, all by personal intervention. His idea
of bliss is to have three telephones ringing, one face at the
window, another at the door, all needing him, at once. Then
he feels indispensable, powerful, valuable.*

*He is a Zeus sabotaging the steady-state. An asterisk in a
square. A mismatch of cultures equals expense, in this case
Bill running unnecessary errands in his van.*

So it is that organisations often, even usually, end up with
the wrong cultures in the wrong places, with jobs defined by
favourite gods rather than gods assigned to jobs. Even as
individuals, in our daily lives, we are guilty of this theistic
favouritism. As a confirmed Dionysian with streaks of Athena
I cannot find it in my heart to do the routine tasks of household maintenance which I designate as 'suburban trivialities'.
Inevitably our house is prone to endless emergencies calling
for creative solutions and personal inspiration. The steady-

state is minimal, asterisks and cells abound.

More instances of mixed-up management:

● Developmental cells may be required to solve the co-ordination problems of the steady state with all its systems. If they don't, then asterisk situations arise and Zeus-style action is needed. Too much of this however, and the steady state becomes pitted with cells and asterisks, depriving it of much of its strength. Reverting to earlier symbols, the pillars of the temple get affected by a sort of cultural dry rot. A plethora of projects is a danger sign in a Greek temple organisation.

● In an attempt to minimise costs Apollo organisations may attempt to standardise and systematise *everything*, even developmental jobs. An Apollonian will tend to use the past to forecast the future. Apollonian planning, for instance, will be a euphemism for 'projections'. Initiative will then be stifled by 'proper channels', and the energies of the Athenian or Zeus characters diverted into beating the system.

● In the 1960s there was a vogue in large organisations for corporate planning departments. In many cases these rightly become creative cells with an Athenian task culture. Staffed by young, talented and enthusiastic individuals, scenarios, alternative futures and forecasts poured out of them. Unfortunately these had often little impact on the mainstream organisation (the steady state of manufacturing and marketing, or of administration and services). The cells were rather like hornet's nests hanging from the gutters of the Greek Temple. Often the departments were housed, territorially, at the edge of the Headquarters' building and attached, structurally, to the management through the most junior of the Directors. Often they found it easier to communicate with other creative cells, even those in competing organisations (at conferences or courses or conventions), than with their own steady-state colleagues. But this 'organisational irrelevance' made it easier to amputate the cells when economic stringency was needed in later years.

● In a competitive talent hunt, large organisations tend to try to restock their manpower bank with an annual intake of young graduates, or MBA's, or professionals. Rightly or wrongly these people have often been educated in a problem-solving mode, the Athenian task culture. If the interest and commitment of these individuals is to be retained, they need to work on developmental tasks in problem-solving cells. But for many organisations the key managerial posts lie in the steady state. The transference is not easy. Athenian notions of project teams, participative management and every man an expert can actually get in the way of routines and administration. The alternative – putting the young Athenians in as apprentices at the bottom of the steady-state pillars ('get their hands dirty', 'learn the ropes the hard way', 'a few months on the road never did anyone any harm') – can be a huge culture shock to the new recruit, breeding a disillusionment with life in organisations which he may never lose.

Asterisk situations are interesting ones. They properly occur where you might least expect them. Not at the *top* of organisations but in the *middle*. At the top the decisions have long-term implications – they are developmental problems which are more appropriately and productively solved by Athenian cells. Asterisk situations usually get thrown up by dilemmas in human relationships – which are of all situations the least amenable to prediction or programming. Personal conflicts, imminent disputes, inter-group rivalries, private crises, crucial selection or promotion decisions – these are the sparks which start an asterisk job. Of course they can occur in the board-room or the council chamber as well as in the factory or office, but numerically and proportionately they will be of less significance. It is at supervisor and middle management level that Zeus should reign, or out on the road where the salesman, or driver, has to act on his own and use his initiative when the rule-book runs out. Unhappily, it is at the middle and edges of organisations that Zeus figures are least tolerated. They are most numerous at the top, although times are changing in some organisations, where the idea of President's office, a triumvirate or quadumvirate of top talent acting as a team (or cell), is becoming more frequent, as an adaptive recognition that the prime task of the Directorate is one of development, not of personal intervention. (There remain of course the ritual and ambassadorial duties of a tribal head. A Zeus figure is appropriate here – to represent the organisation on formal or external occasions, a sort of constitutional monarch.)

Differences, then, are necessary and good for organisational health. Monotheism, the pursuit of a single god, must be wrong for most organisations. But the choice and blend of gods cannot be haphazard. The wrong god in the wrong place means pain and inefficiency.

Apollonians At Work

Chapter 3

THE GODS AT WORK

You have now been introduced to the current Gods of our organisations. An introduction is, however, only an invitation to get better acquainted. One would be foolish, on the basis of so short an acquaintance to start restructuring one's organisation. The ways of each culture need further exploration and explanation should anyone want to act on them. Our next tasks will be to unravel the differences between the cultures and then to suggest how the cultures can be knitted together again to make up the balanced and efficient organisation which would solve the first level of problem in our organised society.

Balance and efficiency eliminate SLACK. SLACK in organisations, as I have defined it, means the waste of resources, be those resources money, men or materials. SLACK is today the slow cancer of our organised society. It is explained in more detail later.

But efficiency is not enough. The elimination of slack only brings us into the second and third dilemmas of the organised society. The impatient reader may want to jump forward straightaway to the introduction to the second dilemma, returning later perhaps to this section with its implications for immediate action.

I have argued that each organisation needs a mix of cultures, a different culture or god for each major activity, process, or job. But *within* each activity or section of the organisation cultural purity should prevail. The cultures must be *internally* consistent, for whilst *organisations* need more than one god, *individuals* are monotheists, they want one god at a time, cultural purity.

Apollonian assumptions, for instance, applied to Athenian individuals produce resentment, cynicism and reluctant conformity, like the signs of guilt in an individual who knows that he denies himself. A healthy organisation is therefore one that is culturally true in its parts. Where Apollo is needed and where Apollonians work, Apollonian ways are healthy. But if the *work* demands Apollo and your *people* are Dionysians, what then? Do you change your clothes to suit your job or change your job to suit your clothes? Which is an organisation's true culture? The one that the logic of the work demands, or the one that exists in the existing complex of the individuals and their cultures?

Each culture makes its own assumptions as to how individuals *think and learn*, can be *influenced*, may be *changed* or might be *motivated*. These assumptions result in theories and practices of individual development, in philosophies of change, systems of control and mechanisms of reward. But what works in one culture will not work, or not work so well, in another. Cultural harmony is health as well as happiness. Fashion, that insidious agent of change, may bring Management by Objectives, or Appraisal, or Team-Building into vogue. These however are all mechanisms best suited to their own culture. Transplanted to another they are ineffective – worse, they generate artificial behaviour, the rituals and rites of organisations that so often are the outward signs of corporate malaise. Without cultural awareness, organisations too easily find themselves genuflecting to false Gods. The only universal sin, it is held, is to be untrue to oneself. Organisational 'sin' is committed when a culture is untrue to itself. We shall look then at each culture in turn, at its assumptions and practices in the three critical areas of

thinking and learning
influencing and changing
motivating and rewarding.

The Club Culture (Zeus)
WAYS OF THINKING AND LEARNING

Zeus individuals tend to think intuitively and in wholes. They move fast to a possible solution and test that, moving to another if the first solution looks unsuitable. A logical step-by-step analysis is not their way, for they like responding to stimulus and get bored easily. Thus they like a jumble of events (nine-minute shots, as one research study shows), and days which are full of maximum variety. They rely a lot on impressionistic, 'soft', data and set little store by the conventional hard data of reports and analyses. They think holistically or in totals, seeing the full picture and assessing that, instead of building it up bit by bit from its parts.

CHIEF EXECUTIVES IN ACTION

Henry Mintzberg watched five chief executives at work.* He concluded:

1. *The chief executives strongly favoured verbal communication, rather than written communication.*
2. *Analytical inputs – reports, documents, budgets – seemed of relatively little importance to these chief executives. They attached more weight to the soft and speculative data – impressions and feelings, hearsay, gossip. Given this data they synthesized rather than analysed.*
3. *The chief executive is usually the best informed member of the organisation, but has difficulty in disseminating that information to the rest of the organisation, perhaps because his information is soft, intuitive and not formalised.*
4. *The chief executives had a simultaneous, experimental, hectic, unplanned work pattern. Half of their activities were completed in less than nine minutes, there were no evident patterns in their days, they preferred interruption (leaving*

* Described in his book *The Nature of Managerial Work* (New York: Harper and Row, 1973.)

*meetings, keeping doors open), and disliked routine (only
7 per cent of verbal contacts were regularly scheduled).*
5. *'Leader', 'Disturbance Handler' and 'Liaison Man' were the
words that best described their main roles.*
6. *In only 14 of 25 decision processes observed was there an
explicit diagnosis stage. Chief Executives preferred to jump
straight to the solution.*
7. *'Timing' was of great importance in the chief executives'
assessment of actions.*
8. *In only 18 out of 83 choices made by the chief executives
did they mention using explicit analysis. 'Intuition' and
'Judgment' better describe what they did.*

This Zeus-like behaviour is typical of many chief executives.
The question we must ask is whether it is *appropriate* at the
top of that organisation.

Zeus individuals do not learn logically or analytically or
sequentially. They learn by *trial and error* or by *modelling*.
And that is how they expect others to learn. The methods of
training and development which Zeus cultures apply to their
youth can be categorised as *apprenticeship* methods: 'work
with me for a while, see how I do it, and when I think it's right
I will let you have a go.' In Zeus cultures one will find systems
of Personal Assistants, or a Chief Executive's cadre of young
hopefuls. People will speak of protégés and crown princes, of
heirs to the succession who will be tested out in some organisational proving-grounds, by giving them their own small
commands where they will be free to demonstrate their ability
without causing too much damage to the parent concern.
It is possible to succeed whilst still young in these cultures,
given a strong patron and success in early trials. Choosing
your models is perhaps the key to successful learning, for a
man will then model the kinds of behaviour and values which
lead to success in that business or trade or profession.

The senior figures in a Zeus culture will find *their* models
in other organisations. A Zeus man will not inquire 'what is
current theory?' but rather 'what is so-and-so doing?' He will

use the luncheon tables of conferences and the receptions of society to unearth new models for his own development. Above all, to Zeus men learning must be secret. To a Zeus man an admission of a need to learn is an admission of a deficiency. I was once asked to advise the Zeus-type Board of an organisation: 'but come after the office closes,' they said, 'and use the rear entrance if you wouldn't mind'. A professor on the premises might be an omen of disaster! After all, these are club cultures, clubs where like learns from like and outsiders have little to contribute.

WAYS OF INFLUENCING AND CHANGING

In the club cultures it is the control of resources and personal charisma that count. If you own the club you can tell people what to do. If you have a track record of success, then you have that certain smell which gets called charisma. A rather charming piece of leadership theory talks of 'idiosyncrasy credits', earning the right to do what you want the way you want. But the credits have to be earned, since there can be no overdraft of idiosyncrasy credits, while any man's bank balance of credits can get used up by too many idiosyncrasies and need renewal by another run of success. Wise men in Zeus cultures do not overspend their credits.

From those power bases of resources and charisma the Zeus culture creates change by changing *people*. Individuals are the link pieces in these cultures. If a link is failing – replace it. A Zeus thinker will instinctively respond to an organisational problem by saying 'whose job is that? Change him.' Change *can* mean reform or education, but often in these organisations it means, literally, replacement. Clubs can be tough, and Zeus cultures do not always respond to the logic of the argument so much as to the signature at its end. 'Who said that?' is a more pertinent question than 'What was said?' Results speak louder than reasons and actions than arguments, for you do not change the course of these organisations by reasoning, but by reasons in the mouths of *credible persons*.

Hence the reputation of Zeus cultures for organisation politics. If the source of the argument counts more than its logic, then your choice of individuals and of clubs within clubs will be crucial. You will succeed or not, and be judged, by *whom* not *what* you know, although whom you know will depend on what you *do*. Inevitably these cultures are therefore political. But that word 'political' is only a sneer when used by men of other cultures. Zeus people accept and enjoy a world of personalities and of power based on credits and ownership.

CREDIBILITY WINS

I had been asked to investigate the economics of a possible investment in North-west Africa and to advise the chairman on what action the board should take.

After a week of careful research, two late nights and much analysis, I had produced a report, full of charts, estimates and calculations. At the front was the mandatory half sheet of paper with a summary of my conclusions, summed up (conclusively, as I thought) in the properly discounted annual rate of return of 15.7 per cent after tax. It must be a good thing.

The chairman looked at it.

'Thank you,' he said, 'you've put a lot of work into this. You think we should go ahead?'

'Of course,' I said, 'no doubt about it.'

'I see, I think I'll just have a word with Aubrey,' said the chairman (mentioning the name of a well known merchant banker). He contacted him on the phone, briefly stated the situation and there followed a five-minute conversation of which all that I heard was

'Yes . . . I see . . . Really? . . . Hm . . . Naturally . . . Quite so . . . Thank you very much, Aubrey'.

He put the phone down.

'No,' he said, 'It's not on. Aubrey says "wrong place, wrong time, wrong company". Thanks all the same, old boy.'

I was grossly offended by this victory of old boy network over rational analysis. In time however I came to recognise that the credibility of Aubrey, with much successful experience in overseas investment, was rightly going to be more important in that Zeus organisation than my untested technical reasoning.

MOTIVATING AND REWARDING

Zeus characters look for power over people and events. They like to see things happen as a result of their personal action or intervention. It is their desire that, personally, they should make a difference.

The implications are fairly clear. They enjoy situations where they have a great deal of discretion, where they have power over resources, and where personal intuitive decisions are important. To be confined in their responsibilities, or to preside over an area where technical expertise alone provides the answer to the crucial questions, are to them constraints upon their potential and therefore de-motivating.

In Zeus cultures money is highly valued; but it is, usually, money as an enabling factor or money as a symbol of results achieved. Many a Zeus will not think to spend heavily on personal goods, regarding this as the wasteful use of a means of power. People, or information, as well as money can be the object of their collector's instinct, knowing intuitively as they do that these commodities are often at least as powerful as money. To this end they will invest considerable time in creating and maintaining *networks*, potential sources of useful people, useful information, or even cash. Such men seldom rest from their labours, because they do not work for rest but for zest: in resting they might miss an opportunity to make a difference. They like uncertainty (including gambles) because uncertainty implies freedom to manoeuvre.

It all fits well into the club culture: trust and empathy backing up intuitive decisions; personal charisma based on a track record of success; money as a thermometer of success; politics, people and networks as a way of life. Reward these people with responsibility: give them resources, a challenge and your trust. Control them by results, or the look in their eyes, not by pension schemes or titles or even office cars.

PERCY AND THE POTATOES

After the long hot European summer of 1967 potatoes got expensive in the shops. One Saturday I went shopping with a friend – a successful ship broker, one of those men who was clearly very wealthy but always needed to borrow money, for his own was all committed. We were staggered by the price of potatoes and walked out refusing to buy any.

Two weeks later I saw him again:

'Remember those potatoes,' he said, 'what did you do about them?'

'I went home and ordered my wife to buy rice instead,' I replied; 'Why, didn't you?'

'O no, I rang up a contact in Calcutta, ordered 2,000 tons of Indian potatoes at £100 per ton, arranged freight and insurance for £30 per ton and sold them in advance to a London merchant I knew for £230 per ton.'

'But, Percy,' I said, 'that's £100 per ton profit and on 2,000 tons . . .'

'Don't worry,' he said, smiling, 'it didn't come off. The Indian Government stopped the shipment on the docks, but for three phone calls it was worth the chance.'

I switched to rice. He nearly made £200,000. But he maintains an extensive network. I would not have known who to ring even if I had thought of it. Besides, what would I do with £200,000 – invest it? He would have staked it all on another deal.

The Role Culture (Apollo)

The role culture is quite different. Apollonians think differently and therefore make different assumptions about influence, control and the motivation of others. It may have something to do with which side of the brain got developed first (see below), the environment of one's youth or even the first organisation encountered in life. Apollo followers will find Zeus people crude, irrational, unpredictable, frightening at times, certainly different. The two cultures do not mix. A Zeus will chafe under an Apollonian regime and forget to trust his intuition or his network. An Apollo can be useful to a Zeus superior, but his more logical ways must be understood and tolerated by the Zeus figure if his true capacity is to develop.

ARE YOU RIGHT OR LEFT BRAINED?

There is an emerging consensus that our talents may have something to do with which side of our brain got developed first. Scientists have known for some time that the brain has two distinct hemispheres. In the left hemisphere of most people's brains are located the logical thinking processes. This left side of the brain works sequentially, in a linear manner. Language is one common example. The right hemisphere looks at patterns, complete images or relationships.

Speech seems to belong to the left side, but movement and emotions to the right, logic to the left, inspiration and creativity to the right. Much of education is linear or sequential or verbal—stimulating the left side but perhaps neglecting the right. Those who are bad at logic may be good at art. Lawyers, scientists, accountants may have a developed left brain; artists, politicians – and some managers? – a developed right brain.

Henry Mintzberg has suggested* that successful chief executives rely more on 'feel' and intuition than systematic reasoning (right more than left), that they 'synthesise' rather than 'analyse', that they know, intuitively, more than they can communicate, revel in ambiguity and dislike regularity. He goes on to propose that planning is a left-brained activity, which can be made systematic, but that creative strategy needs right-brain thinking, which usually comes from one man.

Are Apollo and Athena Left-brained,
Zeus and Dionysus Right-brained?

WAYS OF THINKING AND LEARNING

Apollo definitely prefers the left-hand side of the brain. Apollonian thinking is logical, sequential, analytical. Apollonians would like to believe in a formally scientific world where events move according to predetermined formulae. They like to proceed from problem definition to the identification of the appropriate solution mechanism ('this is a logistical distribution problem, therefore apply the appropriate operations research technique'). On the whole, the more of these mechanisms you know, and can use, the more problems you are likely to be able to deal with. Efficiency tends to mean simplification, getting things down to the bare but essential features.

Intelligence is a useful indicator of ability, but it will be intelligence of the convergent rather than divergent kind – straight rather than lateral thinking.

Learning, therefore, in Apollonian cultures, is to do with the acquisition of more knowledge and skills, it is additive, and it is acquired by a *transfer* process (called 'training') in which those who possess the desired knowledge or skills pass them on to those who don't. It follows that individuals can, to a large extent at least, be classified according to their possession of knowledge, experience (another sort of knowledge) and skills, and allocated to roles which require particular sets

* Mintzberg H. 'Planning on the left side, managing on the right,' *Harvard Business Review* July-August 1976.

of these. If the requisite skill is lacking it can, by training, sometimes be provided.

This way of looking at thinking and learning fits routine predictable activities very well. These activities *can* be broken down into sets of required knowledge, skills and experience. It is therefore in Apollonian cultures that you will find individuals spoken of as 'human resources' – resources which can be planned, scheduled, deployed and reshuffled like any other physical asset. To this culture then belong the formal techniques of manpower planning, assessment centres, appraisal schemes, training needs diagnosis, training courses, job rotation: in fact all the paraphernalia of traditional management development.

The contamination arises when these attitudes and approaches are used in other cultures. In fact, in most organisations these techniques peter out as the higher echelons are reached; for most organisations will have a Zeus-cum-Athena culture at the apex, with individuals who have the power to ignore amongst themselves the rules they set for others. The mechanisms of Apollo thus are often confined to the lower and middle regions. Though many might mutter about one law for the rich and another for the poor, there may be intuitive wisdom in this apparent flouting of democracy.

WAYS OF INFLUENCING AND CHANGING

It is in Apollonian organisations that 'authority' becomes a recognisable concept. 'With what authority do you do that?' is a meaningful question in the steady state, whereas in a Zeus culture it would be seen as ritualistic mumbo-jumbo. Power in the role cultures stems from one's role or position or title. Written into that role is a list of rights as well as responsibilities. The organisation chart (an indispensable piece of equipment in role cultures, although often unheard of in club cultures) is a diagrammatic way of showing who can give orders to whom or via whom. If you don't have the title you can only *ask* not *tell*. The authority of your position not only entitles you to tell someone to do something, it also allows you to create a complex of rules, procedures and systems for your own domain. These rules, procedures and systems are the railways of the steady state. They direct and steer the flow of information and activities which turn inputs into outputs. And, as with railways, the driver (manager) is there to influence the speed, not to control direction. In an Apollo culture the manager is the person *in* authority whereas the Zeus manager *has* authority (his own, not that of the organisation).

It is a misconception to believe that managing means decision-making in the role culture. Decisions are in fact few in number and are very much of the processing category ('do we let that go, start this one, direct that one?'). It is the design of the organisation's railway system which is crucial: its operation only requires an adherence to timetables. Administration is a word that fits Apollo cultures but is anathema to Zeus.

It follows that to change Apollonian systems one must change either the sets of roles and responsibilities (the *structure*), or the network of rules and procedures (the *systems*). Changing any individual (the engine driver) has a minor impact compared with changes in the structure or systems (the lines of track or the timetable). Astute Zeus men trapped in an Apollo culture will adapt their own cultural instincts, and use the rules and procedures and role descriptions of Apollo to lock in their competitors and to free themselves. In so doing they distort the logic of the organisation, and so contaminate that culture and their own. This is an example of the unconstructive politics of organisations – the manipulation of the Apollonian systems for personal advantage.

BUDGETS IN APOLLO

Budgets in Apollo cultures are one way of defining one's organisational territory and personal discretion. It is tempting to any man of self-conceit to enlarge his domain by bidding for an increased budget. But one man's increase must be

*another man's decrease unless an enlarged budget for the total
organisation is accepted.*

*An enlarged total budget has of course to be accompanied
by a matching increase in output – if not, then organisational
inflation occurs, an increase in the 'money supply' of the
organisation without an accompanying increase in productivity. In organisational terms the 'money supply' is activity.
Under budget inflation, activity or 'busyness' rises but output
remains constant. In physics it is known as Brownian motion.*

*Apollonians prefer compromise to conflict. The mechanics
of compromise breed budget inflation. It takes a tough, and
ruthless new arrival, or the imminence of catastrophe, to slash
budgets. Apollo cultures when thriving tend therefore to be
prone to a creeping inflation, with 'activity' increasing faster
than output.*

*Are budgets, one must ask, an underlying cause of the pro-
gressive paralysis of large organisations?*

WAYS OF MOTIVATING AND REWARDING

Apollo men are tidy men. They value order and predictability
in their lives as in their affairs. Things need to fit into place,
with contracts precise and honoured, roles prescribed and
kept to. 'Duty' is an important concept to them, as is the
notion of obligation, or responsibility to keep one's own part
going. They are seldom curious, believing that the world
around them is on the whole organised by people who should
know what they are doing (even if the evidence is sometimes
lacking!).

It is not easy to describe the motivation of Apollonians
without making them seem dull. That is because they pursue
certainty as avidly as a Zeus man shuns it, and because the
role, or the job to be done, is at least as important as the
deeper purpose behind it all. If it sometimes seems remarkable that life goes on with its seed-time and harvest, buying
and selling, fetching and carrying, despite the eruptions of
economic crises or armed rebellions, it is Apollonians that we

must thank for it. Head down in their role, they prefer to assume the certainty they cannot always see. This gives them a particular slant on life. An Apollonian believes in life insurance and pension funds, confident that life has sufficient predictability for it to be sensible to make long-term provisions for the future. A Zeus sees a pension only as a source of realisable assets. An Apollonian finds sense and security in the budgets and job descriptions of a formal organisation even if he may debate the details, whilst a Zeus will view them only as constraints on his opportunism.

Again, these characteristics fit the requirements of the role culture, which relies on predictability to be effective. The complex of long-term careers, pension schemes, career planning, role descriptions, rules, procedures and operating plans which a role culture needs to do its work, all fit the 'psychological' contract required by Apollonians. They are very contractual people, in fact, and are more inclined than most to formalise that psychological contract, turning it into a full legal contract in many cases – a tendency which can frustrate the Zeus personalities who often sit at the top of their organisations.

Because Apollonians value the power that is conveyed by the formal authority of their role, Apollonians are appropriately rewarded by an increase in formal authority and its outward visible sign – status. It is in role organisations that people most avidly compare and compete for the status symbols of the organised society: the company car, the expense account, the executive suite. It is appropriate that they should, though to another culture this would seem a meaningless and petty game.

The Task Culture (Athena)

This is the culture of the group, the group of experts focusing on a common task or problem. It is the organisational culture which most suits those who have been rationally educated in a democratic society, people who would like to think that they are living in a meritocratic society and who would not be offended to be called meritocrats themselves. Success, to organisational Athenians, is desirable if it has been earned. Such men will see Zeus people as over-privileged, or lucky, or unduly thoughtless. They may admire the forcefulness of a Zeus on occasion, but would wish it had been preceded by more counsel and deliberation. Apollonians will be seen by Athenians as useful but boring people, desiring to perpetuate the present rather than explore the potential of the future and of change. Most of the new professionals in organisations, those who think of themselves as 'marketing men' or 'corporate planners' or 'product managers' will see themselves as task culture people, Athenians. It is in fact the form of management that most people accept and aspire to. Unfortunately, as the last chapter indicated, it is an expensive and luxurious way of running organisations, so it is frequently contaminated: a problem solved by Athenians has to be administered in Apollonian ways. But the people are often the same, and there lies the *rub*.

WAYS OF THINKING AND LEARNING

Athenians are problem-solvers. Problems are solved best, they think, by a mix of creativity with some applied logic. Fundamental too to the process of problem-solving is the ability to work with others. Many brains make better solutions, as long as they work with, not against or for, each other. Learning therefore is acquiring the ability to solve problems better. Some technical aids may help and a little Apollonian instruction can sometimes be useful, but the crucial learning is by continual exploration or discovery, successive problem-solving of the hypothesise-test-rehypothesise variety. Mix with this the requirement to learn to work with others, and you get the kind of group problem-solving, discovery learning, project-based approach of so many schools, courses, and training centres. The case study of law schools and management courses is the most frequent vehicle for this type of learning, supplemented by 'group-effectiveness' training embracing such devices as 'T-Groups', 'Power and Influence Workshops', and 'Team-Building Laboratories' – all admirable in their own cultures.

Athenian cultures tend to think of individuals as resourceful humans rather than human resources, regarding them as people who are responsible for their own ultimate destinies but who at the moment are available for assignment to particular problem areas. In these cultures therefore there is more likely to be a bidding system for jobs and positions than in the Apollonian steady state. Leaders recruit teams, or individuals apply to join groups. Assignment is usually subject to the agreement of both individual and leader. A commando unit where the commander has had no say in the choice of his men will not be very effective. If there are appraisal and development schemes in these cultures, they will be likely to be so devised that the *individual* initiates any discussion or action. Self-development will be encouraged and mobility between organisations will not be frowned upon.

WAYS OF INFLUENCING AND CHANGING

Organisational Athenians bow down to wisdom and expertise. To command in a task culture you must have earned the respect of those you command. This command can then be exercised through the socially acceptable form of *persuasion.* Obedience is replaced by agreement. There is a lot of talk, argument and discussion in task cultures, where discussion documents abound and it is expected that what is written is read. Here, in this culture, unlike those of Zeus and Apollo, you begin to rely on the rational strength of your case to win your way. To do so, however, it is first necessary to define the problem and win agreement to that definition and to its priority for the group. 'Problem-solving', say Athenians, 'starts with problem-finding'.

Task cultures work best when a heterogenous group of

talents finds its homogeneity through identification with a common cause, task or problem. The first step to influence in these cultures then, is to change the definition of the focal *problem or task*. Change the problem and you change the direction of activity. Only in cases of imminent disaster can the new problem be *imposed*. More usually it grows out of a changed consensus in the group. Any newcomer wishing to change things must first remember that he cannot even raise the problem of the critical problem until he has the respect of the group. But this respectability can be imported. It can be earned in one place and transported to another. Athenians are cosmopolitans to a degree – that is, they believe that expertise travels, and that one is a citizen of the world, not of one organisation.

The task culture is beloved of the 'new' professional (the marketing, production, planning and development experts of modern corporations), because of this transferability of expertise. In a task culture you can gain the credibility of an expert without the kind of personal charisma necessary in a Zeus culture. These qualifications act as an introduction in the Athena culture, whereas you need a patron or a track record in the world of Zeus. Of course, if your subsequent actions give the lie to your qualifications these quickly get eroded, while in time a track record amounts to a qualification and can then be transported to another organisation.

Athenian task cultures tend therefore to deal with change by 'boxing the problem'. This is an organisational technique which consists of identifying the problem, allocating staff time to dealing with it, and recognising this new distribution of resources and priorities by putting a new *box* on the organisation chart: a box whose title is, in effect, the problem. If, for instance, the problem is one of Co-ordinating Subsidiary Plans, a group (permanent or temporary) can be set up to deal with this dilemma, and legitimised by the allocation of a box on the chart and the appropriate title of Division, Department, Unit, Group, Committee or Task Force (depending on its size and permanence). In a task culture it is usually possible to identify its major concerns by examining the titles of its current committees or study groups.

A predominantly Apollonian or role culture will, sensibly, surround itself with many task culture groups to attend to its needs for change. A Greek temple organisation, finding itself in a changing market or technology, will rapidly become cross-strutted with a whole variety of co-ordinating teams, planning groups and investigating committees. This is fine. The confusion arises when such groups believe that the effectiveness of their reasoning will influence the Apollonian part of the organisation, or when the steady-state Apollonians ignore the task groups because they are inadequately enmeshed in the formal authority structure. Problem-solving, you see, is fine as a method of influence *inside* the task culture, but to influence another culture you have to play its games.

ATHENA INTO ZEUS WON'T GO

The top echelon of the consultancy company was being re-organised. Times were leaner and a new, tougher and more directive style of management was, probably rightly, thought to be required at the top. The four chief barons conferred privately, off-site, meeting in their own homes. The large, consultative top management group was to be disbanded. Its leisurely, reflective, debating style would be too cumbersome for the new urgency they wanted to implant. Instead these four would comprise the Chairman's Group, which would be the top power group in the consultancy.

Then there would be an Administration Committee to look after what we would call the steady-state activities. Although very necessary, this was, in this organisation, very much the housekeeping role and consequently of low status.

But the consultancy had other longer-term problems: its future, for instance, and the question of standards and product quality, of talent, development and recruitment. In a typically Athenian fashion part-time committees were set up to 'deal with' these matters, and the chairmanship given to the most appropriate people in the firm.

One of them refused the task – to the amazement of the chairman (after all, the appointment was by way of being a compliment). 'You do not understand the nature of power in this organisation,' said the refusing manager. 'Unless the chairmen of your committees are also members of the Chairman's Group their work will be ineffectual and I do not want to be busy being ineffectual.'

The Chairman was puzzled, angry and hurt. A proper Athenian by nature, he saw the other's response as a greedy and irresponsible bid for personal status. The manager, probably rightly, saw a Zeus culture forming at the top of a rather fuzzy and extravagant task culture, a Zeus culture in which membership of the club would be an essential prerequisite to the exercise of influence at the top. Talking from different, but undeclared, cultural assumptions the argument degenerated into a personal quarrel.

The committees exist. They do not matter very much – Athenian appendages to the new Zeus club. The Chairman is contemplating joining them 'to beef them up a bit'. The manager, like Achilles, sulks in his tent. A cultural misunderstanding clutters up the organisation.

WAYS OF MOTIVATING AND REWARDING

Athenians like variety and get bored by certainty. But they are problem-solvers rather than difference-makers, looking for a dilemma rather than a vacuum. In this way they differ from Zeus, although, just as in the myth Athena sprang fully-armed from the head of Zeus, so, in a way, the Athenian culture can provide the brains to Zeus' impulse. Athenians, however, also respect expertise and professionalism and are concerned therefore with their own self-advancement, self-advancement in a professional rather than hierarchical sense, although promotion can often be the outward sign of professional success.

When Athenians talk of 'getting the job done', they bring a different flavour to the phrase than when Apollonians say it. Athenians imply a problem solved and dealt with – something finished once for all;. whereas Apollonians work in a continuous present and might more commonly say 'getting on with the job'. Thus it is that an Athenian prefers the task to be defined rather than the role, for he wishes to keep discretion over the means to any given end. 'Objectives' he will buy, not 'Role Descriptions'. Teams, the personalities and talents who make them up, interest him greatly, whereas the Apollonian would prefer to know the rules governing their interaction. The Athenian is content to be judged by results, whilst in Apollo cultures the results can seldom be attributed to any individual or set of individuals, so that it must be means, the performance in a role, which has to be judged.

Athenians therefore flourish under conditions of variety, problem-solving and opportunity for self-development. They respond to payment by results, to group assignments and to 'defined uncertainty' – the solution of identified challenges. Appropriately, they work in the development areas of organisations, in predominantly task cultures such as consultancies, research groups, advertising agencies, or, increasingly, at the very top of very large organisations. They get restless in the steady state and can be indecisive in crises.

MONEY OR . . .?

Lisl Klein* tells of an experience which illustrates the difficulty of pinning down the precise nature of motivation.

A maintenance mechanic in a chemical process firm was being interviewed. It was an unstructured interview during which he talked freely for two hours about his job. At first he took a fairly instrumental line: 'All I'm interested in is the money. This firm pays well and that's the only reason I stop here. What a working man wants from his job is the pay

* L. Klein, *New Forms of Work Organisation*, Cambridge University Press 1976.

packet, and don't let anybody kid you about other fancy notions.'

Half an hour later he was talking about the firm, and discussed various things which he thought were wrong with it. The interviewer said nothing, but the mechanic seemed to think he was being inconsistent, because he stopped himself. Then he said, 'Well, you see, when you get a bit older, and the kids are off your hands, and you've paid for the house, and your wife's got a washing-machine – you don't need money so much any more. You find you start noticing the firm. And by God it can annoy you!' (Some Athena urges?)

Half an hour after that he said, 'You know – what I really like is when the machine goes wrong and I'm the one who knows how to put it right.' (Zeus in a crisis?)
(Klein comments that any definition of his motivation would depend on where the interview finished).

The Existential Culture (Dionysus)

Dionysians, of course, are very different again. It is anathema to a Dionysian to be classified except as *not* belonging to another classification! They like to be individuals, exceptions to all generalisations. It is therefore very difficult, and perhaps mistaken, to describe them as a class. Nevertheless the growth of individualism in organisations is becoming one of the central dilemmas of society, and I have defined it so in this book, so the difficult must be attempted.

WAYS OF THINKING AND LEARNING

Dionysians, for example, defy rigid classification in their thinking habits. These depend a bit on their chosen profession: scientists may well think like Apollonians, artists like Zeus. To be a Dionysian however is to think, whether it be true or not, that you have nothing much to learn from any man. Only from life. For those at the top of their profession this may well be true in fact as well as in perception. In others, less eminent or less skilled, it can seem like unfounded arrogance, disrespect or, at times in youth, downright rudeness.

Dionysians therefore prefer to learn by immersion, by new experiences. It often happens that a Dionysian will give up a job or a post or a project when he is total master of it, just because he is a total master of it and therefore has nothing left to learn. It is a habit infuriating to employers and clients alike.

DIONYSIAN MASOCHISM?

André Previn, the conductor, was being interviewed on the radio. 'Why,' asked the interviewer, 'did you leave Hollywood and the composing of musical scores for the films just when you were doing so well and had that world at your feet?' 'Because,' said Previn, 'I began to wake up in the morning without any pain in my stomach. I was no longer unsure of my capabilities.'

A publisher said, 'Academic authors are always bored by the books we want them to write, which build on their established reputation, while publishers are always worried by the books academics want to write, which are about fields and topics new to them.'

'What I hate about careers,' said the young arts graduate, 'is that you know what's going to happen to you. Its so boring. Its the unexpected that develops you, swimming out of your depth.'

Dionysians will resent any attempt by others, particularly an organisation, to plan their futures or develop their abilities. They want opportunities, but demand the right to choose between them. They will talk of sabbaticals, of second or third careers, of dropping out or dropping in. In one or two organisations the notion of 'educational credits' has been developed as a way of meeting the developmental needs of Dionysians.

Educational credits are, like paid holidays, made a legal entitlement of the individual. A credit is one week's leave plus expenses for development purposes (usually a 'course'). An individual might qualify for two credits per year which could be accumulated for up to five years. He can spend his credits any time, subject to the agreement of his superior on the exact dates and on the 'developmental' character of his proposed activity. In this way opportunity is provided by the organisation but the choice and final decision is the individual's.

WAYS OF INFLUENCING AND CHANGING

It is hard to influence Dionysians. Since they do not acknowledge the power of the organisation, or conceive themselves as working *for* the organisation (as opposed to *in* it), there are no organisational weapons to deploy against them. Dionysians respect only *people* – but there is no predicting what they will respect them for. It can be for their talent, or for their faces. Or it may be talent one month, and personality the next.

It is this very unpredictability that gives them the personal freedom essential to the culture. Even the words 'influence' or 'change' smack of an infringement of liberty to a Dionysian. It follows that any attempt to influence or change a Dionysian is going to be much more a *contracted* procedure than in the other cultures, although in a sense any process of change or influence involves some notion of 'exchange', in which one person or persons do or get something in recognition of something else.

A Dionysian negotiation always starts with the stated or implied opener 'what will induce you to . . .?' Only from an intimate knowledge of the person involved can one begin to make predictions as to what the particular inducement will be. As in all Dionysian situations, everything is particular, peculiar to the time, place and person, not general. Dionysians are therefore very difficult people to 'manage'. To anyone used to working on broad assumptions of similarity between similar people, it is very confusing to find that what works with A does not produce the same results with B, who is apparently a doctor, or architect, or activist, or professor in exactly the same situation.

Of course we all have Dionysian streaks in us, but most people confine these to certain portions of their life – their gardens, their social life, their holidays. To carry them into organisations of work can make it very difficult for those in charge, for the endless series of individual negotiations involved make life both unpredictable and exhausting. It is for this reason that Dionysians have to put on the cloak of another culture, or to be irreplaceable, if they are not eventually to be evicted or discarded by their employer.

Dionysian organisations (partnerships, usually) are therefore managed in a one-on-one fashion. The 'leader' interacts with each individually, meetings being called only for the dissemination of information or to ask for ideas on a situation of common interest.

WAYS OF MOTIVATING AND REWARDING

In these areas Dionysians are, of course, the most individualistic of the lot. Once again, they are hard to characterise as a generality precisely because they insist on, almost exaggerate, their individuality. Like Zeus characters, they want personally to make a difference to the world, but it does not have to be through power or people or resources. It does not even have to be noticed. A poem in a corner, a picture unseen, a patient healed unnoticed, can also be reward enough to Dionysians. It is interesting that the true Dionysian professions actually forbid any form of advertising, whilst the more Athenian professions (consultants, estate agents, architects) find more or less discreet ways to promote their fame.

Dionysians value personal freedom above all, freedom to act and speak as they wish, but particularly freedom of their time. Obligation to a community or organisation they recognise as a necessary part of the social contract, but they will, without rancour, try to incur as little of it as possible in return for their own rights. They like to be consulted, with a reserve right of veto, but not to participate; to be asked for their views, but not obliged to give them.

If this seems an essentially selfish view of the psychological contract, one must remember that these people do not really want to work in organisations at all. They are loners who gather in organisations or communities or partnerships purely for convenience, their convenience. As part of a larger and more culture-mixed organisation these Dionysian values, or psychological contracts, can only be tolerated if the individuals have great personal talent, if they are full professionals. As we shall see, the problems arise when the untalented begin to demand Dionysian contracts.

The first essential then of organisational efficiency is cultural purity. To each god his own. Harmony is health. It is when the gods compete within one activity that confusion results, for then the law of cultural propriety is infringed.

If harmony is health, the healthy (happy) organisation is one that uses the appropriate methods and assumptions of influence in a particular culture. Thus persuasion, logical reasoning (Athenian), is effective in a Zeus culture only if it comes from a member of the club; in an Apollo structure if accompanied by the requisite authority. Techniques and rule-books (Apollonian) get ignored by Zeus figures unless it suits their purpose to use them, or they respect the author (if he can be identified). Changing people around has little impact on an Apollonian organisation although it can be a major learning experience for the individual. Hence 'job rotation' as a fav-oured form of individual development in Apollonian organ-isations – it develops the individual whilst leaving the organisation untouched. Conversely, changing the structure or the procedures (Apollonian) has little effect on Zeus organ-isations if the key people, the club, remain the same. In these organisations structural change is often only a means to changing key people without too much trauma.

My descriptions of the motivational contract were of course

drawn in stereotype. As I have already pointed out, we are none of us, individuals or organisations, culturally pure. All of us like a little predictability in our lives as well as a little variety. All of us want at some time to make a personal impact. But if we are honest with ourselves (and who has more incentive to be?) we can admit that the proportions of the cultural mix differ in each of us. And there lies the problem of motivation. There is no one answer, no universal panaceas to be found in piecework systems, in job security, in lowered taxation, in job satisfaction.

Harmony, as always, is health. Reward systems designed for Apollonian role cultures, linking role performance to hierarchical promotion, can be ineffective if the psychological contracts operating are those of a Zeus culture. Apollonians understand deferred gratification – they can wait a longer time for their ultimate glory. Zeus and Athena people want quick results and rewards, discounting the future at a high rate, living for today or tomorrow rather than the year, or the decade, after next.

DISCRETIONARY DIFFERENCES?

Elliott Jaques has plausibly suggested that individuals differ in their innate capacity for discretion.* He measures discretion by the maximum time that the individual can operate without a review of the quality of his performance. Simple tasks usually have a short 'time span of discretion', maybe even of hours, whilst senior management roles have discretion spans measured in years.

A large number of studies has pointed to a consistent number of strata of discretion spans in organisational roles, as follows:

---

* See further E. Jaques *A General Theory of Bureaucracy*, Heinemann London 1976.

Time-Span		Stratum
(?) 20 yrs	————	7
10 yrs	————	6
5 yrs	————	5
2 yrs	————	4
1 yr	————	3
less than 3 months		1

Giving people work that requires more discretion than their current capacity is very stressful. Jaques goes on to argue that large organisations have most jobs at the fifth, sixth and even seventh strata but that there are few people around with those capacities.

It is intriguing to speculate whether the cultures, and cultural types, differ in the levels of strata involved. Maybe Zeus cultures operate with short time-horizons and levels of 4 and below? If so, such individuals would find the top of large organisations very stressful places. Athenians too may not feel comfortable with time-spans longer than two years. And Dionysians? And some Apollonians?

We don't know, but Jaques' research may be yet another reason to explain why cultures don't mix.

The confusion between Zeus and Dionysus is a very real one. Both act as individuals in situations which, whether real or imagined, demand their personal intervention. The difference lies in the power behind their action. Zeus relies on his control over vital resources and the force of his character, or charisma, backed by his experience and record of success. Dionysians are accepted because of their professional competence, because they are unique craftsmen whose skills cannot easily be replicated. A bad Zeus can make things happen, albeit wrong. A bad Dionysus is ignored. A Zeus can be incompetent in the eyes of others. A Dionysus depends on the respect of others to have any impact. On the other hand, nature is fair. Zeus needs power and wants impact. Dionysus often does not care. 'Take it or leave it' is not a Zeus remark, but it could be a Dionysian one. Dionysians are more self-contained, inner-directed and concerned about their craft. A Zeus without people to interact with will die, and the entrepreneur who claims that he will retire to his orchard when he has made his pile, is usually lying: his need to intervene in the affairs of others is not going to be satisfied with apple trees. The Dionysian on the other hand can be happy cultivating a garden visited only by himself. Yet because both Zeus and Dionysus characters intervene personally, relying on their personal prowess, it is often hard to distinguish them by their behaviour. The dedicated scientist, intent on an idea, can be just as dominant, even ruthless, as the Victorian mill-owner. Many a Zeus will define himself as an organisational craftsman, an enthusiastic professional, and be both surprised and hurt by accusations of dictatorship.

Formal documented schemes of Management by Objectives will turn into time-consuming rituals in Athenian cultures, who will find their own ways of defining the common purposes of their groups. To apply the 'group-effectiveness' training of the Athenian culture to the steady state is only to foster insecurity and uncertainty, or, in Zeus cultures, outright rebellion. The notion of patron and protégé is anathema to Apollonian cultures, who regard crown princes as disruptive to their grading schemes. Yet, in their proper place, these devices work. You cannot run a factory like a trading company, nor a trading company like a consultancy. So the habits of thought and of learning are just as unlikely to be identical. They are in fact very different and need to be seen to be so. Cultural propriety must be preserved.

THE MISSING REFUSE BAGS

In one local authority area it was the practice to collect refuse in plastic bags, which were distributed to householders for this purpose by the drivers of the refuse-collecting lorries.

These plastic bags had a value on the open market, as some of the lorry drivers apparently discovered. At least it soon became clear that many of the new bags were not reaching the house-holders for whom they were intended.

It was, therefore, decided to set up a separate unit with its own vans to distribute these bags independently of the refuse vehicles.

Now lorry drivers are a special breed. Their cab is their kingdom, the road their territory. Once on the road, they answer to no man. They are the Dionysians of the motorways or the Zeuses of the delivery services. In their own spheres they wield dictatorial power, as any housewife who offends the delivery driver will know. Refuse collectors are no exception. They are individuals with their own freedoms. Leash them if you can, and dare.

Private marketeering can be one of the side attractions of this mini-buccaneering. This is often more a game than a crime, and losing is getting caught. To stop the game as a penalty for catching some losers is seen as unjust, even, per-versely perhaps, as an infringement of liberty. Zeus is humiliated, Dionysus snubbed. Their interventionist energies, their wish and ability to be noticed, will now be turned inwards on the system instead of outwards. Their power will be negative.

In this case the local authority sought to reduce the num-bers of drivers to compensate for manning the van. The drivers retaliated by working to rule and threatening a strike. The action of the authority brought the drivers together as nothing else ever had. From now on muttering increased, morale decreased.

Zeus will not willingly, or cheaply, submit to Apollo.

ENTER ATHENA

The new chief executive – the radical son of his more tradi-tional founding father – was keen to put more life and humanity into his father's viable but unspectacular dye-manufacturing company. This company employed 150 people and produced a range of dyes from base-stocks for a number

*of long-standing customers. Their methods, both of manu-
facture and of accounting, were old-fashioned but reliable,
and adequate in a world where things did not change very
much, where growth was slow but steady, and where the labour
turnover was under 5 per cent.*

*'Groups,' he announced, 'were the way to work: groups
where we earned respect from our colleagues by an honest
sharing of both problems and perceptions, where the pursuit of a common goal by equals would produce a new
synergy.'*

*Although most of the managers and supervisors did not
even understand the words he was using, he did after all pay
them, so they reluctantly agreed to attend a weekend 'Group
Dynamics Workshop' to find out about these new ways of
working. A Group Dynamics Workshop is a T-Group, a
method designed to help the individual explore the way groups
work and how he can work in them by a mix of discussion,
exchange of perceptions, small tasks and a shared reflection.*

*By the Saturday night, Bill had revealed his true feelings
about Fred, who was unlikely to forget them in a hurry; the
chief executive found that the group could discover at least
one common enemy – himself; Tom, the accountant, had
withdrawn behind a wall of silence; and overall a new sense
of unease and defensiveness had entered the usual bantering
conversation of the group.*

*The young chief executive was puzzled. It had worked so
well at college and in that consultancy group he had been
attached to for a while. What had gone wrong?*

*Athenian ways do not, however, fit the more staid and
formal roles and ways of an Apollo organisation which, like
it or not, was what he had inherited.*

The questionnaire at the end of this chapter provides one
way of analysing and codifying the cultural preferences of
your organisation and yourself. Questionnaires, of course, are
fallible, particularly when one fills them in for oneself about
oneself. Add to that the fact that organisations are not hard

objective realities like chairs, which can be objectively measured and described; nor is your character or personality (in spite of the attempts of some psychologists to define them). So it is clear that the scores that you arrive at can only be your view, from where you stand at this point in time, of the organisation and yourself.

The interesting thing would be to give the questionnaire to a variety of people, and then to compare their ideas of the organisation (and of you?) with yours. A lot would depend on where they worked in the organisation, whether they were looking up or down or across it when they filled in the questionnaire, and how satisfied they were in their own lives. To some extent they probably change their cultural behaviour as they do different parts of their job. And so they should.

Questionnaire on the Cultures of Organisations*

To complete the questionnaire proceed as follows:

a) Consider the organisation you work for, the whole of it. What sets of values, what beliefs, what forms of behaviour could be said to be typical of it? Look at the four statements under each of the nine headings in the questionnaire. Under each heading rank the four statements in order of 'best fit' to the organisation as you see it (i.e. put '1' against the statement that best represents the organisation, '2' against the next best, and so on). Put the figures in the column under 'Organisation Ranking'.

b) When you have done this for the organisation, then go through the whole process again, this time for yourself, reflecting your own preferences and beliefs. Try not to look at your rankings under 'Organisation' while you do this, so that your second ranking is truly independent.

When you have ranked all the statements under each of the two columns, add up the scores for all the statements that are marked (a) under each heading, then the scores for all the

* The questionnaire is adapted from one originally developed by 'Dr Roger Harrison of Development Research Associates.

statements listed (b), and so on (e.g. a total score of 9 for all the (b) statements would mean that you had ranked the (b) statement '1' in each of the nine headings).

You should now be able to complete the following table.

	All (a) Statements	All (b) Statements	All (c) Statements	All (d) Statements	Total
The Whole Organisation					90
You					90

As in most questionnaires, you will want to qualify all your answers with the remark 'it all depends . . .'. You will find it hard in some instances to find any great difference, in your own mind, between some of the statements. Do not let this deter you. The questionnaire results will not be precisely accurate, but they should provide useful indications. You will find that the best way to proceed when trying to rank each set of statements is to trust your first, almost intuitive reactions. Do not linger over them too long.

When you have completed the questionnaire and added up the scores turn to page 88 for an explanation of the total scores.

Own   Organisation's
Ranking   Ranking

1.   *A good boss*

(a)   is strong, decisive and firm but fair. He is protective, generous and indulgent to loyal subordinates.

———   ———

(b)   is impersonal and correct, avoiding the exercise of his authority for his own advantage. He demands from subordinates only that which is required by the formal system.

———   ———

(c)   is egalitarian and influenceable in matters concerning the task. He uses his authority to obtain the resources needed to get on with the job.

———   ———

(d)   is concerned and responsive to the
                                        personal needs and values of others.
                                        He uses his position to provide satis-
                                        fying and growth stimulating work
———————   ———————   opportunities for subordinates.

Own Ranking	Organisation's Ranking	

2.   *A good subordinate*
(a)   is hard working, loyal to the interests
                                        of his superior, resourceful and trust-
———————   ———————   worthy.
(b)   is responsible and reliable, meeting
                                        the duties and responsibilities of his
                                        high job and avoiding actions which
———————   ———————   surprise or embarrass his superior.
(c)   is self-motivated to contribute his
                                        best to the task and is open with his
                                        ideas and suggestions. He is never-
                                        theless willing to give the lead to
                                        others when they show greater ex-
———————   ———————   pertise or ability.
(d)   is vitally interested in the develop-
                                        ment of his own potentialities and is
                                        open to learning and receiving help.
                                        He also respects the needs and values
                                        of others and is willing to give help
———————   ———————   and contribute to their development.

Own Ranking	Organisation's Ranking	

3.   *A good member of the organisation
                                        gives first priority to*
(a)   the personal demands of the boss.
———————   ———————

(b)   the duties, responsibilities and re-
                                        quirements of his own role, and the

		customary standards of personal behaviour.
(c)		the requirements of the task for skill, ability, energy and material resources.
(d)		the personal needs of the individuals involved.
4.		*People who do well in the organisation*
(a)		are politically aware, like taking risks and operating on their own.
(b)		are conscientious and responsible with a strong sense of loyalty to the organisation.
(c)		are technically competent and effective, with a strong commitment to getting the job done.
(d)		are effective and competent in personal relationships, with a strong commitment to the growth and development of individual talents.
5.		*The organisation treats the individual*
(a)		as a trusted agent whose time and energy is at the disposal of those who run the organisation.
(b)		as though his time and energy were available through a contract having rights and responsibilities on both sides.
(c)		as a co-worker who has committed his skills and abilities to the common cause.
(d)		as an interesting and talented person in his own right.

6.　　　　　　　　　　*People are controlled and influenced by*

(a)　　　　　　　　　the personal exercise of rewards, punishments or charisma.
———— ————

(b)　　　　　　　　　impersonal exercise of economic and political power to enforce procedures and standards of performance.
———— ————

(c)　　　　　　　　　communication and discussion of task requirements leading to appropriate action motivated by personal commitment to goal achievement.
———— ————

(d)　　　　　　　　　intrinsic interest and enjoyment in the activities to be done; and/or concern and caring for the needs of the other persons involved.
———— ————

7.　　　　　　　　　　*It is legitimate for one person to control another's activities.*

(a)　　　　　　　　　if he has more power and influence in the organisation.
———— ————

(b)　　　　　　　　　if his role prescribes that he is responsible for directing the other.
———— ————

(c)　　　　　　　　　if he has more knowledge relevant to the task at hand.
———— ————

(d)　　　　　　　　　if he is accepted by those he is controlling.
———— ————

Own　　　Organisation's
Ranking　Ranking

8.　　　　　　　　　　*The basis of task assignment is*

(a)　　　　　　　　　the personal needs and judgment of those who run the place.
———— ————

(b)　　　　　　　　　the formal divisions of functions and responsibility in the system.
———— ————

(c)　　　　　　　　　the resource and expertise requirements of the job to be done.
———— ————

(d)　　　　　　　　　the personal wishes and needs for

———— ————	learning and growth of the individual organisation members.
9.	*Competition*
(a)	is for personal power and advantages.
———— ————	
(b)	is for high status position in the formal system.
———— ————	
(c)	is for excellence of contribution to the task.
———— ————	
(d)	is for attention to one's own personal needs.

Interpretation of Questionnaire Scores

The (a) statements represent a Zeus 'Club' culture,
the (b) statements represent the Apollo 'Role' culture,
the (c) statements represent the Athenian 'Task' culture,
the (d) statements represent the Dionysian 'Existential' culture.
The *lower* the total score for any set of statements the *more prevalent* that culture is in your organisation or in you. A score of 9 for the (a) statements (the lower possible total) would mean a totally pure Zeus culture. You are unlikely to have any totals as low as that.
A table that reads, for example:

	(a)	(b)	(c)	(d)	Total
Whole Organisation	14	12	27	37	90
You	29	24	16	21	90

would mean that your organisation was a mix of Apollo and Zeus while you prefer to be Athena backed up by Dionysus.

First – Balance Your Gods

Chapter 4

THE GODS IN BALANCE

It is now necessary to look a little more closely at the forces that influence the balance of gods or cultures in any organisation, at the problems of changing the mix of cultures when necessary, and at the way of holding that balance without contaminating the individual cultures. If the mix is wrong, or badly balanced, or is not changed when change is needed, the result, as we know, is this phenomenon called SLACK, which we have defined as the disease of the organised society.

Effective organisations have usually formed their own balanced mix by experiment and continual adaptation. They have achieved cultural propriety and minimised slack. But success, if it is to continue, must be understood. History, the story of how it happened, is an inadequate explanation for others to use, for history cannot be relied upon to repeat itself. I shall therefore attempt to explain, functionally rather than historically, how it is that effective organisations achieve the proper balance of gods. The organised society needs more cultural propriety in its organisations, and it needs it now: it cannot wait for some Darwinian process of evolution to get there in the end.

We shall look in turn at the *forces* that influence the *choice* of mix, and the ways of *changing* and of *managing* that mix.

HOW DO YOU EXPLAIN YOURSELF?

An American visitor to Europe commented that every time he asked the reason for something in Europe, he received the historical explanation: 'Because the King met with his nobles in this way;

or

'Because my grandfather liked to see the mill from his bed-room;'

or

'Because my family did not approve of schools;'

or

'Because originally they got free travel when this firm was owned by the railway.'

'In my country,' said the American, *'I normally get a functional explanation, perhaps that's why you all are so interesting while we are more efficient.'*

The Influencing Forces

Organisations have to live with the pressure of several countervailing forces. 'Management' is the act of reconciling these forces in some blend of jobs and cultures. There can be no universal formula, for the pressures will be felt differently by each organisation. The best way to express these forces is to describe their effects as tendencies: 'the greater the force, the more likely . . .'.

The principal forces are:

Size
Life-cycles
Work Patterns
People

If we describe their effects briefly we can then come back to a discussion of what one can do about them.

Size: How many people can you relate to as individuals at any one time? Fifty? One hundred? One thousand? It all depends on how well you want to relate to them of course, but for most people the answer must be nearer fifty than one thousand. All the cultures except the role culture (Apollo) depend on the people within a work group knowing each other. Knowing each other implies an awareness of personality, talents and skills as well as just a name.

THE BIGGER YOU ARE THE MORE LIKE APOLLO YOU WILL BE

That is the general tendency. My own inclination is to follow Antony Jay's empirical rule of ten as the breakpoint. Once you have more than ten individuals in a group, ten groups in a division, or ten divisions in a company, you have to rely on formal methods of control and co-ordination. The farmer with his three farmhands has no need of the Apollonian devices of managerial textbooks. It can all be done intuitively and personally. The small Grammar School can run perfectly well with a minimum of impersonal co-ordination, hierarchies and forms. Not so the large inner-city comprehensive. Small is non-Apollonian, which is not the same as saying it is beautiful, but many a small company takes growth as its goal, achieves it and hates the changes it brings. From Zeus or Athena to Apollo is quite a violent transition. Parkinson's Law that the administrative component always grows faster than the rest, ignores the influence of other factors which we have yet to examine; but, if translated and downgraded from a law to a tendency, it does emphasise that increasing size means an increasing proportion of the steady state, a large square. □

RESEARCH AND SIZE

*As with much descriptive research on organisations, the conclusions of research on the effects of increasing size cause little surprise:**
- *As the size of the organisation increases, so does the need for co-ordination and supervision.*
- *As co-ordination and supervision increases, so does the bureaucracy.*
- *As bureaucracy increases, so do impersonal controls.*
- *Impersonal controls are accompanied by increases in absenteeism and turnover.*

* Based on Indik B.P. 'Some Effects of Organisation Size on Member Attitudes and Behaviour'. *Human Relations* 1963, 16, No. 4 pp 369-84.

- *The larger the size, the smaller the average amount of communication between members.*
- *As size increases, so does specialisation.*
- *As specialisation increases, the complexity of each job reduces.*
- *It is NOT always true (in spite of Parkinson's Law) that the administrative component increases faster than the rest.*

Apollo thrives on size.

Life Cycles: This is another way of referring to the old chestnut of management, 'rate of change'. The tendency can be expressed as *'The higher the rate of change the larger the influence of Athena'*.

The difficulty is that it is very hard to assess the rate of change. As overall measures of societal tendencies, it may be appropriate to use indicators such as speed of travel or quantities of data processed. But these are of little value to an individual organisation, to which it is more useful to think in terms of life-cycles – products, technologies, systems. How many years will each last? When the solutions of the fathers were good enough for the sons – a generational life cycle – the Athena component in organisations was very small. When, at the other extreme, the useful life of any idea is shorter than the time it took to create it (as in some very new technologies), the Athena influence is huge.

The idea of life cycles, too, should not be confined to industrial or commercial products. Diplomatic rules, educational policies, housing plans, co-ordination systems – all have their life cycles. When you get to minimum life cycles – only one of anything is ever made (in consulting firms, some architects' offices, art studios and the like) – there is an almost pure Athenian culture, with the Apollonian methods reserved for the housekeeping duties of the 'services and administration'.

It is impossible to quantify the proportions in general terms. It would be nice to be able to state that if the life cycle equals the creative cycle, Apollo will equal Athena, if double then double Apollo. Life is not that simple, but such a rule of thumb will do for a start, as a quantification of this tendency alone. Remember however that there are other factors at work to influence the final mix.

In practical terms, this tendency means that organisations adapt to shortening life cycles by, for instance:

pulling people out of straight production into production development, or from sales to market development;

setting up task forces or study groups;

calling in consultants;

cutting down the production or administrative component, leaving development groups intact;

creating a top management group removed from operational responsibility.

In all these cases the *problem-solving capacity* (Athena) is increased, not the *administrative capacity* (Apollo).

Work Patterns: There are three different ways to arrange the work to be done in an organisation:

as *flows* (where one section's work is the input for the rest);

as *copies* (where the work of each section is identical);

as *units* (where the work of each section is independent).

An assembly line is the most familiar example of a *flow pattern*. It is a logical way of organising complex repetitive work, allowing specialisation and economies of scale at each stage. A chemical process plant is an automated flow pattern. A local government office is often a clerical flow pattern, as a particular piece of paper goes through successive official stages in the office. A school, or a hospital, can also be regarded as a flow pattern, with students or patients as the pieces.

Branch banking, multiple stores, gasoline stations are familiar examples of *copy patterns*. Economies of scale and co-ordination depend on each unit being a replica of the others. If airline tickets were not filled in, identically, in every ticket agency it would be much more difficult to arrange interchanges among airlines, or communal booking facilities. If every outlet of a multiple store did its own purchasing and pursued its own billing procedure, the economics of mass purchasing and of centralised accounting would be impossible.

Unit patterns apply where standardisation is impossible or unnecessary. Trading and dealing activities, craftsman manufacture (pottery, painting or architecture), the self-employed, small organisations such as farms or independent shops, are all familiar examples of this pattern.

The tendency is for flow and copy patterns to require Apollonian (role culture) methods.

Unit patterns can be Zeus-like (most frequently), or Athenian (if the collaborative work of a group is needed), or Dionysian (as with most professionals). Teachers for instance are Dionysian in their own approach and prefer to operate as single units, yet often find themselves part of a flow or copy organisation. Dilemma! And the recent experiments at Saab and Volvo automotive plants have been attempts to create unit patterns in a traditional flow pattern industry.

It is not, however, only the economics of standardisation that drive organisations towards flow or copy patterns. The concept of *control* is also at work. Control is important if you need to regulate or inspect quality *before* the event. It is very hard to do this systematically or efficiently in unit patterns, because quality control in unit patterns is a post-factum feature. If you make a bad deal, or a bad picture, or sell the wrong item in your store, the mistake will not be discovered until *after* the event. In many businesses and offices this is not critical. Although errors are always undesirable, it is often impossible and unnecessary to avoid them altogether. We can and do learn by them. But some errors are too critical to be left for post-factum discovery. This particularly includes errors which might cost human lives, and in such cases antecedent checking is usually required by law (e.g. in aircraft manufacture, the drug industry, housebuilding and food manufacture). Even when it is not a legal requirement, an organisation can decide that the financial cost of an error is punitive and must be stopped before it happens. It will then find itself insisting on copy or flow patterns of work, and an increase in the role culture (Apollo).

The takeover of a small firm by a larger one can often result in the unit pattern of the small firm changing to conform to the copy pattern of the larger one. This causes a culture change, usually from Zeus to Apollo. Once again the culture shock to the individuals can be severe, the more so because it is not understood.

THE KALMAR PLANT

Volvo's Kalmar car-assembly plant is the most visionary experiment in job redesign yet.

The shape of the building is designed to provide a lot of sides and corners. Each corner provides a home for teams of 15-20 workers with their own workshops. There are more than 20 of these small shops, each with its own entrance and facilities such as change room, sauna bath, coffee and conference room, coffee machines and even a view. Duplicate facilities are built in to provide for a possible second shift with its own territory. Employees are allowed free use of phones for local calls to keep in touch with the outside world.

A true little village.

Around these villages glide wagons, silently controlled by electronic impulses from under the floor. A wagon, a low platform carrying the chassis or body, can be called in by one of the workshops when the workers are ready for it. The wagon can be tilted to any angle, stops instantly if it bumps into any person or thing, and is constantly checked by computer for work faults which are fed directly back to the workshop for rectification.

Teams are required to produce a daily quota, breaks and idle time are not monitored or controlled. The quota was fixed by union negotiation, not imposed by management.

'It all sounds too good to be true,' comments John O'Meara of Witwatersrand University Business School in South Africa after visiting Kalmar, 'but is it really working?' The answer was that the new plant had so far exceeded expectations.

FROM UNIT TO COPY – ZEUS TO APOLLO

The old man was sawing my length of timber for me with quite unnecessary care and precision in the timber yard.

'You look as if you love that wood,' I said, 'were you ever a professional carpenter?'

'Yes indeed,' he replied. 'I used to work for X' (naming a famous furniture designer).

'Why did you turn to a timber yard then?'

'Well X got taken over by YZ Co. (a conglomerate with a furniture division) and everything had to be made to fit their standard designs. Suddenly it wasn't fun any more. All the pride went out of the work. And then they said they didn't need so many people, so the older craftsmen went – the more expensive ones, you see. In the old days, Terence (the owner and founder) used to be around – we all knew him and knew how he wanted things – great man. After "they" came it was all forms and regulations and inspectors. Not the same at all. So now I just work to get money. It's OK here. Just a job.'

People: Much as one may sometimes deplore it, in others, people are different! This is not going to be an excursion into personality theory – that is an unnecessarily complex field for our purposes here. I want only to underline that we all have our cultural preferences. But there is probably a bit of each god in each of us and we are all to some degree adaptable – that is, when we have to, we will live in alien cultures, though usually unwillingly and at a price.

Our cultural preferences are probably thrust upon us by our early experiences and environments. No doubt some are born as Zeus or Dionysus, but since these cultures describe the ways we relate to our fellow men, it is likely that our attitudes to them are due more to our environments than to our genes. There is good evidence to suggest that certain cultures are more popular in certain societies, indicating that there is some kind of societal conditioning.

Japanese are different from Italians, aren't they? But were

they *born* different in their cultural preferences? Our education can bend us towards cultures or away from them, as can the values and customs of our early homes. Father's occupation is still the best predictor of the son's choice of job – and probably of culture as well.

And though people certainly can adapt, they do not necessarily adapt easily. If your organisation is currently manned by Apollonians, wanting a secure life and a fair day's pay for a fair day's work, it will be hard to create a range of developmental cells and Athenian attitudes. You have got to work with what you've got in the way of people. That applies to the organisation, to the catchment area of your work and to society as a whole. Deportation is becoming as rare in organisations as in society (it is almost necessary to prove an illegal offence before dismissing a man), and wholesale re-stocking of an organisation is unthinkable in democratic societies.

The tendencies of the 'people forces' are too varied to be easily summarised. Some of them are obvious:

Youth does not relish Apollo, with that culture's need to play down individuality;

The more you've been educated, formally, the further down the scale of cultures you are likely to be (e.g. doctors and architects, with unusually long training periods, are often Dionysian, the illiterate driver or entrepreneur a Zeus);

Educational philosophies which emphasise the individual and his development (as opposed to the inculcation of received wisdom or values), will produce people with Athenian or Dionysian preferences;

The hungry obey, the contented argue. Apollo cultures rely on an *economic* contract between organisation and employee, a contract that works best where economics matter most;

Personality characteristics affect cultural preferences. A restless intuitive extrovert will find Apollo tiresome. Individualists dislike Athena, with her group emphasis, as much as they do Apollo. Conformists prefer Apollo. And so on.

Remember that these are tendencies, not laws. As humans we

have the delightful ability to be the exceptions to our own generalisations.

DO THE GODS HAVE PERSONALITIES?

In his popular book *Know Your Own Personality*,* Eysenck has related two of the personality dimensions which he uses to categorise personality (Introversion-Extraversion and Stable-Unstable) with the traditional divisions of the ancients. It is interesting to speculate (there is no factual evidence) whether the quadrants provide clues to the personalities which I have associated with the different gods. Dionysus is the difficult one to fit into the picture. A law unto himself, a Dionysian can perhaps be found in any quadrant although some of the characteristics of the 'empty' quadrant (Melancholic) must fit many a 'loner'.

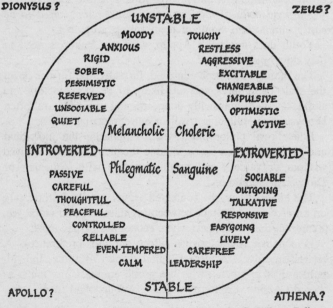

* *Know Your Own Personality* by H. J. Eysenck. G. Wilson, Pelican, 1976.

The Choice of Blend

Where do we go from here? The organisation is a mix of four activities (steady state, development, asterisk and management), each with its cultural god or gods. The proportion of each activity is influenced by the four forces. Thus a *large* organisation with *long life cycles*, operating in a low technology *facsimile pattern* with *minimally educated* workers from a depressed area is very likely, almost certain in fact, to have evolved with a large number of steady state activities and to be dominated by an Apollo role culture. Some canning factories, perhaps; the automobile industry in some of its parts; 'nuts and bolts' manufacturers of any size; the textile industry of yesterday.

A *small* organisation, making hand-made objects *to order* on a *unit* basis, with highly-trained *craftsmen*, will resemble a Dionysian partnership; whilst the account teams of an advertising agency, *smaller*, with *short life cycles* and requiring *talented groups* of people, will be very Athenian if successful; although some agencies have been built up by the careful selection of a few Zeus characters with their own webs (mini-agencies in fact under one umbrella).

If you want to know how you arrived where you are, this method of cultural analysis will explain it. If you want to know why there are more creaks and groans in the organisation than you would choose, this may provide the clue (a culture-mix out of line with the principal forces). If you, individually, are unfulfilled or uninspired or underpaid, this analysis may show you why (an Athenian trapped in a Temple?). More generally, cultural analysis will indicate the underlying reason for much of the incompetence in our organised society.

WORK-TYPES AND PEOPLE-TYPES

Is your work pattern recurrent (a repeating schedule of events) or fragmented?

Is it trouble-shooting or long-term requiring sustained attention? Is it responding or self-generating?

These questions come from Rosemary Stewart's investigations into the pattern of managerial work.* She finds three basic patterns, and some mixed.

Pattern 1 – Systems Maintenance *(Works Manager, Production Manager, Branch Manager)*
Exception-handling, responding to problems, monitoring performance. A fragmented work pattern, particularly in a variable market or work-flow situation, more crises than predictability. Frequently found in middle and junior management positions, not usually found in senior management except in small companies or with individuals who like to work this way. Will suit individuals who are energetic, resourceful, decisive and perhaps restless. Zeus perhaps?

Pattern 2 – Systems Administration *(Financial Accounting, Staff Manager)*
Concerned with the accurate processing of information and the administration of systems. The more formalised the organisation the more of these administrative, recurrent, time-deadline jobs there will be, particularly in the middle of junior levels. Suits those who like security and dead-lines. Apollo?

Pattern 3 – Project *(Research Manager, Project Leader, Product Sales Manager)*
Long term tastes, often of a one-off nature. Little recurrent work, more need for sustained attention. There will be a greater need for self-generation and any fragmentation will be self-imposed. Found at all managerial levels. Suits those who can sustain a self-generating interest over a long time. Athena?

Pattern 4 – Mixed *(General Manager, Production Engineer)*
A mixture of the previous three. The occupant of the job has to vary his work pattern. Management?

---

* See further STEWART R. *Contrasts in Management* McGraw-Hill June 1976.

Changes in the Balance

Any balance of gods and cultures, once achieved, is bound to be only temporary. Organisations must respond continually to their environment, even if they do not themselves set out to change that environment. Growth is one typical, self-induced problem of cultural change.

A small pottery of craftsmen inspired by its success to grow and mechanise, will run into conflicts as Dionysians are confronted with Apollonian systems. The people will resent the new need to keep count and to record, to itemise and to cost. They will dislike the necessity of employing non-potters at comparable salaries to sell or keep the accounts. They may hire an 'administrator' and hope that these new features of their life will go away. They won't. Although they themselves have created these new forces, their creatures have lives, or at least cultures, of their own.

This 'stage of growth' problem is a common one. Zeus begets Apollo as the system grows. Then Athena is needed to maintain the development. 'Management' comes to mean the co-ordination of all three, and sometimes four gods in one whole. Previously 'management' meant 'Zeus'. Now it only sometimes does. Naturally people find it hard to realise that a way of behaving which worked yesterday does not, cannot, work today. Self-imposed culture change of this sort is very stressful. It seems to carry with it a loss of identity as the culture shock gets personalised – 'I can no longer make things happen, what has gone wrong with *me*?'

The irony of success often lies in the fact that the methods which brought success are not those which are best suited to maintaining it. The commander who won battles was often the wrong person to administer the territories he had conquered. The planners are often the wrong people to implement their plans – culturally wrong, I mean – as the saga of the Bosco Chemical Factory demonstrates.

THE BOSCO CHEMICAL SAGA

Bosco Chemicals UK Ltd had been doing well. Their eight lines of imported pharmaceutical products had produced an annual growth of 25 per cent in turnover and profits. Hitherto they had been essentially a field sales force based on a warehouse in London, but they decided in 1970 that their turnover now justified doing the blending and formulation in a factory of their own. Based on estimated factory costs and the expectation of a continued growth in sales, the economics of the venture appeared good, for the base stock was available locally and the imported finished products had been expensive.

Being historically only a distributing organisation they had no manufacturing competence. So they bought some, the best. They hired a group of nine people to oversee the design and construction of the factory and then to be its first management team. The nine were young, highly qualified, well paid, and between them they covered the range of competences required. They were headed by Martin, 34, the factory manager designate. Martin typified his team. He was idealistic, enthusiastic and saw this job as an opportunity to show that factory work could be meaningful and interesting as well as profitable to individual and organisation.

For two years the nine worked together in one large room dominated by a model of the new factory in the centre. They were planning everything, from the layout of the machines to the decor of the refreshment room; from pay scales to uniforms. They sat in a circle. This in itself mirrored Martin's approach to management — a collaborative problem-solving activity spurred by mutual respect between colleagues. Hopefully the whole factory of 400 people would work like that. The room, when you visited it, was bubbling with excitement, ideas and lively good fellowship.

In the autumn of 1973 the factory opened, only a month behind schedule. There was a backlog of orders, piled up in anticipation of own-manufacture. But there was also a start of worldwide recession in the industry and a consequent tightening of margins. Inflation in the UK was starting to rise. The first months were difficult (teething problems, they called it) with machines breaking down, operators without experience, unanticipated quality problems. 1974 was a disaster. Sales were falling and the sales force were putting great pressure on the factory for immediate delivery, shorter production runs, special orders etc. But the factory was planned on the assumption of long, computer-calculated, standard production schedules. The planned system could not cope. Instead endless interim arrangements had to be made. Day was lived by day. Costs escalated. Tempers flared. The planned room for expansion (in staff and facilities) now looked like overcapacity without the expected increase in sales. Redundancy was ordered. Unions moved in.

The 'nine' met in almost constant session. In accordance with their tradition every problem was classified as a project and assigned a project team. In June 1974 there were 47 projects, and Bert (the production engineer) was involved in 23 of them. Martin was losing his hair and getting divorced. There was a general feeling in the group of puzzlement, dismay and irrational anger at fate. 'How could it be going wrong? We are all talented, young, hard-working, committed people, Why isn't it working?'

The company boss blamed Martin. He should get tough. Kick a few people. Shout more. Less of this endless committee work. Martin wanted time. You can't start up a factory in under two years. Participative problem-solving must be the best way. Mike (Production Manager) blamed participative problem-solving. 'It's just a pill factory,' he said. 'You don't need brains, only blokes, and some system.' Everyone else blamed the 'nine'. 'Why don't they do their job?' they said, 'always asking us to help with their problems. It's their business to manage, not ours. We knew there was a catch to all these fringe benefits and luxury coffee rooms.'

And then they started leaving. Three of the nine left for other companies, seeing no promotional prospects in Bosco. Martin fired one after an argument (which did a lot for his self-confidence). Redundancy slimmed down the workforce.

*Experience began to keep the machines working. Martin was
unexpectedly offered the job of New Product Manager in the
US parent company and accepted. Mike took over. Systems
superseded projects. Participative problem-solving was replaced in the jargon by 'role and responsibility'. The nine was
now three reporting to Mike. There were regular monthly
meetings for information exchange. Mike solved the problems
and told the others.*

*They say it's boring, but the results look good. Athena for
creating, Apollo for running a factory. But it's hard for the
same men to excel in initiating and in steady-state activities.
Organisations do adapt, but with pain and time unless they
understand what's happening to them.*

The general pattern is that change of any magnitude involves
a subsequent change in the balance of cultures and gods. If
that cultural change does not take place, there is a mismatch
between the demands of the work and the ways of managing
it – success has bred inefficiency through cultural imbalance.
But cultural change of the order needed in these situations is
hard to bring about deliberately. We are creatures of cultural
habits and do not change gods easily, particularly when those
gods have served us well in the past. It need cause us no surprise therefore to find that we have to be frightened into
cultural change – a kind of organisational culture shock is
needed. The sequence of major change in organisations is well-
established. It goes like this:

THE CHANGE SEQUENCE

*An analysis of the recorded major organisational changes of
recent years reveals an almost invariable sequence of events:*
*FRIGHT: The organisation is faced with unmistakable signs
of alarm – imminent bankruptcy, slump in sales, major strikes,
massive operational failures might be some of them.*
*NEW MEN: The new men set up a process of search and in-
vestigation into the major aspects of the organisation's activi-*

ties, usually through a newly-created set of study groups and task forces which tap new sources of talent and energy in the organisation.

RE-GROUPING: The study groups and task forces produce the data, and often the manpower, for a restructuring of the organisation and the introduction of new methods, systems and norms.

Only in additive *change, where an organisation adds on a significant new component, usually by purchase, is this sequence avoided. The new addition can in time begin to dominate the old and then impose its culture on the old.*

If we have to wait for fright to change us, it cannot be surprising that our organisations conceal so much inefficiency and slack due to a cultural imbalance in their ways of managing.

Linking the Gods

Given the right mix, the organisation still needs to be held together. The gods need to be linked. Failed linkages in institutions show up most dramatically in the scrapbook of 'goofs' held in the institutional memory of any organisation – the creations of the research department developed by someone else, the sales drive that ran out of goods to sell, the product switch which no one mentioned to the purchasing department; and so on. More insistently they show up in the arguments, bickerings and tribal wars that proliferate in organisations, particularly the bigger ones.

Cultural harmony within one part of the organisation is often nurtured and supported by deliberately distinguishing it from the other parts. Enmity without encourages harmony within. But this cultural isolation can destroy the total institution. Linkage between the cultures is essential, and effective linkage has three elements:

cultural tolerance;
bridges;
a common language.

When these fail, a fourth element, *slack*, will cover up the cracks, but slack is only the thermometer of inefficiency or incompetence, the outcome of mixed-up management.

CULTURAL TOLERANCE

Each culture has its own preferred ways of co-ordinating and controlling. The club cultures rely on trust, empathy and personal inspection. The role culture links defined jobs or roles by rules and procedures, and an inspection system to make sure that the rules and procedures are enforced. Task cultures, dealing always with new problems, plan and re-plan, using past data to correct future estimates and forecasts. Existential cultures relegate and delegate the co-ordinating function, calling it administration (a denigrating term for them).

But since, as I have shown, the ways of one culture are anathema to another, the personal visitation of a Zeus seems to an Apollonian an intrusion on private territory, reeking of distrust: 'Does he not believe my reports or understand the figures?' Zeus people, on the other hand, are bored by the formalities of Apollonian co-ordinating mechanisms and find them hard to use. The discussions and committees that lie behind the planning of Athenians seem like inefficiency to Apollonians, just as the disregard of Dionysians seems like irresponsibility.

But to impose your ways on others is bigotry, cultural sin. The first step, then, to effective linkage is to allow each part of the organisation to develop its own appropriate methods of co-ordination and control and to tolerate differences between the cultures. Otherwise one enters the 'Spiral of Distrust', when what seems sensible co-ordination to you appears intrusive control to the other.

THE SPIRAL OF DISTRUST

The principle of 'balance' keeps cropping up in life. There seems to be a reciprocal 'balancing' relationship between trust and control, so that where trust is increased control diminishes, and if you increase your control the perceived trust is decreased, as on a balance:

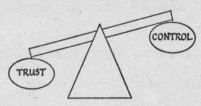

The farmer had been successful, he now operated three smallholdings (each of about 120 acres) in addition to his own home farm. Each smallholding was managed by one of his three sons (indeed he had bought them for this purpose). Clearly, he thought, good management required that he co-ordinate the work of the four farms so that he got optimum use of the central pool of capital equipment, better purchasing and sales deals, etcetera. The principle was so obvious that he didn't need to discuss it, he merely asked his sons for a weekly detailed advanced schedule of their work, followed up a week later by a matching report on work done, with, where appropriate, details of quantities.

The sons met in the house of the eldest. 'Father has been conning us along,' one said. 'He told us that he trusted us to run our own farms and would finance the start-up. Now it's clear that he wants to check on everything we do both before and after we do it. We are just employees – not his trusted sons. I propose that we demand that he hand us over the legal ownership of our farms, otherwise he is quite likely to sell them over our heads once we've put them in order.' 'And another thing,' said the third son, 'he's deliberately adding together all the proceeds so that we can't tell whose is what.'

The father was astonished. His attempts to start his sons off as independent farmers had resulted in outright rebellion. It must, he muttered, be the result of this new mood of distrust and independence in the youth of the country.

The possibility that his well-meant attempts at co-ordination looked like control, *which suggested, in that Zeus-like culture, a measure of* distrust, *simply did not occur to him.*

The spiral of distrust starts with good intentions and is often invisible.

But cultural tolerance is only the *prerequisite*, the necessary condition, of a balanced organisation. Much more, of a more positive nature, is needed to link the cultures.

BRIDGES

Some well known work in organisation theory* has demonstrated that the more 'differentiation' there is between the people, the work, ideologies and time-horizons of different parts of an organisation, the more methods of 'integration' are needed. The idea of balance again. Like many of the precepts of organisation theory, this is blindingly obvious once it has been stated. In our terms, the more diverse the cultures the more bridges you need.

Bridges range from copies of correspondence, through joint committees (with appeals to superior courts or umpires), to co-ordinating individuals, liaison groups or project teams. In between them are what might be called pontoons, or the temporary bridges of task forces, study groups or 'confrontation meetings' between the arguing groups.

Without bridges the cultures go their separate ways (resulting usually in lowered efficiency and the occasional goof), or they have to be held together at the top by imposed directives, decrees and referee-like decisions. Using the top of the organisation as the principal 'bridge' not only distorts the structure and corrupts the cultures, but occupies an undue proportion of the top people's time.

* Lawrence, P. R. and Lorsc J. W., *Organisation and Environment,* Boston. Harvard University, 1967.

THE PARADOX OF DELEGATION

The Chief Executive was explaining his way of management.

'I've taken my job,' he said, 'which is running the organisation, I suppose, and then I've split it down into its constituent parts (such as Planning, Financial Control, Sales etc) and then put a man in charge of each. That way I've delegated my total work and am free to act as a counsellor, consultant or arbitrator to any of them as and when needed. Look,' he added, 'an empty desk, an empty diary: perfect delegation, wouldn't you say?'

Three months later I saw him again.

'How's it working?' I asked.

'The system's fine,' he replied, 'it's the people, they're not up to it. They are very blinkered, can't take an overall perspective. Do you think they can be educated to think like Directors of the Company?'

'How do you mean?' I asked.

'Well, everything I push down to them seems to come back to me as an argument to be resolved. Our Board Meetings consist of a set of functional viewpoints leaving me to take the company view and make the decision. They can't see beyond their own function, yet in their position every functional problem concerns others as well as themselves.'

'But that's what you wanted wasn't it?' I said, 'you delegated everything except co-ordination, compromise and linkage, so that remains your job.'

'I suppose that's true,' he said, ruefully. 'But it wasn't what I intended. Now I'm busier than I ever was before I delegated it all so neatly. I'm so busy I don't have time to think, let alone be counsellor, consultant and all those other things I talked about. I've got back more than I gave away, it's like delegating into the wind.'

'Perhaps you should try delegating some of your linkage responsibility as well as your functional supervision. After all, if you can only cross the river at its top it will not only be a

*very busy bridge but other people are going to have to do a
lot of walking.'*

The 'matrix organisation' (in which the demands for co-
operation between functions are met by full-time project groups
made up of representatives from the functions, operating under
project leaders) is the ultimate 'bridged' organisation. In this
design the cultural priorities of the functions are exported into
the project groups. In these groups much depends on the
leadership capacity of the project leader to make an effective
bridge, bonding the capabilities of the functions to a common
good. He is helped in this task if he has the power of *selection*
and/or promotion, if the projects control the allocation of
new investment, and if the project group has full use of each
individual's *time.* On the other hand, putting too much
emphasis on the 'bridge' may be to weaken the individual cultures or functions. The balance can be restored by giving some
of the powers (of appointment, or production) back to the
functions, or retaining them for the centre or top of the organisation. This will weaken the power of the projects but
strengthen the functions. It has been argued that projects
pursue the practical, functions the ideal, in a matrix organisation. Balance would suggest the need for a constantly shifting distribution between these two.

Few organisations will find that the complexity justifies the
cost of a full matrix organisation. Few will be content with
a bridge only at the top. Most will locate a bridge at the points
of major interaction between the cultures – where research
meets production, for instance, or where purchasing, production and sales combine in a production schedule. Some will
include bridges between policy management and executive
supervision. The first question clearly is – how many bridges
and where? The temptation for management is always to
overdo it. It feels lonely at the top when you don't know what
is going on or know who does know. The danger of too much
co-ordination is not only its cost, but the ever-lurking 'spiral
of distrust'. The danger of too little is, of course, the goofs and

sub-optimisation referred to earlier. On balance, experience would suggest that we should make do with as little as we can, even at the risk of a goof. There is an established connection between the *quantity* of co-ordination and the degree of apathy in organisations. The more co-ordination the greater the apathy. The invisible apathy may well cost more than the occasional but visible goof. If, of course, goofs are either illegal (e.g. in hospitals or government) or extremely costly, the apathy may have to be endured.

The second decision to be taken on bridging is the method. There are essentially *three* ways of achieving formal co-ordination in organisations, by *grouping, central information,* or *liaison.*

Grouping. Essentially this means putting all the functions concerned with a problem into one group with one objective. In a factory, instead of having a production unit serviced by engineers quality control, maintenance, and production development, there is one of each of these in the unit, so that all the bits to be co-ordinated are represented there. The matrix organisation applies this method in the extreme. It is effective but clearly very expensive, since to work it properly you need to have an engineer, quality controller, maintenance officer and development officer for each group or problem.

Central Information. By this method, all the information necessary for co-ordination is routed, by manual documentation or computer, to a central point, usually at that position in the hierarchy which could be called the lowest cross-over point in the organisation chart of the points to be linked. In a predictable world it is quite possible to work out what information is needed when and where, in order to allow particular decisions to be made. One can even state in advance the criteria for these decisions, so that they can be made automatically by the computer when the decision is at hand. The impact of the computer on organisational decision-making (as opposed to record keeping) is here – in this form of bridging. The airline booking operations, the computerised stock-control systems, even the automatic entry gates to car parks, rely on this vertical information system of linkage. Central information works well in predictable situations, if the humans involved can live up to the accuracy required. Most systems however are over designed and very vulnerable to human error. One fool can gum up the whole works.

Liaison. This is the most tenuous form of bridge. It relies on one man telling another what he is doing, wants to do, or cannot do. Liaison can be helped along by the disciplines of committees, by formally circulated information, or by permanent liaison officers (a sort of human bridge), but ultimately it does depend on the willingness of individuals to talk, discuss and compromise on both means and ends.

There are cultural affinities to these bridges. The Athenian culture prefers liaison, with its flexibility and emphasis on trust and informal ways. Apollo cultures like Central Information and the kind of certainty and predictability that this involves. And Zeus cultures, quite properly, like the Group, with all that they need under their own command.

But organisations remain a cultural mix and require a mix of bridging mechanisms. The temptation is to overdo one's preferred mechanism and to attempt to apply it to the other cultures. The tidiness of the data and the forms of Central Information cannot apply throughout the organisation without reducing its flexibility. Apollonians must show some cultural tolerance in their bridges with the task cultures. Zeus cultures must allow more systematisation than they are comfortable with. One must, in short, resist the instinctual pull of one's own culture if the bridge is with another culture.

The cultural split implied by bridging two different cultures occurs in its most obvious form in the role of the liaison man who must stand with a foot in each. The 'Integrator', as he has been called, has become a prized person in the complex organisations of today – and a special person. The successful liaison man, we know from research, is knowledgeable about each of the areas he has to bridge and is respected by both, is of high status in the organisation so that he can get things done, is skilled in interpersonal relationships and has a high tolerance for stress. Not a job for a weakling! Nor for a very young man, or for someone who has failed in the mainstream. The stress arises, in my view, from the great difficulty of having to live in two cultures simultaneously. It is hard to sustain this dual nationality. Most liaison men become identified in time with one side or the other, thus reducing their efficiency as a bridge and turning liaison into negotiation. A better understanding of the cultures and their preferences might make it easier for these human bridges to carry out their very difficult but necessary role.

Nowadays the supervisor and the junior manager are often liaison men parading under more formal titles. Their job is to link a number of lateral forces, often without the formal authority to do so. It is at their level that the asterisk situations we have referred to earlier arise – situations where the possible is to be preferred to the ideal, where trust and intuition and empathy are quicker than formal communication, and where interpersonal relationships are critical: Zeus situations in fact. Good liaison men are Zeus characters, but they often act as bridges between *Athenian* task forces. They need cultural self-discipline.

Any inhabitant of organisations will have perceived the law of the pendulum at work as the organisation centralises, and then a few years later decentralises, only to centralise again in due course. Here the organisation is intuitively searching for a new balance: it swings from Central Information to a mixture of Groups and Liaison and back again. The search for balance is never-ending. The pendulum is inevitable, but if done with cultural understanding the pain is less.

A COMMON LANGUAGE

The third aspect of linkage is a common language. 'An organisation that talks together walks together', one might say. But the vocabulary of organisations differs from our everyday conversation. What is it that goes across the various bridges in the linking systems? What does the organisation choose to talk about? Is it sales? Or costs? Or productivity? What concealed but central values are revealed by its private codes or the fashionable jargon of the day?

What are the critical figures or columns in the formal reporting system? Do the internal memoranda refer to people, or reports, or departments? What does the private humour reveal as the 'in' buzz-words? What are the failures you mustn't make?

A supervisor was studying the 40 pages of internal information circulated monthly to all departments of the great integrated multi-department corporation. 'Do you use all this?' he was asked. 'O no,' he replied. 'I only look at this figure on page 22. If it's up I'm OK, down and I'm in trouble.'

The choice of what you count, what you compare with what, what you show to whom, has a clear effect on behaviour. Do you compare performance with past performance or with planned performance? Do you count functional results or overall results? It is little point talking profits if the reporting system only counts sales and costs except at the very top.

The code will indicate where the power lies and what method of linkage is most important.

ORGANISATIONAL CODES

An internal memo in a Zeus culture will often read like a private family letter. For example, 'In view of Jeremy's information, JGH suggested that we suggest to Bob H that he try to win over Peter McK in the hope that his support will be conclusive. RTC agreed to follow this up after talking to TStJR and GJS.'

Apollonian communiques bristle with terms like MKR/Z, PROD/EVR/S, JDRs and FSPs which refer to Departments or regular documentary returns.

Task cultures are full of commando language – 'Bill's Gang', 'the Television Group', 'the Forward Planning People'.

Dionysians use professional rather than organisational codes, demonstrating their true allegiance.

All these codes are baffling to the outsider, but serve a function in linking the organisation together, as long as both sides understand them. Language however can be a barrier as much as a bridge.

The slang, the buzzwords and the current jargon will point to current priorities – 'Objectives', 'Participation', 'Quality' or 'Health and Cleanliness'.

It is easy to be quietly humorous about the languages of organisations, but words do affect behaviour. Language is normally but a mirror of its society, but it can be used more deliberately to shape and direct the preoccupations and priorities of that society, or to reinforce new bridging mechanisms. If, for instance, a 'group' system is introduced the reporting mechanism must reflect the new system by producing 'group' data. If quality is more important than quantity, the informal vocabulary should reflect that. And the languages should coincide. It is no use preaching productivity to the unions if the statistical vocabulary does not contain appropriate productivity statistics. You can detect an organisation's heart by looking at its language.

The temptation is to follow one's personal cultural instincts. The quandary is how far to 'sin', to go against the instincts in the interests of cultural propriety, to use new vocabularies deliberately to send new messages, in order to achieve a new internal balance in the organisation. The instinct of a Zeus to rely on informal conversations to inject new values and goals may not carry over to the Apollonian part of the organisation, which will expect these changes to be reflected in the statistics of the reporting system. Athenians won't believe them unless they are incorporated in revised group assignments.

Slack – The Price of Imbalance

If linkage is not achieved, the gaps get filled in by *slack* and organisational slack indicates some fat somewhere in the system. A small degree of slack is no bad thing: a fully lean organisation will find it hard to cope with any irregularities in its planned activities. Slack can be used to iron out bumps, to live through difficult periods, take advantage of unexpected opportunities. But slack that conceals poor linkage, or a mismatch of gods, is a cancer in the body of the organised society. Like cancer it can grow unnoticed until it gets so bad that the whole body begins to decay. By then it is too often too late to intervene.

Now slack takes various forms:

Investment. Equipment and facilities are provided to cope with the peaks of quality or quantity, leaving 'slack' in the troughs. Seasonal industries (e.g. soft drinks, photo-finishing, tourism) invest for summer peaks. Quality-conscious industries tool up for the highest quality even if such small tolerances are required only for a small portion of their work.

Staffing. Many organisations staff up to meet all contingencies, including sickness, holidays as well as peak-loading. Industries which peak daily (catering, commuter transport) have a daily slack problem. Slack in staff can create self-fulfilling prophecies: over-recruitment to cover wastage can actually encourage it, as people see a visible excess and leave before they are pushed.

Systems. Systems can be designed to cope with an expanded operation; but do not flex with the varying size of the operation, so that a small workload incurs the full weight of co-ordination, systems and controls, or trivial decisions get the full boardroom policy routine.

Time. The more time you have at your disposal the less you need of other forms of slack. In the quality furniture trade it is customary to manufacture only against a firm customer order. This practice allows one to carry minimum stocks (no investment slack), but makes production planning very difficult so that one probably has to carry excess personnel (staffing slack).

Margins. High margins permit one to carry other types of slack, including error slack. Technologies where speed is more important than accuracy (e.g. trading) often carry high margins to allow for error slack. It is an established fact that stock-market ratings of earnings per share rise in relation to the likelihood of risk, or error. It is then the customer who pays.

Errors. Error slack usually accompanies high margins on the assumption that the errors will be corrected. The existence of room for errors in the tradition of the industry allows one to skimp on systems, but of course results in poor quality and shoddy work if the errors do not get corrected in time.

We can choose our slack, although usually we fall into line with the traditions of our industry, occupation or society. It can be argued that it is Britain's tradition of using staffing slack rather than investment slack that has been a major contributor to her successive economic crises. Labour has historically been cheap in Britain, and investment more lucratively routed overseas to the old Empire. As a result British firms tend to be over-manned and underequipped, compared with, for example, the USA where capital was readily available and labour scarce. Now of course the labour slack in Britain is no longer cheap. In cutting down that slack, a pool of unemployment is created, but, and possibly more serious, the slack has not been replaced by investment slack, margin slack is seldom possible in the conditions of international competition (although continual devaluations can help), leaving any needs for slack to be met by time (overdue delivery dates) or error (poor quality), or high domestic prices. The organised society pays for its slack through its consumers.

On an organisational scale there are cultural preferences for slack. Club cultures prefer margin slack. This gives room for experiment, allows people to learn by their mistakes without ruining the institution, and permits flexibility. When appropriate they would like to back this up with investment slack as a form of equipment back-up to their key resource – individuals.

Role cultures believe in system and staffing slack. In their way of thinking, the capital assets of the operation can be used efficiently or inefficiently depending on the way the work is planned and carried out. They like to play on the slack of 'human resources' (believing these to be the most flexible of resources) and on chains of systems. The ability to draw at will on a pool of retained labour has, for instance, long been at the heart of the automobile industry's way of working.

Task cultures like investment slack, again as equipment for their talents to work upon, and time. Where time is unavailable they will tend to staff up – more brainpower will produce good results quicker.

Luckily, existential cultures have small linkage requirements. Luckily, because these cultures seldom have the resources to create investment slack, they abhor systems slack and are unlikely to add deliberately to their number to create staffing slack. When therefore the Dionysians of an existential culture have to be co-ordinated there are usually delays (time slack) or mistakes (error slack).

It is when the comparative costs of the different forms of slack change, as in Britain in the 1970s, that management has to reconsider, and often to act against, its cultural instincts. Club cultures, for instance, are often accustomed to working in a mini-monopoly situation where, for reasons of geography (they are in a regionally distant market), size (they are too small to bother with) or custom (the norms of the cartel or industry or occupation), they have price discretion and could use the slack of high margins. When they expand, they encounter competition and have to cut slack in order to compete. If they do not at the same time improve their linkage they will have to find another form of slack. If they are not careful, that slack will be of the time or error variety. Thus it is that growth in Zeus cultures can often result in inefficiency.

Role cultures, used to a pool of cheap labour, and with decision routines which examine investment projects with a microscope whilst overlooking major staffing decisions, may have to change their ways if the pool gets expensive and can no longer be fished at will. Investment may then be the appropriate form of slack if linkage fails.

LABOUR AS 'A' FIXED COST

A friend was attending an international management course in Belgium. The British executives were complaining loud and long that management in Britain had become impossible due to the burden of legislation and the impossibility of moving your labour force around, or reducing it, as you wanted.

'Aw shucks!' said the American, 'We've lived with that situation in Scandinavia for years. It's easy. You just treat your labour as a fixed cost.'

There was a perplexed silence.

'And so . . .?' asked a timid voice.

'Why then your investment is your variable. You build lots of small plants and close down or open whole plants. Play around with the operation, not the people.'

It's only a change in slack.

The Role of the Missionary Manager

Cultural propriety might appear a rather obvious virtue. Surely every organisation intuitively reacts to the influencing forces in its environment and seeks to minimise inappropriate forms of slack? Indeed, if it does not, will it not be starved of profit and therefore of its prospects for survival? Why then should not a purely mercenary approach be in fact the best way of securing that cultural propriety which will in turn remove any unwanted slack or unnecessary incompetence?

This is the essential premise of capitalism. I shall argue at more length later that this premise will not hold much longer. Here we can at least recognise that the principle is fallible even now. It is true that *gross* incompetence or excessive slack usually results in a loss of clients and thence in organisational death, given a free market. But how many markets are free? For a start, all professions have a protected market, as do all Government agencies. These are organisations just like any others, and often affect one's lives more deeply than those of commerce and industry. Incompetence or slack in these areas is protected by regulation – a slow-moving and ineffective device, particularly where, as in the case of the professions, the police and the civil service, it is self-policed. Then the industrial and commercial organisations owned by the state normally have protected markets, at least in their own countries. There are exceptions, notably the automobile industry in France, Britain and Germany, but the exceptions are rare enough to be noticeable. Finally, in the private sector of commerce and industry, how effective a policeman is competition among rivals? Where monopoly is outlawed most businessmen would prefer an oligopoly where a number of firms run *parallel* businesses, competing in defined ways in defined areas but usually mirroring each other's cultural patterns. True competition comes from outside, from another country or another technology carrying with it different assumptions about cultures and slack. And when that true competition arrives, there is no shortage of squeals of anguish, pleas for tarriff barriers and for technological protection (once it was for textile workers, now for shoe-makers).

Profit – the major mercenary objective – is more easily guaranteed by seeking to win an area of price discretion than by eliminating slack. In these days where profit margins are increasingly regulated, decreased costs can actually result in decreased profits. Indeed, profit can be the result of inefficiency rather than efficiency in a situation where *margins* are controlled but not the final price.

PROFIT AS THE MEASURE OF INEFFICIENCY

In my early days in the oil industry, a marketing cartel still operated in various parts of the world, a cartel in which the major companies agreed to preserve their existing market shares in each territory (the 'As Is' agreement).

Under this arrangement, the oil companies became essentially monopoly distribution systems for a vital commodity: justifiable, perhaps, in an age when oil supplies were limited and capital could have been wasted in unnecessary fields at the

*consumer end. However, profit was still used as the measure
of efficiency.*

*One of my first tasks was to compile the price lists for
lubricating oils. It was a simple task, actually. There was a
printed list of cost items for each brand. I got the relevant
figures from Accounts and added on the 15 per cent profit
margin (not excessive, the companies saw themselves as non-
exploitative), and put the final total down as the new price.*

*After a couple of weeks, I commented to the Sales Manager
that this system was a recipe for inefficiency since the higher
our costs the higher would be the 15 per cent margin. He
was horrified at the thought. Conditioned to believe that higher
profit was always good, he could not bring himself to consider
that it might only indicate inefficiency in a monopolistic service
industry.*

*This particular cartel ended soon afterwards when oil
supplies increased and the companies went on the search for
new markets. The counterparts to this story continue however in many industries and trades in many pockets of society.*

In most Western countries over 50 per cent of Gross Domestic
Product is already in the public sector with protected markets.
If an honest evaluation were made of the remainder, a large
part would consist either of professional fees, practical oli-
gopolies of parallel businesses, or territorial monopolies
equivalent to the small regional equipment rental operation,
or the village store whose monopoly is too small for others to
wish to intervene. All these areas have price discretion to some
degree. The discipline of competition and the whip of profit
will punish only *gross* incompetence or *excessive* slack. No,
cultural propriety, like social propriety, cannot be enforced,
only desired. Mercenary organisations and mercenary managers are not in themselves enough. They must be missionaries
too if incompetence, mixed-up management, that first
dilemma of the organised society, is to be resolved.

THE SECOND DILEMMA: EFFICIENCY VERSUS INDIVIDUALISM

The Apollonian Crises and The Organisation of Consent and Contract

The three preceding chapters have suggested that if organisations sorted out their managerial philosophies and got all their gods in the right place, with the right followers, all would be well. And so it would be – in theory. But unfortunately the sorting out process itself raises another problem, the one I have called the second dilemma.

This section of the book looks ahead over the coming five years or so, to the time when it looks as if there must be an inevitable confrontation of organisational gods. Expressed in my metaphor, there will be (already are?) too many followers of Athena and Dionysus (experts and individuals) in society just when organisational logic requires a growing supply of Apollonians (bureaucrats). The resulting conflict, which will increasingly take place inside organisations, is destructive for both individuals and organisations.

As I explain in the next chapters the pressures of a growing individualism are not going to go away. Organisations and the organised society as a whole are already reacting to this confrontation particularly in Britain, but also in Scandinavia and increasingly in other Western countries. I will argue that these reactions are misjudged or inadequate, and will not in themselves be enough to stop or even diminish the likely conflict.

A more radical approach is needed, a new vision of the management task, involving a realignment of the gods. Apollo cannot win, and if efficiency is to live with individualism we must find other ways of managing.

If we do not urgently revise the way we design and run our organisations the decision will be taken out of our hands, because they will, many of them, self destruct. No one will enjoy the resulting trauma.

Negative Power

Chapter 5

THE DILEMMA OF APOLLO

The Drift to Apollo

If you are sitting near the top of an organisation, responsible in whole or in part for its continued success or at least survival, there is a strong urge to want to make it *bigger* and more *internally consistent*. There are good reasons for each of these tendencies which need owe nothing to the supposed egos, lust for power or dictatorial ambitions of those in authority.

First, bigness. The bigger you are, the more able you are to influence your own destiny. A small organisation has to ask others for money: banks, other lenders, the stock-market, the government. The more money you, as manager,* can generate internally, the less you are dependent on others, and if and when you need their money, the more likely they are to believe your estimate of your future. The bigger, therefore, the easier.

And bigness brings clout: clout in the market-place, enabling one to offer comprehensive ranges or services, to launch sales drives, price offensives or massive advertising campaigns; clout in the research laboratories, allowing adequate finance for adequate research and development, all of which is insurance against the future (93 per cent of the research in Britain happens in large (over 3,000) firms); clout in recruitment, offering scope for varied careers within the protection of one organisation.

And finally, bigness brings flexibility and a built-in insur-

* Of course, pure capitalist theory would have all surplus earnings returned to the owners who would then decide where it was appropriate to re-invest. But this 'city-state' view of the capitalist notion implies a more perfect market, better information and speedier decision processes than could in practice exist, so the managerial prerogative has become enlarged until managers have acquired the right to re-invest their earnings in the continuation of the business. Due payment must be made, in dividends or interest, for the *use* of the capital, but the capital itself is seldom returned voluntarily to the owners.

ance. A loss in one area can be offset against unusual profits elsewhere. Resources can be taken from one use and given to another without the need for anyone outside to know or be concerned. It is no accident that the big corporations are private universes, revealing only the tips of their icebergs to their shareholders in their balance sheets or to their employees in their internal communications. Privacy carries its freedoms and as the custodians of the organisation's future, its managers and directors understandably want as much discretion as they can retain, and bigness to provide that discretion.

WHY DO FIRMS GROW?

A recent analysis of the evolution of Giant Firms in Britain was made by S. J. Prais.*

He pointed out that the share of net output contributed by the 100 largest manufacturing firms in Britain rose from 16 per cent in 1900 to 22 per cent in 1949 and to 41 per cent in 1970. But whilst the size of firms has increased, the size of plants has remained relatively static. Prais argues that it is economics in marketing, transport and the likelihood of cheaper finance that encourage growth, not economies of scale at the plant level.

Does it work?

Leslie Hannah and John Kay** in another recent work agree that while firms grow plants remain small, but found little evidence that the new giants performed better. The giants certainly export less, and have higher labour costs than the overall average.

In search for the 'clout' of size have we lost efficiency?

The second urge is towards *consistency*. Consistency is desirable to a manager in two ways. If the future is consistent with

* S. J. Prais: *The Evolution of Giant Firms in Britain*, Cambridge, University Press, 1977.
** L. Hannah and J. Kay: *Concentration in Modern Industry*, Macmillan, 1977.

one's expectations of it, then planning can be tighter and all the provisions for that future taken care of – in that way things will happen as they were expected to happen. A catering firm once claimed that the *predictability* of its operations was such that it could forecast to within two dozen the number of eggs that would be consumed by its 250 London outlets in any given day. This consistency over time allowed it to run a more cost-effective purchasing and delivery system than its competitors.

Most organisations seek to achieve the *consistency of predictability* by choosing the kind of future they want and then setting out to achieve it. That is not quite the way they put it, of course. They talk instead of forecasts, long-term plans and corporate objectives, but essentially these plans are intended to be self-fulfilling prophecies. J. K. Galbraith, the American economist, has found alarming portents in the ability of large corporations to create self-fulfilling prophecies, seeing this as a corruption of democracy. Others have deplored the way the consumer becomes just a part of the corporation's plans, the patient an 'input' to the hospital's operations. We need not, at this stage, take sides on the rights and wrongs of this managerial urge for predictability, but only take the plaints as evidence of its existence.

Managerially, consistency over time, or predictability, is highly desirable. The longer one can guarantee predictability, the more scope there is for tightening up the operational side of the organisation. Consistency over time is an entirely normal and appropriate instinct for those seeking managerial comfort.

UNPREDICTABILITY AT HOME
Have you ever stayed in an unpredictable household?

> *'Is there anything for supper?'*
> *'How should I know, have a look. There may be if the children haven't eaten it all. There isn't anything? Well, don't blame me, I've had other things to do.'*
>   *or*

'Where's Alan, we've got to leave now?'
'He's gone off on his bike.'
'Did he say when he'd be back?'
'No idea.'

or

'I need the car today, dear.'
'You can't have it, I'm afraid, I'm driving to Gateshead.'
'Well, then, how do I get to mother's?'

For a time, the feeling of spontaneity carries its own brand of charm. On a holiday the charm can linger for days, even weeks. But slowly the irritation mounts, and its costs. It is impossible to plan in these conditions. Time is wasted as people stand around. Activities cannot be co-ordinated or days organised in advance. Every joint venture becomes a major event. Instead of everyone doing his or her own thing, everyone begins to feel thwarted by the others. Tempers flare. Stress mounts.

Organisations demand predictability.

Consistency across activities, *comparability*, is also highly desirable. In any case, it is being pressed upon us in organisations whether we desire it or not.

Comparability is desirable, even essential, for the *dovetailing* that lies at the heart of most organisational activities. One task depends on another and contributes to another. Seen at its most obvious in the automated assembly-line, the principle of dovetailing applies to the accounts department and the despatch warehouse as much as to the factory.

Comparability is necessary for *control* from the top. Without a proper basis for comparison, control becomes arbitrary, governed more by whims and impulses than by rationality.

Comparability is imperative in certain *work-flows*, particularly the copy or flow types. The arrival of new expensive technology which demands high throughput to justify its existence drives organisations to flow or copy work-patterns, and the consistency or comparability which these demand.

The high technology of process industries is one example of a technology demanding a precise standard of consistency between inputs in order to operate efficiently. More commonly, the computer, with its insatiable appetite for input data, has imposed copy conditions across organisations which did not need them or want them.

Consistency is also forced upon organisations from outside. The spate of legislation, of government regulations, of union bargaining mechanisms, all encourage consistency, a comparability across activities. In some organisations, this consistency is achieved initially through *centralisation*: by, for instance, establishing a central negotiating office to deal with union negotiations. But centralisation is only one way, and can be the most costly, to achieve the consistency which is often the driving force behind the apparent need to centralise.

There are, then, these twin pressures towards *bigness* and *consistency*. They are not only understandable, but, viewed from the standpoint of operational efficiency, much to be desired. In the original sense of the word, things are more 'manageable' if they are under our control. Bigness and consistency both increase control. Unsurprisingly, ambitious managers concentrate their attention on opportunities for growth and on improved systems of control.

However, both bigness and consistency imply an *Apollonian culture*. Size, as we have already shown in an earlier chapter, brings formality, impersonality and rules and procedures in its train. There is no way out of it. When a man cannot rule by glance of eye and word of mouth because there are just too many people, he has to lean on formal systems of hierarchy, information and control. Similarly, consistency implies budgets, forms, standardised methods, fixed reporting periods, common documents and the whole barrage of bureaucracy. The ineluctable logic of efficiency drives organisations towards Apollo and the role culture.

It has been suggested that by the end of the century fewer than 200 companies will control more than 70 per cent of private sector activity in the Western democracies. In Britain the 100 largest manufacturing companies accounted for 22 per cent of total net output in 1949, but 41 in 1970.

The consistent trend in organisational reform in the British public sector has been towards amalgamation and standardisation. The comprehensive schools have typically been created by a merger of one 'grammar' school with one 'secondary modern'. The McKinsey reform of the National Health service amalgamated into one regional organisation the remedial, preventive and service activities that had previously run their own separate affairs. The Maud reforms of local authorities created larger and more all-embracing units. The Water Authorities have decreased in number but increased in scope.

A recent piece of research by John Child of Aston University shows that in the faster growing and more profitable large companies, as total size increases, so do certain types of systems and procedures: sophisticated financial controls applied to a wide range of activities, a precise definition of operative tasks by management, the application of work study and methods, the use of labour turnover statistics, the planning of recruitment, and the regular updating of company forms and documents.

The Resistance to Apollo

Unfortunately, logic no longer reigns supreme. Psychology also counts, and these Apollonian systems are managed and worked by humans. And from these humans comes an increasing resistance to the inexorable advance of the Apollonian culture. One strand of this resistance suggests that we are creating systems that are simply too complex to be managed by humans, that logic has outdistanced psychological capacity.

A second strand argues that the extreme specialisation of the work role is alienating, that it deprives man of control over his destiny and splits his work off from his other lives: family, recreation, community.

A third strand says that, rightly or wrongly, the new norms and values of society expressed through our schools and traditions of child-rearing, do not encourage the kind of obedience and subordination to imposed methods which are required by Apollonian organisations.

THE FIRST STRAND OF RESISTANCE

Size brings complexity, and it may well be that we cannot humanly handle the complex decisions of the mammoth corporations within the time available. Professor Elliott Jaques believes that individuals of immense conceptual span are needed, and that there are too few of these around in any generation. The evidence of mergers has been that bigness on its own does not lead to increased efficiency but rather the reverse, as we import more administrative 'slack' to handle the increased complexity. Computers have immeasurably increased our capacity to handle information and complexity, but they have also added hugely to the information that we have to handle. Some multi-nationals, looking at the incredible complexity of trying to manage a wide range of national subsidiaries in a constantly shifting environment, have, in a sense, abandoned the pursuit of 'the one best' solution and left their subsidiaries to go their own way. Most managers would agree that the apparent logical pull of bigness and consistency does not seem to make their job any easier.

A cultural analysis according to patron gods would suggest why. The Apollonian culture demanded by bigness and consistency will work as long as the work is routine, the environment stable and change infrequent. Unfortunately, as an organisation gets larger, it *imports* uncertainty when it begins to get involved with more and more outside groups, and becomes exposed to a wider range of forces. Ironically, as an organisation gets larger, it *ought* to attempt to make do with *less* of Apollo's culture rather than more. This is the first glance at the Apollonian paradox: the tendency for Apollo to self-destruct. For just as size creates an *internal* need for Apollonian methods, so the very increase in that culture tends to make the total organisation less responsive to its environment, less capable of changing, more dinosaur-like than ever – impressive but out of touch, and often out of control.

The first consequence of the excessive complexity of large Apollonian systems is what Derek Sheane of ICI has called the 'symptomology of bureaucratic breakdown'.* His list of symptoms includes:

1. The invisible decision: no-one knows how or where decisions are taken;
2. Unfinished business: too many tasks get started but not finished;
3. Co-ordination paralysis: nothing can be done without checking with a host of other interconnected units;
4. Nothing new: bureaucracies polish but do not invent. This applies to both processes and products;
5. Pseudo problems: bureaucracies seem to magnify some issues until they become an internal organisational epidemic, for no apparent reason;
6. Embattled centre: the conflicts between the centre and the local or regional units increase as the centre battles for consistency;
7. Negative deadlines: the dates for reports and historical explanations become more important than doing the work. He who carries bad news gets priority over good news;
8. In-tray domination: individuals react to their inputs rather than impose their own initiatives.

THE COSTS OF WAITING

Specialisation ought to make things change, but the costs of co-ordinating specialised activities can hugely outweigh the savings.

---

* In his stimulating booklet *Beyond Bureaucracy*, 1976, available from Management Research.

Take batch production.

The component to be manufactured is split down to a set of operations on machine tools. There may be as many as twenty separate operations. Each operation will involve a different tool, or at least a different setting of the same tool. In between operations, the component has to wait. It has been calculated* that out of the average 100 days it takes a component to go through a normal efficient factory, it will spend 99 days just waiting. The cost in work-in-progress can be huge if the material of the component is expensive.

In the name of consistency, we specialise, then we co-ordinate, and so we pay.

The second consequence of excessive complexity is that the burden of holding the thing together now falls upon the manager – typically the middle manager. In a straightforward Apollonian role culture, he would be an ordinary man in a straightforward routine administrative job. Instead, today, in the oversized organisation, he receives all the imported *uncertainty*, yet is equipped only with the (Apollonian) methods for dealing with *certainty*. Lashed in by the rules and procedures dictated by the pressures for consistency, he has to find a way of coping with the inconsistent. He can only do it, Zeus-like, by ignoring the rules and procedures, by playing organisational politics, by taking organisational risks, and by working enormously hard. Many succeed in doing this, but the costs can be high, both to themselves and to their organisations. It is understandable if they feel themselves underrewarded in a society that depends on the organisations which they seem to be carrying on their shoulders.

The cost of coping with imported uncertainty in an Apollonian system designed for certainty is overload. When the overload gets too much, ways of coping with it have to be evolved. All of these 'coping mechanisms' in effect create slack or inefficiency in the organisation.

* By D. T. N. Williamson in 'The Anachronistic Factory', Personnel Review, 1973.

COPING WITH OVERLOAD

Think of yourself when tired, when there is more to do than you can easily cope with.

Do you ever:

Polarise – Push problems into extremes of black or white, good or bad? Do you find yourself saying to a subordinate 'I don't want to know that there are pros and cons, I want to know it is viable or not?' (It is easier to decide between black and white than shades of grey).

Shorten Time-Horizons – Put off to tomorrow that which does not have to be done today, leave the five-year plan till the week after next, think about the growing apathy over the Christmas holidays. (Postponement of longer-term decisions is one way to lessen the load).

Search for Routines – say 'What did we do last time?' or 'PO requirement' even if the situation doesn't neatly fit that box? (Finding a routine avoids a decision).

Delight in Trivia – when baffled, turn your attention to an easy problem or delve into some issue of minor importance? (Taking the easy things first does at least reduce the load).

React not Proact – Deal with the In-tray before going out to change the world, cope with events as they arrive rather than seek to influence them before they arrive. (Re-activity reduces the list of things to be done, pro-activity adds to it).

Flare Up – Show irritation, anger, emotion over matters of relatively minor importance, often to illustrate that you are still around and matter. (Emotion acts as a relief valve).

Withdraw – Either physically or emotionally take yourself away from the centre of action – shut yourself in your office, go on a trip, claim that 'it's all unimportant anyway'. (Withdrawal puts the load into a reduced perspective).

Hammer Away – Do what you normally do only more of it. Work longer and harder, write more reports, hold more committees, make more visits. (More effort will reduce the load).

Escape – Into excess behaviour, often accompanied by un-

necessary humour, drink, drugs etc. (These are forms of sublimation).

Breakdown – *Collapse, usually into hospital. (An extreme form of enforced withdrawal).*

All of these mechanisms do cope with the overload, for you. But they either export it to someone else, or they reduce the ultimate efficiency or success of the operation. Some of them (Escape and Breakdown) have unwanted consequences for oneself.

THE SECOND STRAND OF RESISTANCE

The second strand of resistance to Apollo arises from the emphasis that the Apollonian culture of management gives to the 'role' as distinct from the 'individual'. Here lie the ideas of 'organisational sin' and 'corporate slavery'.

We have already glancingly noted that traditionally 'sin' meant 'denying oneself', being false, in word or deed or thought, to one's true beliefs and true self. The concept of sin has these days been so downgraded to a list of mere peccadilloes that it is even socially respectable to boast 'I am a confirmed sinner'; but one would still be unlikely to *boast* 'I do not believe in what I do, nor does my behaviour reveal the kind of man I am'. That is simply not a boast. Instead it is a kind of bleat, and it is heard often enough. A man's job or official role can become his private crucifixion, as he finds himself forced to act and speak in ways which do not reflect his real beliefs in order to do his job.

George Orwell has described how once, as a minor colonial official in Burma, he found himself, an apostle of non-violence and a lover of living things, raising a gun to kill a harmless elephant because he lacked the will, or perhaps the courage, to deny the demands of what others called his 'duty'. It is a moving description of a private shame, or sin.

For many people, organisations seem to reek of this kind of private sin. It is not that employees are forced to cheat, or bribe, or lie – although such dishonesties are not unknown in

organisations – but in smaller ways they feel pushed to sub-
merge their identity in the job, to argue cases of whose merit
they are not convinced, give priority to rituals they know to be
charades, be charming to those they despise, appear fierce
when they feel sympathy, and act committed when uncon-
vinced. Perhaps it is not profit that makes youth shy away
from organisations – but sin?

The idea that organisations deprive individuals of the right
to express their values and their personalities in their work
has a long and distinguished pedigree. William Morris and
D. H. Lawrence in England, Thoreau and Marcuse in America,
Brecht in Germany, Simone Weil and André Malraux in
France, and, of course, Karl Marx, have all sung this song.
The IBM young men are but the latest exponents of the idea.

THREE QUOTATIONS

Karl Marx: '*In his work, therefore, (the worker) does not
affirm himself but denies himself . . . does not
develop freely his physical and mental energy
but mortifies his body and ruins his mind . . .
His labour is . . . not voluntary but coerced;
it is forced labour. It is therefore not the
satisfaction of a need: it is merely a means
to satisfy needs external to it.*'

Frederick Taylor (originator of 'Scientific Management'): '*One
of the very first requirements for a man who
is fit to handle pig iron as a regular occupation is that he shall be so stupid and so phleg-
matic that he more nearly resembles an ox
than any other type.*'

Adam Smith: '*The man whose life is spent in performing
simple operations . . . has no occasion to
exert his understanding . . . He generally
becomes as stupid and ignorant as it is possible for a human creature to become*'.

RUNAWAY SLAVES

In 1970 IBM France had a new experience – they lost a team of softwear specialists who decided to leave to found a business of their own. The manager of Computer Services, the new company, said 'Never has man owed more to a private business enterprise. Without IBM the economic level of our planet would not be what it is today. Why then did we quit? To perform a more interesting work, and above all for moral reasons. Tomorrow, the real power will belong to those who master software. Whereas this firm has dominated the world's information-processing market, the French engineers participating in IBM's activities have by no means been involved with decision-making. They are in some ways nothing but "golden slaves".'

All these people see Apollonian organisations as inevitably alienating places. Alan Fox has demonstrated that low levels of discretion lead to low levels of trust. Apollonian organisations cannot tolerate much discretion – it would violate their consistency. They will not, cannot, be high trust organisations. One can redesign jobs to allow marginally greater discretion, introduce flexitime or autonomous groups, create Works Councils, but these all remain placebos, temporary pills to relieve the pain and alleviate the inherent incompatibility between man and this type of work. Today, they point out, more than 90 per cent of the working population are in organisations and many of them, the majority probably, in a bureaucracy of one sort or another. One hundred years ago, fewer than 30 per cent worked in any form of organisation, and very few of those institutions that did exist would have been classified as bureaucratic, even if they had other flaws and faults. The bureaucratic phenomenon is, then, of fairly recent origin. Only today, they would argue, are we becoming aware of the extent of the malaise. When it afflicted only a minority it could be ignored, or the minority could be regarded as volunteers, prepared to suffer the so-called indignities of organisational work because they wanted the money, the security or the promise of higher status in time to come. Now that it is the majority that is involved, 'sin' is no longer a voluntary option but a built-in requirement of life.

THE THIRD STRAND OF RESISTANCE

This problem is not concerned so much with rights and wrongs, as with the way things are. A new generation has grown up in the Western democracies, a generation that is less frightened (it has experienced no major wars), is less hungry, less insecure, and perhaps less greedy than preceding generations. But not only have external conditions changed (improved?) for the new youth, so have the ways of rearing and educating children. Education is as much about the nature of authority as it is about information and skills. When the parents of the young currently in their twenties went to school, most of them sat in rows and copied down what the teacher said, only to write it back to him in due course as a test or examination. Whether or not this was an efficient method of learning, it certainly conveyed the message that the younger, or more junior, or less clever, did what their elders and betters said. The message from the home matched that of the school, obedience and conformity to those in charge were a prerequisite of life. Today it is different. My young children sit in groups in their school. They work on projects. They think of themselves as learning rather than being taught. They are encouraged to express their own personalities in stories, poems and paintings instead of memorising or imitating those of the great. And again, for better or worse, the home mirrors the school. From an early age, due partly to the exigencies of small houses and communal living, the young are treated as equals in the family, with a right to their own views and attitudes. In adolescence, the new affluence, the increased ability to earn marginal income, allows the growing men and women to be rapidly independent of their elders. The result is predictable, and is summed up by David Yankelovitch's survey, summarised below.

'AUTHORITY' TO THE YOUNG

In 1971 David Yankelovitch carried out a survey for the IDR Third Fund to investigate the changing views of American student youth.* Amongst many other facets of their attitudes, he looked at the increasing resistance to authority:

In 1968, six out of ten students (59 per cent) found that they could easily accept the power and influence of the police. In 1971, that number had been reduced to 45 per cent. Many fewer students than formerly (15 per cent) find it easy to accept outward conformity for the sake of career advancement, and to abide by laws with which they do not agree.

The greatest single erosion of relationship to authority is in the 'boss' relationship and the work situation. In 1968, over half of all students (56 per cent) did not mind the future prospect of being bossed around on the job. This number fell to 49 per cent in 1969, 43 per cent in 1970 and down to 36 per cent in 1971. The result: today, two out of three students do not easily see themselves submitting to the authority of the 'boss'.

A student's relationship to authority of all kinds – including the boss – is at best one of grudging but not easy acceptance. Students see the major barrier standing in the way of securing desirable work to be their attitude to authority. No obstacle comes even close to this one, including political views, style of dress, or unwillingness to conform.

This random concatenation of words and phrases capture as well as any formal definition the things which students in 1971 do not want in their world:

Professional . . . . system . . . . planning for the future . . . . conceptual framework . . . . experiment . . . . organisation . . . . detachment . . . . management . . . . verification . . . . facts . . . . technology . . . . cost-effectiveness . . . . theory . . . . rationalisation . . . . efficiency . . . . measure-

---

* D. Yankelovitch Inc., *The Changing Values on Campus*, New York, Washington Square Press, 1972.

> *ment . . . . statistical controls . . . . manipulate . . . . mechanisation . . . . institutions . . . . power . . . . determinism . . . . intelligence testing . . . . abstract thought . . . . programming . . . . calculate . . . . objectivity . . . .behaviourism . . . . modification of the human environment . . . . literal . . . . moulded to specification . . . . genetic planning . . . . achievement.*

Dionysians all?

Gordon Rattray Taylor, in his book *Rethink,* has drawn attention to the difference between what he terms patrism and matrism in our society. The values and attitudes of patrism might be called traditional, or tough, as opposed to radical, or tender. Patrism believes in order and discipline, wishes to maintain the traditions of the past and respect for authority; it values self-control and rational behaviour, distinguishes male and female roles, puts more faith in experience and age than in youth. Matrism, on the other hand, is optimistic about the future, decries the past, believes in openness and likes emotions, makes little distinction between the sexes, wants discussion rather than orders, places reliance on expertise rather than experience, values youth and imagination more than age. Rattray Taylor is convinced that there is a marked swing towards matrism in our society.

In my cultural terms, we are bringing up the young in a Dionysian tradition – individuality and personal expression – with Athenian overtones – groups, projects and shared values. It is not surprising that they then reject the Apollonian culture when they begin to meet it at work, or that they look increasingly to the established professions for their careers (the schools of law and medicine are those in most demand in universities everywhere), or to the new professions in the media, in writing or design or fashion. These are the Dionysian occupations, and today they are overcrowded.

In some countries, Japan perhaps most obviously, the educational and family systems are still Apollonian. There the bureaucratic organisation is more readily accepted, even welcomed as a natural and necessary part of life. In Germany, France, Switzerland and parts of Italy, the Apollonian tradition in schools and homes is still strong but weakening. In these countries, the Apollonian culture is still viable and cost-effective, but perhaps not for very much longer.

Efficiency or Individualism then is the second dilemma of the organised society. There is an organisational imperative (size and consistency) which drives organisations towards a preponderant amount of Apollo in their management mix. 'Bureaucracy is inevitable', some have said. On the other side we see the groans of individuals who cannot *manage* these giants that they have created, who find them *alienating* or who cannot tolerate the *obedience* and *conformity* that are required of them. Here is the Apollonian dilemma, the crossroads for organisations.

Individuals may change or organisations may change. We shall look at both possibilities. Until they do, individualism has its own weapons – the organisational hijack.

Organisational Hijacks

This is how it works. Organisations get designed logically, according to the precepts of Apollo. As in a clock, each wheel fits the next in a hierarchical dovetailing of systems. One part depends on another and in its own turn is essential to the proper functioning of its neighbour. But take one cog out of a large clock and the whole apparatus is halted. Clocks are not designed with alternative relief systems, that would be an expensive and seldom utilised form of *slack* for a mechanism that can count on its cogs always being there. But it is not so with organisations. The cogs cannot be relied upon. Indeed, the power to stop or remove a cog is actually given to the cog itself. In organisational terms, the cog is a work-group, a sub-assembly unit, a department. Should the members of these groups decide to withhold their labour, skill or talent, they can bring a tightly designed organisation to a halt.

In many organisations this hijack capacity has been unwittingly handed to the very people who are most likely to be resistant to the Apollonian tradition. They may feel bruised as individuals, but into their hands has been thrust a weapon with which to hold their enemy to ransom. Increasingly they will use it, indulging in a walk-out or a spontaneous strike, often in support of some quite trivial incident.

The incident itself can be merely the product, the symptom of a deeper discontent. The mini-strike or walk-out will often fail to win the support of the union (which can perceive the longer-term consequences of supporting hijackers), or even of fellow-workers whose earnings can cease if the whole system grinds to a halt. But in the short term, it will usually pay the organisation to bribe the group back to work, even though the longer-term precedents are likely to be punitive in terms of higher rates across the board.

The monolithic over-tight design of our organisations is an invitation to hijack and a major contributory cause to wage inflation. We have given what is called *Negative Power* in huge amounts to those people most likely to use it. Apollonian cultures come equipped with this time-bomb which will destroy the whole temple if it is not defused.

NEGATIVE POWER

In 1974, a Turkish Airline DC-10 crashed north of Paris killing over 300 people. A ground mechanic had failed to close the door of a luggage compartment in the appointed manner. He was probably the lowest paid member of the ground staff. Reputedly, he was illiterate. Yet he had the power to destroy one of the most sophisticated and best cared-for of man's creations. He had little or no positive power, but immense negative power. In this case, he used it unintentionally. It can always be used intentionally.

All members of interlocking systems can find some negative power to use. Its conscious use, often by lower officials in bureaucracies, is a way of reminding themselves, and the organisation, that they do exist and do matter. Negative power is therefore fertilised by unhappiness, low morale or a feeling of powerlessness.

Travelling in India, I needed to hire a bed-roll for an overnight train journey. This is a complicated procedure at the best of times, involving filling in a document with seven separate copies, so I allowed plenty of time. Nevertheless, on arrival at the desk of the key functionary responsible for the hire of bedding, I was informed that he was closing the office for one hour for his statutory meal-time allowance. I pointed out that by the time he reopened my train would have departed. He expressed regrets, but assured me there would be a later train. I begged him, yes begged him, to deal with my request before he closed the office but he was adamant. His time was already overdue. Had he no assistant? 'Not today, he is absent attending his sister's wedding.' 'Can I talk to your superior?' 'He is not, alas, available until tomorrow morning.' 'Would this (showing some money) help?' 'Ah, no, sir, I'm not that sort of man, sir.' By this time, we had used up more time than the actual issue of the bedding could conceivably have required. The desire to exercise his negative power, for whatever reason, prevailed over logic, economics and human charity. I spent a very uncomfortable night.

Less perceived, less dramatic but more pervasive than the active use of negative power to hijack organisations is the stealthy threat of *absenteeism*. So stealthy is this threat that figures are hard to collect, even in statistics-conscious Britain. Some estimates, however, suggest that absence due to sickness, family need, or just unexplained, is as much as *100 times* greater in the UK than days lost through strikes. This silent stilling of the clock is the real threat to Apollonian cultures. It is countered by over-employment, by sufficient over-manning to cope with any anticipated absenteeism, manpower slack. But this remedy exacerbates the disease. If it is obvious that you are not needed, you may the more easily be absent. And the cost? Immense. Here is the 'concealed unemployment' in industry, here the true nature of the 'English Disease'. Maybe it is not after all a disinclination to work, but a silent expression of negative power in reaction against the Apollonian cultures of organisations, that saps the energy of Britain's productive machines. And the disease is not confined to Britain. It is estimated that the *net* average working day (after sickness, absenteeism and holiday) of the Italian worker is only four hours (instead of the formal eight), while Swedes each take an average of 24 days a year sick leave.

Overcoming the Resistance

If the efficiency of Apollo is to triumph, the resistance to it must be overcome. We have identified three strands to this resistance, and now we must examine counters to each. How effective these counters may be is a question to which we must continually return while we consider them.

The first strand had to do with the unmanageability of the complexity of large Apollonian structures. But perhaps we should not accept defeat: cannot we increase the comprehension span of selected individuals and equip them with further computational aids? Already the computer is in the board-room. There are programmes which will evaluate the likely outcomes of any combination of strategic decisions, and flash them almost instantaneously on to screens in front of the decision-makers. Cannot this kind of facility be taken farther? Using another approach, is not management education the solution to the comprehension span problem?

Certainly the computer's ability to explore the effects of changing assumptions is potentially of great assistance to management. Just as the effect of different economic options open to government can be checked out on a computerised model of the total economy, so, notionally, could all options open to a manager. There is much work in progress attempting to find a generally applicable way of modelling the flows of information, of goods, activities or money within organisations. No doubt in time these models may become close enough to the reality to be more useful than the oversimplifications of the present. Whether they will ever be able to replicate the emotions, needs and beliefs of human beings which lie behind the equations in the models, is another matter. The essence of being human lies in our ability to over-ride our own predictions. This 'essential humanness' may be the unbridgeable gap in the modelling approach to management.

So far the attempt to educate for conceptual span has been another of those searches for the elusive Holy Grail. Techniques can be taught, information transferred, skills acquired by practice and coaching. But the ability to embrace complexity, or the cathedral mentality (to envision or start something whose completion you will not live to see), are rarer things. Some will maintain that they have to be inherited or at least acquired in those precious first years. Others argue that one can learn to think conceptually, that the study of history, economics, business case-studies and even literature can bring out whatever latent abilities there are to see patterns in things, and to look beyond the particular to the general. Yet there is little evidence for this. And if the ability can be acquired at a mature age, then assuredly it requires more time and attention than the four-week course which is the most that any practising manager would feel justified in devoting to it.

We must conclude that, *at present*, neither computers nor education offer a likely or a quick way out of the Apollonian impasse.

DOES EDUCATION HELP?

To most people education means learning useful things, be they facts or techniques. In that sense, most further or higher education has an effective usefulness of about ten years maximum. After that, either the knowledge is outdated by advancing technology and new discoveries, or the individual has moved to a level or an occupation where he no longer needs it. How many 40-year-olds are still using anything they learnt at school or college?

But it may be that higher education creates or improves the ability to cope with complexity, to deal with issues rather than facts, and the abstract as well as the particular. Watch what people talk about. Can they reason? Do they deal only with facts, turn opinion into fact, shun logical discussion? Is this related to their educational background?

Dunning, in a study* of the relative profitability of US subsidiaries in Britain, writes 'Table 13 . . . reveals quite decisively that US and UK firms in which executives possess degrees or equivalent formal qualifications earn considerably higher profits than those who do not. It is noteworthy too that, whilst this relationship is broadly the same for both the US and the UK firms in the sample, a much higher proportion of executives in US firms possessed university degrees or equivalent formal qualifications.'

The cross-cultural comparison does not apply only to the US. Fewer executives have degrees in Britain than in any other Western European country or Japan.

Does this mean anything in terms of relative managerial ability, or is it only a reflection of different cultural fashions?

The second strand of resistance had to do with the essential 'sin' of the Apollonian culture, which makes it an alienating place for the individual. The counter to this strand is not a denial, but an acknowledgement that in any society and in any organisation there must be a lot of boring jobs. Roles have to take priority over individuals. Work, for most people, is something that has to be done in order that the rest of life may be enjoyed. There are, of course, those fortunate few whose work is their hobby. Was not happiness once defined as 'being paid for your hobby'? For the rest, it is obviously important that work be made as painless as possible, that the physical conditions of work are congenial (but how can you make a foundry congenial?), and that the contractual side of employment is fair. And most importantly, the rewards of

* J. H. Dunning, 'U.S. Subsidiaries in Britain and their U.K. Competitors', *Business Ratios*, June 1968, p. 16.

harder work, whether they be in money or increased leisure time, must be seen to be adequate. Here, it is argued, is the modern rub. The equation is not clear, more money is not linked closely enough to more work when clever negotiating or hijacking tactics can win the money without the work. Even when increased rewards do flow from increased productivity, penal personal taxation robs the individual of most of the fruit of his labour. If today the game of work is no longer worth the candle, the fault lies in the candle, not in the game.

There is, however, a fatal flaw creeping into this age-old argument. One man's rewards are too often now another man's grudge. Fred Hirsch, in an important book called *The Social Limits to Growth*, calls this dilemma the false promise of the affluent society.

It works like this: as long as you don't mind everyone else having what you've got, then you can offer the same carrot all round and it works as a universal incentive. So far so good. Plentiful food, better heating, more leisure – these are things that all men might want all others to have as well as themselves. But there are a whole lot of things we want which, *by definition*, all others cannot have because they depend on *comparative* advantage. Private education is one of them in Britain – give it to everyone and it ceases to be desirable. Servants used to be another but we cannot all be masters for who then would serve? A house with an unspoilt view? If all had them, we would end up looking at each other in that view. Once we move from universal goods to comparative goods, we come up against the endless paradox – 'When you've got what you want, you don't want what you've got, because everyone else has got it too.' The majority cannot enjoy a minority right.

When people are hungry, incentives work universally. When they work for comparative advantage, then increasing the incentives for some will only make others discontented. As they catch up, the effort from the first group will fall away. It is like walking up the down escalator. Apart from anything else, it is a built-in inflationary pressure.

'Let them go hungry, then.' Indeed, a dose of massive deflation, unemployment and siege economy conditions would soon bring back the universal incentive side of money. The counter-argument to the second strand of resistance to Apollo would then be justified. But to use hunger as the lever to organisational efficiency is not politically acceptable today. We should be glad.

DOES MONEY MATTER?

Studies in both British and American organisations have shown that a substantial pay rise (over 10 per cent in net pay) does produce increased effort, energy and enthusiasm – for an average period of six weeks. Thereafter, the new pay becomes the new base line.

Questioned by Nancy Morse and Robert Weiss in America, 80 per cent of 401 employed men said that they would continue working even if they did not need the money.*

In a study of British managers undertaken by Harry Hansen in 1971,** the personal objective 'to earn a substantial amount of money' ranked well below the other objectives:

'Have freedom to carry out your own ideas, a chance for originality and initiative;'

'Belong to a growing, successful organisation;'

'Work with associates whom you personally like.'

The third strand concerned the changing values and norms of society as revealed in our educational methods and our child-rearing habits. The attention given to personal expression, to the development of one's own talents, to group activities, to influence through persuasion and a search for common purposes – Dionysian and Athenian attitudes – is antithetical to the impersonality, conformity and obedience required in Apollonian systems. The counter to this strand might be to revert to

---

* Morse N. and Weiss R., 'The Function and Meaning of Work and Job,' *American Sociological Review*, 1955.
** Hansen, H. *The British Manager*, Harvard University Press, 1976.

more traditional ways of bringing up our young. In Britain, as in France, the Netherlands, the US and parts of Germany, education has been in the forefront of public attention during the last ten years, heralded by the student unrest of 1968. In all these countries, there are many who argue for a return to former ways, and their arguments are based as much on the need to re-establish the traditional patterns of authority as on the efficiency of the learning methods. They maintain that the young, the less extrovert, the ordinary majority of working folk, need and appreciate structure and discipline in their lives. Too much, it is claimed, has been given and promised to the young. The pendulum must swing back and the disappearance of the 'youth bulge' in the population statistics of all countries during the next decade will help to push youth back in their place as a minority apprentice group in society.

To a degree they must be correct in their predictions. In 1965, over half of the population of the United States was under 25. In 1985, over half will be over 40. Society will be middle-aged, youth will be in a minority, middle-aged values of stability and security will prevail. There are even some worries that in the late 1980s there may not be a large enough working population to fill the available jobs.

Nonetheless, there does seem to have been a radical shift in society's attitude to the individual – a shift of which our educational philosophy is only a mirror, even if a slightly distorting one. If that is so, then organisations cannot ever again expect to rely on an obedient, complacent, dependent workforce. Democracy has worked its way through to the workplace, but Apollo prefers to ignore the democratic process. The clock cannot be turned back, even if its rate of change is slowed down, even if it is halted for a time. Our organisations are increasingly going to be populated by people who are Dionysians and Athenians at heart, with the occasional Zeus to flavour the mix. Necessity will make Apollonians out of many of them – at least on the surface. Many of them will not have the talent or abilities to sustain a Dionysian or Athenian job, inside or outside the organisation. Hunger will breed conformity in some, but it will be a reluctant conformity, one that fertilises negative power, absenteeism and hijacks. And though some there will be who are true Apollonians – the tidy-minded, those prepared to subordinate self to system – they will not be enough to staff the mega-bureaucracies pushed on us by the pressures for bigness and consistency.

The conclusion begins to seem inescapable. The three strands or tendencies that frustrate the Apollonian logic of the large organisation will neither fade away nor be overcome in today's world. The visible result is expense – the expense of buying off hijacks, of staffing up for absenteeism, of compensating for the incapacity of the humans at the top: *slack*. For a time, in monopoly or quasi-monopoly situations, when your competitors are in a similar state, the extra expense can be concealed by higher prices. In some few cases, a technological breakthrough, or a giant step up the economies of scale, will so lower the cost of production or service that the expense of the Apollonian system is absorbed – for a time. But there is no end to the possible costs of Apollo. In the end, the inflationary pressures of over-pricing force themselves into the wider society. In competitive situations, the collapse comes sooner and is confined to the individual enterprise.

The railways can offset their reduced numbers of passengers for a time with increased fares, but society in the end will repudiate the sight and the cost of endless empty carriages whistling through the stations.

This, then, is the crossroads for the organisation, particularly for the mega-bureaucracies of government and industry. Do they commit themselves to the ultimate victory of bigness and consistency, heads down as they go, believing that the resistances are little local difficulties? Or do they change course? Although the resulting decisions will be hugely important for the 90 per cent who work in organisations, and are therefore crucial decisions for society, the issue is not a political one, or an ideological one, but a practical question of the design and management of organisations. It is not that the mega-bureaucracies are irresponsible, corporations taking over from the state: the truth is that they may be too expensive because they have become, literally, unmanageable.

Today's dilemma was foreseen, of course. Keynes, the economist, perceived that his theories of economics were the economics of scarcity. Once scarcity had been eliminated, the central theories might lose their validity.

KEYNES THE POST-KEYNESIAN

In 1930, John Maynard Keynes looked forward in an essay to the 'Economic Possibilities for our Grandchildren'.* He prophesied that his grandchildren (who would be adults today) would discover that the 'economic problem is not the permanent problem of the human race.' He went on, 'If the economic problem is solved, mankind will be deprived of its traditional purposes. Will this be a benefit? If one believes at all in the real values of life, the prospect at least opens up the possibility of benefit, yet I think with dread of the readjustments of the habits and instincts of the ordinary man, bred into him for countless generations, which he may be asked to discard within a few decades. . . .

'The strenuous purposeful moneymakers may carry all of us along with them into the lap of economic abundance . . . but the rest of us will no longer be under any obligation to applaud and encourage them for we shall enquire more curiously than is safe today into the true character of this purposiveness . . . for purposiveness means that we are more concerned with the remote future results of our actions than with their own quality or their immediate effects on our environments.'

Gurth Higgin has argued convincingly that since the Middle Ages the whole thrust of society has been towards the elimina-

---

* Published in *Essays in Persuasion*, New York, The Norton Library, 1963, and quoted by Professor Gurth Higgin in his inaugural address (1975) at Loughborough University of Technology entitled 'Scarcity, Abundance and Depletion.'

tion of scarcity. Now that this is potentially a solved problem in the industrialised world, society is searching for a new thrust, and old values and systems and codes of behaviour come into question. When scarcity was the enemy, then much could be tolerated in the name of efficiency. The organisation was the instrument of society and men, machines and money the instruments of the organisation. When scarcity is no longer a common enemy, except in time of war or natural disaster, the costs of efficiency begin to seem high.

Never will so many Owe So Much to so Few

Chapter 6

REACTIONS

The Apollonian dilemma is not new. We have all been aware for a long time that the disciplines which efficiency seems to require are not always palatable to free men. Marx may or may not have exaggerated in comparing industrial organisations with the institutions of slavery, but he has always had many sympathisers, many of them vehement. For a long time society could afford to ignore the dilemma. The results of efficiency in terms of more to eat and spend, of years lived and comforts enjoyed, were so obviously worth the costs of organisational discipline for society as a whole. Of course, the benefits were not always as well distributed as they might have been, but political pressures could be relied upon to put that right in the end. But that cost-benefit equation is no longer so obvious today, when there appear to be diminishing returns to the individual from increased efficiency. The game is no longer worth so much candle, and the dilemma of Apollo gets more urgent as a result.

We can detect in society various attitudes and responses to the dilemma. None of them seem to me to be adequate. Some of them even compound the problem. Yet we need to examine them, if only to dismiss them, because they, between them, make up the conventional wisdom in this field. Let me describe them briefly.

One attitude relies on a staunch belief in the inexorable logic of efficiency. More growth will once again make the game worthwhile. In effect, if the theory of cultural propriety succeeded in eliminating slack, we should once again be swallowed up in a common objective of material growth. Others, however, would accept that we should need impossible rates of growth to keep us all profitably employed. To them the solution lies in the creation of a sort of industrial meritocracy, who would create wealth that the rest of us might live. The pre-conditions of their view are that the meritocracy be properly rewarded and that the rest of us be educated for leisure, or life without employment. Both of these views have, of course, a lot of popular support, but I will argue that they do not present us with a long-term solution to the need to blend efficiency with individualism for the whole of society.

Then there are those who see organisations as inevitable, and as inevitably diminishing to the individual. The pressures of efficiency need, as they see it, to be balanced by pressures for individual rights in organisations. Democracy must apply within work as well as in the wider society. Many of these democratic enthusiasts would have their cake as well as eat it, by maintaining that increased democracy would bring increased efficiency. Others are more realistic, recognising that democracy has never been known for efficiency, but maintaining that it is a necessary precondition of human relationships in a civilised society (cost what it may, they might add). There is, finally, a lower key variant of full democracy which argues for practical participation and organisation on a human scale. I would have more sympathy with this last approach if I felt that it was genuinely concerned with the dilemma of human dignity at work, and not merely tinkering with the distorting effects of excessive alienation.

The arguments between the exponents of these different viewpoints are often violent. The diverging perspectives of the 'industrial meritocracy' view and that of the 'full democracy' stance do in fact colour the whole of our political debate. To call it a debate is to dignify it, for usually the advocates of each view cannot understand or even hear what the others are saying. Society sometimes seems to be tearing itself apart over this Apollonian dilemma. The debates go on in private, too, as the following example demonstrates.

WHEN AUNTIE CAME TO DINNER

My aunt by marriage is a splendid character, but from a bygone age. Her father never worked, nor his father before him, nor, of course, had she ever earned a penny in her life. Their capital worked for them, and they managed their capital. Work was done by workers. She sees all governments today as insanely prejudiced against capital, all workers as inherently greedy and lazy, and most managements as incompetent. No wonder the world is in a mess and she getting poorer every day.

Tony is a friend from work. His father was a postman. He started life as a draughtsman in a large engineering firm. He grew up believing that inherited capital was socially wrong. He had never met any man who did not or had not worked for his living.

They met, by chance, at my house over a meal. It started quietly, politely. Then she inquired what he did. It transpired that he had recently joined his staff union. Auntie had never met a union member.

'Good heavens, how could you?' she said.

'It makes very good sense,' said Tony, 'to protect your rights.'

'What rights? What poppycock is this? If people like you spent more time at their work and less looking after their own interests, this country wouldn't be in its present mess.'

'Don't you,' said Tony, 'spend your time looking after your rights?'

'Of course,' she said, 'but then, I've got rights. I provide the money that makes it possible for people like you to live.'

'I provide the labour that keeps your money alive, although why I should work to preserve the capital of rich people whom I've never met is something that puzzles me.'

'You talk like a Communist, young man, although you dress quite respectably. Do you know what you're saying?'

'You don't have to be a Communist to question the legitimacy of inherited wealth.'

My aunt turned to me.

'You see why I'm worried about this country?' she said.

Each regarded the other as an example of an unnatural species. Given their opposed 'core beliefs', no proper argument or dialogue was possible, only an exchange of slogans or abuse. It is a score which is replicated at negotiating tables as well as dinner tables.

Let us now examine these unavailing responses in a little more detail.

The first response relies on the inevitable imperative of growth, and the eventual recognition that organisations are both the necessary means of growth and the inevitable price that we must pay for it. In this view, the problems of the distribution of wealth are regarded as separate from the problems of the creation of wealth. The distribution of wealth is a political issue, but the creation of wealth is a management issue, and after all there is no point talking about the distribution of wealth if there is none to distribute.

The advocates of this view would have us remember once again that growth makes it easier to divide the cake more fairly because there is more cake. We can therefore be united at least in deciding how to make the cake, even if we are opposed in debating how it should be divided. If we could only persuade people of the importance of the creation of wealth, and of the need for greater efficiency in our services and in our administration, then the Apollonian organisations could rely on their human resources once again to do what the rules say they ought to do.

When advocacy fails, and the wolf cries of newspapers get ignored, this response falls back on the discipline of the economic pendulum to return people to their (Apollonian) senses.

It may be, they will say, that in the short term one must envisage the progressive over-pricing of our outputs because of the cost of large Apollonian systems operating amid current popular values. This over-pricing can be sustained artificially for a time by lowering the exchange rate, by large external borrowings, by import controls, by selective earnings. In the end, however, we shall run out of mechanisms, and the threat of scarcity will no longer be a threat but a perceived reality. Efficiency in the face of this common enemy will then once again be seen to be worth its costs, in terms of lost individualism. We shall no longer take things for granted but will start to instil the virtues of discipline, conformity and obedience into our children. In return, the organisation will on its part revert to the obligations it used to have to provide work and careers for life. Look at Japan. For a time after the war, they embraced American ideas of individualism and American practices of management in their organisations. After a period of vicious inflation and political immobility, they returned to an organisational contract that exchanged protection for commitment, supported it with more traditional educational systems, and arranged for their own form of participation at work, the unique concept of 'Groupism'. It could happen here in the West, but only if we get hungry enough. Maybe, the travellers on this road would argue, things will have to get worse in every country before they get better. The Apollonians who argue this way believe it is the country, the people who make up the country, who are out of step, not them. Time, with some pain, will bring them back to their rightful culture.

Alas, the pendulum swings both ways. Maybe hunger would make us Apollonian once more, but as soon as efficiency returned us to abundance, would not the problems recur? Is this not a route to a generational stop-go cycle of a more traumatic kind than the minor economic ones of the past twenty years? There are signs already of a return to individualism in Japanese society.

The second danger is that as they seek to delay the sweep of the pendulum and the ultimately inevitable hunger, governments may make changes that will be more fundamental and more long-lasting than any mere import controls or rationing procedures. It is doubtful, for instance, whether any stock exchange would be willing or able to provide the desired quantities of new investment in the desired areas under the conditions of over-pricing envisaged in the first part of this scenario. Government would then be forced to step in, first as banker of last resort and ultimately as the prime source of new investment. This is the economic road to totalitarian rule, with the increased bureaucracy that would inevitably accompany it – compounding Apollo everywhere. Governments, furthermore, in an attempt to hold back the damaging costs of organisational hijacks, will be forced to collude with any who can guarantee labour peace, even at the long-term cost of over-manning. This temporary by-passing of the democratic process may leave permanent damage behind it by downgrading the whole notion of electoral democracy. Thus, by a process of successive expedients, without conscious aim, a nation can be forced into government by edict. And once the economic and political mechanisms of a more responsive democracy have been allowed to wither, they may not bloom again for a long time. Democracy might be the price one has to pay for underwriting Apollo as the principal god of the organised society. Is our hunger great enough?

The second response is based on the view that organisations and the work of organisations is not loathed by everyone. In fact, given free will, most people would still go to work for the companionship, the variety and the chance to feel useful. The trouble lies in our own insistence that everyone, now including women, should contribute to the money economy. The truth is that there is not room for them. Most organisations could work more efficiently with fewer people, particularly if those remaining were then paid more and if more money was available for more supporting facilities and for more advanced technology. Organisations should become *meritocracies*, with the responsibility of maintaining society as the price.

Work, it is argued, is open to all and should be expected, of all. For some, it should be in the so-called 'gift' economy, where work is done for its own sake and not for economic reward. We need not wait until we retire to serve on the local council. The theatre and the arts in general could only prosper by a greater infusion of talent that was not dependent on earnings for total livelihood. A society with a thriving gift economy is a more varied and interesting society than one which invests all its talents and energies in the money economy. A famous economist once told me that he enjoyed living only in countries where the economy was on the way down, because that usually meant that talent was directed to non-material objectives. England, he added, was his favourite country for *living* in, though he worked in America. It is *employment*, not work, which needs to be voluntary and limited. It is therefore a great mistake to undertake political commitments to full employment, even to call it by such a denigrating name as *un*employment. The theatre, a more Dionysian occupation, at least calls it 'resting'.

At the moment, it is argued, there is a lot of concealed unemployment in the manpower slack of the large organisations. It would be cheaper to pay these people pensions, to send them to school, even to pay them higher welfare benefits, as long as they were not replaced in their organisations. In fact, therefore, the unemployment figures might not increase. Instead, the enrolments at the various places of continuing education would rise, more and more people would define themselves as self-employed, even if their output were mostly in the gift economy and they kept body and soul together on a package of early retirement annuities, state benefits (perhaps via a negative income tax), and on a more self-sufficient existence (growing one's own food, for instance). The compulsory retirement age (from employment) might fall, but the *average* retirement age would fall even faster. People would stay at school longer, or go on to higher education more often, partly because the jobs would not be available for school-leavers, but partly because qualifications would be necessary for almost every job.

The following table speculates on the various ways the USA could *get rid of* the unwanted man-hours if productivity continued to increase, and if we employed only the people we need to do the work. The alternatives are quite dramatic.

Prospective Growth in Productivity and Possible Uses of Released Time (U.S.A.)

| Year | Possible increases in real GNP (1960 dollars) | | | Alternative uses of potential nonworking time | | | | |
	GNP (billions) $	Per capita GNP $	Total number of years	Retirement age	Length of workweek (hours)	Vacation time (weeks)	Labour force retrained[1] (per cent)	Education and training Years of extended education
1965	627.3	3181	—	65 or over	40	3	—	—
1966	655.6	3280	2,245,542	65	39	4	2.9	1.2
1967	685.6	3382	4,655,526	63	38	7	5.0	2.4
1968	707.1	3490	6,910,648	61	36	7	8.7	3.4
1969	745.3	3578	8,880,092	59	36	8	11.1	4.2
1970	779.3	3690	11,263,301	57	34	10	13.8	5.1
1975	973.4	4307	23,135,642	50	30	16	26.2	9.4
1980	1250.2	5059	35,586,729	44	25	21	37.2	13.8
1985	1544.5	5802	47,200,158	38	22	25	45.2	17.5

[1] Figures are in addition to the number of workers now trained in public and private programmes.
Compiled by Juanite Kreps and Joseph Spengler in 'Future Options for More Free Time' in F. Best (ed) *The Future of Work*, Prentice-Hall 1973.

There would still be boring jobs. Underground trains need drivers. Garbage has to be collected. Letters have to be typed, cars assembled. But with more money available from the people dropped from the payroll, technological aids could be developed to take much of the boring element out of these jobs. Where this was not possible, people would be paid high piece rates so that they could, effectively, choose to do a little unpleasant work instead of a lot of more pleasant work.

HIGH PAY FOR LOW WORK?

There was an interesting exchange of letters in one of the national newspapers not so long ago.

The head of one of Britain's newer universities wrote to complain about the low numbers and poor quality of the students applying to enter his university.

'It is, perhaps,' he said, 'hardly to be wondered at. After all, the salary which they are likely to receive on leaving will probably be less than that earned by a new or unskilled recruit to an assembly line in a car plant.'

Four days later, the paper printed a reply from a shop steward in a car plant.

'No doubt,' said the letter, 'the vice-chancellor has never worked on an assembly line. If he had, he would not wish his graduates to find their employment there. As a result of their education at his university, they will find jobs in pleasant surroundings, with an opportunity to use their talents and influence events around them. Is it not fair that my lads, deprived of these things, should get more money by way of compensation?'

A recent calculation showed that already, today, in Britain if one man decided to become an academic and eventually a professor, whilst his brother remained as an engineering fitter, the professor would be 54 before his accumulated life-time earnings would overtake those of his brother.

Fair or unfair?

A pattern might then begin to develop whereby a man's life-time's earnings could often be accumulated in an *employment-life* that lasted from, say, 25 to 45. A proportion of his earnings would go, via taxation or pension contributions, into support-ing him, on a reduced basis, for the remainder of his life so that his subsequent *work* need not be tied to *employment*, or at least not to high income-producing employment. After all, it is argued, the resulting earnings graph relates remarkably accurately to an individual's life-time expenditure graph, when his highest rate of expenditure is normally between 30 and 45 and declining thereafter. Organisations would then be younger and more energetic than they are now. Some employees might stay on after 45, particularly perhaps those who liked the Apollonian aspects of employment with its security and pre-dictability. Others might work part-time after their main energy jobs had been completed. Others still could use the opportunity to develop a second career, with the security of some minimum financial support behind them.

In other words, individuals would make an implied life-time contract with the organised society, in which they would agree, implicitly, to tolerate, and often to enjoy, the challenges and frustrations of organisational work, in return for the roughly equivalent number of years outside the work organisa-tion. There would be some discretion as to when the work years happened and exactly how many there would be. In return for this reduced and more discretionary organisational contribution, individuals would be expected to make the, basically, Apollonian organisations of society more workable; and indeed, thinned-down as they would be, they *would* be more workable, more tolerable and more efficient.

The new system would not be as controlled and organised as that description makes it sound, of course, but that would be the unstated social contract. It has its appeal to many, in that it recognises the Dionysian urges to individualism in many of us and provides more opportunities to indulge those urges *outside* the work organisation.

My worry about it as a useful scenario is that it reverses

the likely sequence of cause and effect. The model that it describes is a very likely *result* of more efficient organisations, but I do not see it as a likely *cause* of those organisations, because I see little evidence that individuals can collaboratively take such a long-term view. They would have, for example, to agree in effect to pay higher taxes and pension contributions, and also themselves work harder to generate the higher efficiency which would in, say, fifteen years, allow them to enjoy the freedom which would meanwhile be given to a proportion of their colleagues. Alternatively, management would be required to mortgage the future of the organisation with higher immediate pensions and sabbatical payments, in the hope that increased efficiency would repay them. I doubt that people trust that much so far ahead.

Maybe this is defeatist. Maybe a courageous society could lower the retirement age, establish a negative income tax to support the low-earners, pay high rates for dirty jobs, and at the same time use taxation devices as encouragement to management to replace the dirty jobs by automation, build more schools, encourage sabbatical education leave, etcetera. Yet it is easy to see how a government could be accused of encouraging idleness with such measures; or how a government might be afraid that employment might not fall, while subsidies grew, efficiency remained unaltered and the total public deficit increased.

Some of it *is* happening, of course. Economics tend to adjust themselves in time to human needs. The bargaining power of unions, utilising the threat of hijack, has increased the pay for dirty jobs enormously – so much so that in some cases straight economics, requiring no outside encouragement, makes it sensible to automate with expensive technology. This has now occurred, for instance, in the printing industry, although the actual jump to lower employment and higher automation is hard to negotiate in times of high unemployment.

The levelling effect of personal taxation in many countries means that the actual loss of spending power involved in moving to a lower income job with lower expenditure needs, is not as great as it may seem at first sight. Through taxation and the welfare state, the gift economy is already heavily supported in most countries. The second, low-income, career is already a well-supported institution.

THE SECOND CAREER

It is no longer difficult to find examples of people who have abandoned good jobs and promising prospects in one field to try their hand in another. Eric Clark, writing in New Society *in January 1973, had no difficulty in finding 30 examples of what he called 'middle-class drop outs'.*

Malcolm X was a typical example. He had become increasingly frustrated working for a large anonymous company. What he wanted was a strong sense of personal achievement. 'I don't want to make cogs. If you ask me to make the whole wheel, that's different.' He had been doing well, too. £10,000 a year in 1972 as managing director of an overseas subsidiary was good British money. A year later he was running a weaving and crafts business, reports Clark, in North Yorkshire. Money was tight. He had given up smoking. But he had no regrets at all. He made the decision at the age of 37. 'I felt that if I carried on I'd be doing the same job for the rest of my life. I could map out the rest of my career – abroad, head office and ending up like so-and-so. It's curious that the people at the top don't seem a very happy bunch of people.' He had prepared himself for the technical aspects of his work by taking a course at Leeds University.

The 1974-6 recession in the industrialised countries gave many organisations the excuse to thin down their manpower. Many will not increase it again when the recession ends. Politicians then found that an increase in unemployment no longer provided the spur to lower wages, or at least to lower wage increases, that had been its traditional result. Wage rates must continue to rise faster than the cost of living when Athenians or Dionysians work under Apollonian conditions, because of their hijack power. The costs of wages can therefore only be held down by cutting the payroll *numbers* whilst increasing the payroll *rates*. Slimmer organisations are on the way. We have not, however, yet learnt to use, in the rest of society, the new residue of talent and effort that is created by this organisational response.

Nor has that residue learnt to capitalise on what this approach to the future would regard as their new-found freedom. For every eager seeker after a second career, there are ten who find freedom and second careers thrust upon them when they would happily have settled for a continuation of the first. Alas, in this emerging Athenian vision of the organisation, it is usually the Apollonian, helpless on his own, who gets cast out, not the self-sufficient Dionysian or Athenian. God preserve us, many will say, from this vision of slimmer, more competitive organisations. Meritocracies are fine for those with merit, but terrible for those without, and this road would create the meritocratic organisation, and a large deprived residue of the population.

PROS AND ANTIS IN AMERICAN COMPANIES

A recent American study* investigated pro-company and anti-company attitudes among organisation employees. The pro-company people turned out to be competent, self-assured and independent. The 'antis' despised and condemned the firm they worked for, although not many ever left it. The disgruntled anti-company workers were found to be personality types who need a lot of sympathy and support from others. When support did not come from the company, they turned to unions and professional associations.

Ironically, it seems to be the Dionysians, or at least the Athenians, who are at ease, not the Apollonians. Who would lose out in the meritocratic organisation? Would they let it happen?

---

* Reported in the London *Sunday Times*, March 6, 1977.

There is *a third response* which accepts the dominance of organisations as a fact. It goes further, pointing out that if 90 per cent of the working population work in an organisation of some sort or another, then the organisation has become one of the principal *communities of our society.*

Already we can see how the state uses the work organisation as its favoured administrative community. Wherever possible, taxes are collected through the work organisation, not the local authority. Legislation on incomes, on equality of opportunity and of treatment, on the treatment of the disabled or the underprivileged, is all enforced through the work organisation. Naturally, because this is where most of the people spend most of their time.

If, then, the organisation is the new community, it is appropriate that the rights of the individual be extended into that community. What does this mean? What are these rights? The normal citizenship rights in a democracy include the following:

> *THE RIGHT OF TENURE (or protection against eviction without due process of law). In organisational terms, it is the right to a job.*
> *THE RIGHT OF APPEAL, if decisions affecting an individual are disputed.*
> *THE RIGHT TO INFORMATION, if that information has any impact on oneself.*
> *THE RIGHT OF FREE SPEECH, as long as neither treason nor libel is involved.*
> *THE RIGHT TO ELECT ONE'S OWN RULERS, and, occasionally, the right, in referenda, to tell them what to do.*

Increasingly, it is pointed out, we see these rights being brought into the organisation. In the smaller organisations they can and have happened informally. It is because they have not happened often enough in enough places that they are now imposed by legislation. It is a recognition of what the EEC in a Green Paper calls 'the democratic imperative'.

These rights are not, this third approach might claim, anything to be unduly alarmed about. They are merely a recognition, in legal terms, of something that has been readily accepted by many managers for a long time: that an organisation is as responsible to those who provide its labour as to those who provide its capital, its shareholders. Indeed, since increasingly the capital comes from retained earnings (i.e. from the labour), the responsibility to the workforce must far outweigh that to the original owners.

Now that scarcity is potentially a solved problem, we are really talking about comparative degrees of abundance. The organisation, therefore, is no longer an instrument of society, it is much more than that, it is part of the main body of society, a fact which has to be reflected in the way it is run. A community is a collection of individuals who must be allowed their individual rights. Life, Liberty and the Pursuit of Justice are not to be valid only in the home or the sports arena – they must be carried into the factory, the office, the hospital, the field, everywhere that man works.

The rights of the individual can, however, be protected another way – by ownership. One version of this approach favours the co-ownership or co-operative organisation, where the work organisation is owned by those who work there. There are today many examples of this pattern of which the John Lewis Partnership and the Scott-Bader Commonwealth are only two of the best known in Britain. But ownership, on its own, does not seem to give the protection or involvement that it should. The sense of ownership that nationalisation was supposed to bring has long since proved to be a myth. Few who work in the large and geographically distant parts of the John Lewis Partnership would feel that it is their share in the ownership of the firm which gives them their protection and their commitment. In the *large* organisation, it seems, some legislation is essential to protect our Dionysian rights.

There are even, it is argued, long-term economic grounds for this legislation for individual rights. The large organisations are essential to maintain our societies in that precarious state of moderate abundance which we have now achieved. The collapse of these organisations would return us to that scarcity from which we have only recently managed to haul ourselves. Yet these organisations are now so powerful, so dominating and often so alienating that people will not work in them, will not join them, or contemplate joining them, unless they can be assured of some countervailing power, of the protection of the law and of the state. There are already quite enough incentives for those who rule these corporations to be efficient. Let there be some pressures for individualism.

The China of the last ten years is seen by some as an example of this attempt to combine the rights and wishes of the individual with the goals of the work organisation. Apart from some of the largest concerns which are owned centrally by the state, the organisations are owned by the province, town, or street, depending on the size of the organisation. There are managers, but they are appointed ultimately by the workforce, and are constantly under the inspection and questioning of a Workers' Management Committee which is elected from all levels of the organisation, meets daily at the work-team level and has to agree all major new proposals before they are implemented. This Committee also acts as the representative of any individual who feels his ideas are ignored or his rights infringed. Full and full-time participation. But it works, or so we understand. The productive efficiency of China's factories continues to increase. But China has, at present, something that we lack – an ideology, an all-consuming purpose. Indeed, it is the principal task of these Workers' Management Committees to reinforce the political message by constant education, discussion and reminder. Will it last or is such dedication to a cause a wonder for a generation? Would we want it here?

* Described by Charles Bettelheim in C. Bettelheim, *Cultural Revolution and Industrial Organisation in China*, London, Monthly Review Press, 1974.

THE GENERAL KNITWEAR FACTORY IN PEKING*

The General Knitwear Factory in Peking was built in 1952, employs 3,400 people and produces fabrics as well as finished goods totalling 20 million items per year.

Before the Cultural Revolution of 1969 there was a division between workers and management. The factory manager was appointed by the central administration. He had considerable powers and could make unilateral decisions, but he had very little contact with the workers. The factory stressed production, bonuses, the importance of experts and technique.

After the Cultural Revolution, all was changed. Workers' management teams were formed – against the opposition of the old managerial staff. These management teams are elected from candidates of various levels. Their aim is not, in spite of their name, to manage their plant. They are not concerned with profitability, but are there to serve the interests of the people. They function as a control on the normal managerial bodies and administrative departments. They have five areas of concern: (1) ideological and political work, (2) production work and technical change, (3) cost control and investments, (4) safety, (5) general welfare. They are also involved in planning factory output, in liaising with other factories, and in quality control (which is a self-control system). There are therefore ample opportunities for everyone to participate in the organisation, whilst at the same time individual rights are carefully protected against abuse through the watchdog role of the same workers' Management Committee.

But above all, the Workers' Management Committee is concerned with the political and ideological education of all the workforce.

All the factories work according to what is called a 'unified plan'. At all levels, and in each production unit, the basic principle is that politics is in command, the interests of the individual factory must be subordinate to the collective interests of China's people.

Bettelheim comments, 'This is the driving force of a new

*kind of economic progress – production is no longer domin-
ated by the pursuit of exchange value, growth, monetary
returns and profit, but by the pursuit of value in use . . . the
regions and the productive units must give priority to overall
interests. This requires each individual at the base to acquire
a grasp of the nature of the general interest, and implies a new
attitude on the part of the masses with respect to overall
political and economic problems.'*

*Can it last? Can the pull of a central ideology keep the
3,400 workers of the Knitwear Factory committed inside
what remains an essentially Apollonian system? The reforms
described are only ten years old.*

Call it what you will – industrial democracy, participation, the
protection of individual rights, this road to the future must
be a Dionysian charter. Even its advocates might admit that
the enforcement of these rights, however necessary, will
hamper short-term efficiency. It may do more than that. It
may tilt the balance of power so much toward the individual
that the management of large organisations will become
impossible. The emerging Bill of Rights will be seen as a
license to use negative power if there is not the opposing draw
of commitment, dedication, service. Yet to create these conditions in a large formal organisation is perhaps to ask too
much of any leaders. Warren Bennis, head of one of those
huge American multi-versities, has written of the 'politics of
multiple advocacies' in which pressure groups spring up (he
has to contend with over 500 in his University alone) to 'represent people who are fed up with being ignored, neglected,
excluded, denied, subordinated. No longer, however, do they
march on cities, or bureaus, or on organisations. . . . Now
they file suit. The law has suddenly emerged as the court
of first resort.' He asks, 'Where have all the leaders gone?
They are all scared', he concludes, 'and who can blame
them?'

This formal enfranchisement of the individual, this organisational Bill of Rights, is, when one thinks of it, an Appol-

lonian response to individualism. 'Codify it, formalise it, institute procedures,' is the Apollonian way. Such a response may do no more than acknowledge the *legitimacy* of individualism in organisations. It will not be enough to contain it. 'Industrial Democracy' which turns out to be a modest attempt to introduce formal representative democracy into the central government of organisations, may well turn out to be as full of false promise as representative democracy traditionally has been in the wider society. It may, as it spreads, signal the complaint rather than cure it – like coloured ointments on a boil – leaving the true disease to fester underneath. In 1977 in Britain, the Bullock Committee on Industrial Democracy published its proposals for the formal representation at Board level of the employees of large industrial organisations. The general reaction has been that the problem (of industrial democracy) is much bigger than the proposed solutions (of formal representation), and that the detailed proposals may actually cause more problems than they resolve.

There is, however, a more pragmatic variant of the democratic imperative. Organisations are communities, true, say such people. But the only communities which mean anything are small ones, communities which have to do with the individual and his personal hopes, fears, activities and friendships. In the organisation, that community must be the immediate work group, the ten or a dozen or twenty people that converge on a particular task. If participation is to mean anything, it is at this level where it matters. If individualism must be expressed, then it is here that it would be most appropriate.

Volvo led the way in a redesign of the engine shop which allowed the group to organise their own work. Why did they do it? Because the workforce which they had traditionally used on the traditional assembly line had to return home. They were Finns, working as aliens in Sweden for the higher wages of that country: hungry, or greedy, people tolerating Apollonian restrictions for the money. Swedes, however, are less hungry or more greedy (depending on how you look at it) and they were less prepared to accept the alienating procedures for that sort of money. So the work was redesigned.

There are now innumerable examples of firms handing over more responsibility to work groups, breaking down assembly lines, increasing job cycles so that each worker does more than one operation. The results nearly always include a lower rate of absenteeism and of sickness, better overall morale, and, often, better quality. In the IBM typewriter plant in West Berlin, for instance, typewriters used to be assembled on two lines, each 150 metres long; individual employees had a repetitive job cycle of six minutes each. It was boring work with social contact limited to the people on either side. The line was then replaced with six shorter lines, each worked by a team. The teams developed a system of 'mutual obligations', which allowed people to take time off for sickness or refreshment. They increased the job cycle to 24 minutes and were allowed to choose their own teams. Morale, turnover, quality all improved.

Often, however, these ideas are sparked by the general thesis that smallness is not only beautiful but also economically efficient. The difficulties in organising larger complex organisations (referred to in an earlier chapter as the first strand of resistance) can be very expensive. H. G. Van Beck of the Philips plant at Eindhoven in Holland has described how he split up the 104-man assembly line into five groups with buffer stocks between each group. As a result, the waiting time caused by lack of material fell by 45 per cent, and the workers experienced the higher morale and lower absenteeism that could have been expected.

SMALL IS EFFICIENT

In the period 1971-1973 time lost through industrial disputes* increased with the size of the plant from 15 days per 1,000 employees in small organizations (fewer than 25 workers), to more than 2,000 days per 1,000 employees in large organisations (over 1,000 workers).

Evidence collected in Wales and England on farm perform-ance* suggests that very small farms are inefficient but that once the three-man unit has been reached, further improvements in performance are small or non-existent.

For most firms the maximum efficient size seems to be when it controls 10 per cent of the market. After that, for all but a handful of companies, the ratio between profit and size does not change however large it grows, although the danger of fluctuations in profit is reduced in a large operation.

When Serck Audio Valves pioneered the idea of manu-facturing 'cells' in their factory (effectively these were self-contained manufacturing units or 'villages'), their sales went up 32 per cent, their stocks (the slack in an Apollo system) went down 44 per cent and the output per employee increased 60 per cent in the first five years.**

There is now a whole movement, grandiosely entitled 'The Quality of Working Life', which seeks to promote, through research and dissemination of results, this approach to the design of the more boring jobs. No one can deny that it is sensible. We know quite a lot about boring repetitive work, or the micro-division of labour as it has been called.

- The micro-division of labour induces fatigue, boredom, distractions, accidents and anxieties. The indirect costs of these things are reflected in spoilage, absenteeism and high staff turnover.
- The true costs of monotony come in very high wages for low skill level, high rates of strikes and wastage.
- Men, unlike machines, work more efficiently at a variable than at a constant rate.
- Moderately complicated tasks resist interruptions and gener-

* Quoted in E. Johns in 'Where Smallness Pays', *Management Today*, July 1976.
** Quoted in D. T. N. Williamson, 'The Anachronistic Factory', *Personnel Review*, Autumn 1973.

ate psychological impulses towards their own completion.

• Excessive specialisation reduces the opportunity for social contact or team-work. Long periods of unrelieved isolation are hard for individuals to tolerate.

It is not then just good sense to put some variety into the job? Are we really dealing with the individual's need to express himself at work? Many of the studies of job redesign show a gradual return to the old norms of morale and absenteeism, once the changes have become adopted as the new routine. A 24-minute job cycle is much more interesting than a three-minute one, but given the tolerance to which it has to be done, the eventual anonymity of the product and the remoteness of the end-use, is it really such a big deal? In one study it was discovered that the workers in small towns and factories responded well to the redesign of their work. The workers in large cities showed no response or reaction at all. The research called them 'anomic', rendered insensitive by large city life. Perhaps they were not duped. It would take more than an enlarged job cycle to get them to put their identities into their work.

A MIRAGE OF DIONYSUS?

The autonomous work group is the nearest that most large formal organisations have got to recognising the pressures of individualism.

The idea of an autonomous group is that a work group becomes responsible for organising its own system of working, job rotation, quality inspection, leave roster, etcetera. The foreman becomes a liaison man with other groups, a provider of information, but not a boss. The following example from Denmark shows how it works, but there are now very many examples from all the industrialised countries.

In a factory producing measuring instruments the assembly section was re-organised into autonomous groups. All groups are made up of skilled and unskilled workers (both men and women). The groups themselves divide the work. The groups co-operate intensively with the quality control section, and now other groups and the control section discuss each batch together. The workers state that they find it more meaningful to work with a whole apparatus rather than a part, as one has no idea what the parts are. Several find that they are more concerned with each other under the work group, and that they learn more. Productivity rose 25 per cent.

No one can quarrel with this way of organising work but is it enough? The workers' final comments speak for themselves.

'The firm is a profit orientated enterprise, and we only come here for the sake of the money, but that does not keep us from making our daily work as pleasant as possible.'

Autonomous groups offer only a mirage of Dionysus. The real thing will have to be much more significant.

It is possible that organisations adopting this approach can hold Dionysus at bay for a time. But today's change so quickly becomes tomorrow's routine. The Dionysian cult is not to do with monotony at work but with the whole relationship between organisation, individual and society. This approach does nothing to change that relationship. It is not therefore likely to be the true road to the future.

Growth, of course, we need, and the efficiency that produces it. But at what price, and paid by whom? Do any of the views discussed contain the true solution? Confirmed Apollonians will stick to their guns, modifying their ways perhaps to accommodate the 'autonomy' of the fourth approach as long as it can be demonstrated to improve efficiency. The meritocrats will continue to work towards their ideal of the slimmed-down voluntary organisation properly rewarded. The more modest and humble will settle for a Bill of Rights: some, behind it, will play their game of economic brinkmanship with the managers and directors, others will settle for a quiet life, keeping their individualism for the garden.

In modern industrialised societies we can see progress down

all four approaches. None of them leads, on its own, to a future which we can want. A four-way split is painful as well as unproductive. If these ways will not work, what might? That is the theme of the next chapter.

The New Professionals

Chapter 7

THE GODS IN NEW ORDER

We have argued in the last two chapters that the *organisational* imperatives (for increased size and greater consistency) in our present society are locked into an inevitable battle with the *individual* imperatives (for greater opportunity for personal expression and choice). It is a conflict that will not disappear. Nor, in my view, is it a conflict that Apollo can win. If our organisations are to survive they must adapt their managerial philosophy to one which is better suited to the needs, aspirations and attitudes of *professionals*. In the new mix of the gods which will result, Apollo will be less dominant and less inhuman. This will mean, however, a massive re-organisation of the structure of organisations and of their work.

This reorganisation calls not only for an adjustment of scale and style (culture) of institutions: it calls for a more profound change, a qualitative change. The model I propose looks back, as well as forward: to the village, the oldest form of organisation beyond the family itself. It is my submission that the time has come for the village to be reborn in the organisation.

Let us look, then, at the various paths that lead us towards this new village, the village of the future, the organisational village, and what it implies.

The Professionalisation of Work

The best way of looking at the combined pressures of individualism is to think of work as becoming increasingly professionalised. It is an ironic consequence of the specialisation so beloved of Apollonian systems that everyone is now a specialist of some sort, and all jobs are skilled jobs, or are so termed. And every specialist, as we know, looks for the personal prerogatives and advantages of specialisation – professionalism.

Professionalism brings with it some advantages and some consequences. The advantages include a protected entry to the profession, agreed fee scales and effective 'tenure'. Moved down a slot in the social scale, these become the closed shop, differentials, and guaranteed job security – all items in the managerial news these days. Only the managers seem to be left as unorganised professionals, as they have recently begun to realise. This emphasis on the terms and conditions of work is normal, even when scarcity and bread for one's family is no longer the critical issue, because to a professional his work is the major source of his identity. If you cease to describe yourself in terms of where you live or who your father was but in terms of your trade, skill or occupation, then the nature and style of that occupation are of great symbolic and real importance. Work is no longer a means of paying for the groceries, it is central to personal identity.

Similarly with earnings. A professional, like a craftsman, is paid for his skill, not for his length of service or his loyalty. Differentials are important, for symbolic as well as economic reasons. The professional worker will be concerned to ply his skill to his maximum advantage, for his commitment will be to his profession before his organisation, and we should not expect it to be otherwise. Professionals therefore will be mobile, with a reference group which spreads across organisations. They will move, and be able to move, when they want to. Organisations have to handle their good professionals gently or they will disappear. The good professionals have effective tenure and may be expected to exploit this.

And professionalism means freedom, the freedom to express oneself and to be true to oneself (the Dionysian virtues). A professional puts his or her mark on the job – his is not an anonymous act, even though it conforms to a set of standards common to the profession. Freedom also implies that you are owned by no man, and by no organisation even though you may lend it your skills. This freedom of the personal service professions is greatly sought after today. It is the personal service professions of law and medicine whose schools have the highest application rates, not the impersonalised professions of the civil engineer or the industrial chemist, whose talents, on the other hand, may be in even greater demand. It is this freedom of the personal service professions which the new specialisms envy and would claim for their own.

Professionalism, of course, carries responsibilities, but they are responsibilities to the practice of one's trade, craft or skill, not to an organisation. Professions are likely, as a consequence, to be jealous of their traditional territories, to resist new developments not initiated by them, and to be generally conservative in many of their attitudes. Demarcation disputes are found in medicine and law as well as in engineering, even if they go under other names. Today, in Britain, the legal profession is fighting to continue its monopoly in property transfers.

To be a recognised professional today, at any level of society, is to substitute the protection and the status of a trade for that of an organisation. Most people want it that way and most people can now get it that way.

A recent study in Sheffield,* England, of 245 school-leavers showed that 85 per cent were looking for skilled jobs. 93 per cent of these got the categories of job they were looking for. Work has become professionalised, and all men want to be treated as Dionysians or Athenians whatever bit of the organisation they work in, or whatever the cultural demands of their work.

This spread of professionalism colours all the cults. Even the true believer in order, predictability and system, the Apollonian, will be influenced by the wish to be treated as a recognised expert in the tradition of Athena, if not of Dionysus. It is this spread of professionalism which in the medium term will *force* us to change our ways of managing, for pro-

* Lucy Paul, 'The Four Letter Word', *New Society*, 17 February, 1977.

fessionalism has added the teeth to the forces resisting Apollo listed in Chapter 5. We may have been able to get away with lip service to cries for more individualism. We shall have to do more in the face of organised professionalism.

Our starting models for the new ways of managing must be the existing organisations of consent and contract.

Organisations of Consent and Contract

'Universities,' I said, 'are the prototypes of the organisations of tomorrow.'

'If that be so,' said a Professor standing near, 'then God help us all.'

Behind my remark was the suggestion that universities, rather like professional partnerships, mountain climbing teams, and theatrical groups or orchestras, have to be managed to be effective, but have to be managed by consent.

What is meant by an *organisation of consent*? In these organisations the 'psychological contract' between individual and organisation is implicit, and has a particular slant. In traditional, more Apollonian, organisations the contract runs something like this: 'the individual is here because he has a particular talent or skill or aptitude or just a pair of hands; he is lending this resource to the organisation in return for some mixture of money, facilities, excitement or companionship, and he cedes to the organisation the right to deploy this resource, himself, as it sees fit, within reasonable limits, often formally defined and negotiated.' If the organisation violates this implicit contract if, for instance, it offers increased excitement or job satisfaction, when all the individual wants is money – then it runs into difficulties.

In the organisation of consent the contract goes beyond this. For one thing, it has a very individual slant. A person sees himself as a valuable *person* which the organisation ought to cherish, not just a resource to deploy. He is very much an individual with a personality, with individual desires and rights which the organisation must respect. The contract also includes some deep beliefs about the way people should relate to each other. Hierarchy is bad. Argument is good. All men and women are on an equal footing.

We are talking, it is clear, about *Athenian* and *Dionysian* attitudes.

Now, the manager in an organisation of consent is meant to manage, to take decisions, set up information systems, to plan and to organise. Each individual believes that he has his own proper and valuable role to play and nobody wants to do anyone else's work for him. But the important decisions, the right to institute procedures, start things, stop things or change major things, must be exposed to possible disagreement before implementation. The individuals may not want to be involved, but they do want to be consulted. They want to be unfettered but not unnoticed. The minority report may never be implemented, it must be listened to.

MANAGEMENT BY CONSENT

Once I had to manage one part of an organisation by consent. I was trying to discuss why my instructions had not been carried out by a colleague whom I thought of as my subordinate.

'You cannot tell *me to do something,' he explained gently, 'you can only* ask *me.'*

'On the other hand,' he went on, rubbing salt into the wound, 'I don't ask *you if I'm going to do something, I* tell *you.'*

Similarly, a friend, moving into an organisation of consent from a traditional hierarchical business, was dismayed to find that his circular memoranda and his published requirements of his associates produced absolutely no result at all, not even rebellion. Just silence. 'Would you believe it?' he said, 'I've had to go along and make an individual personal contact with each of them?'

He got into further difficulties when he assumed that, since his associates rejected his assumption of the right to decide, they wanted to take all decisions themselves. Not so. 'That's

*your job,' they said, 'we have other and better things to do
than help you take your decisions. But we need to be consulted
about those decisions before they go into effect.'*

*It was not authority in itself that they were objecting to, but
his assumption of that authority before it had been given him.
The distinction is tricky – but important.*

The *organisations of contract* are those where *fees* are paid
for work done rather than *wages* paid for time spent. Professionals work for fees. They may calculate their fee on some
time-spent basis but the essence of any contract is money for
work completed. The organisations of contract are therefore
those who rely on contractors to provide particular parts or
services, which they, the organisations, then put into a whole.
Publishers, for instance, are organisations of contract, paying
fees to authors and printers, commissions to retailers and dis-
tributors, employing directly only a minute proportion of all
those involved in the production of a book. Architects, responsible for the construction of a building, will contract out all
the work, apart perhaps from the co-ordination and inspection
roles. It would never occur to an architect to *employ* in his
own organisation all the talents necessary to do a particular
job. Advertising agencies, too, do not employ the people who
actually *make* the advertisements that one sees in newspapers
or on television screens, they employ people only to contract
out this work to others and to co-ordinate the work of the sub-
contractors.

The organisations of contract use the ways of Athena, pulling experts together for particular tasks.

The Implications for the Managerial Gods
THE EROSION OF MANAGEMENT'

Professionals, self-styled or real, do not like to 'be managed'
with all that the word today implies of control, manipulation
and direction. They would prefer to use the word 'manage' in
its colloquial or nineteenth-century meaning, where it is equiv-

alent to 'coping', as in 'how did you manage today?', or 'did you manage to . . .?' It is interesting that our *old*-established institutions or professions do not use the word at all for their *high*-status roles, preferring Governors, Presidents, Directors, Senior Lecturers, Deans, Commanders, or even (in the British Civil Service) Secretaries. Managers, when the word does occur in such institutions, refer to the office-managers or warehouse-managers – the necessary 'coping' roles. Management, in other words, seems to be an Apollonian term. Management began to be a high status-occupation with the rise of the Apollonian corporation, some two generations ago.

The first major implication of the new professionalism in organisations and its Athenian overtones will undoubtedly be a tendency for 'management' to revert to its earlier meaning. In other words, the Apollonian, bureaucratic administrative part of organisations will become culturally subordinate to the professional parts. Managers will no longer automatically be the high-status people in these organisations.

What, then, one must say about all the planning, organising and controlling that is supposed to be of the essence of management and upon which the organisation traditionally depends for its survival? These must still continue. We must remember, however, that only in the role cultures is there a particular person for every task or role. It is not some equation inherent in nature that a task equals a person. There are many jobs that can be done by temporary groups, and it is a feature of the organisations of consent that the professional members wear a variety of hats, sitting in the morning, perhaps, as the planning group and in the afternoon as the adjudicators on standards – the quality control function. The design and use of the planning, organising and control systems will be in the hands of the people whose work is being planned, organised and controlled, although the actual *administration* of the systems, the collection and processing of data, could well be done by others. To an Apollonian it sounds illogical to put the control devices in the hands of those being controlled. To an Athenian or Dionysian, it is insulting and degrading to have it any other way: it would be to treat them as children, deviants or incapable and would start them on the Spiral of Distrust.

THE NEED FOR LEADERSHIP

But whilst Dionysians and Athenians may be happy to sit in various groups wearing their different hats from time to time, when they are not exercising their professional skills in groups and individually, they are not usually culturally self-sufficient. In practice, they need a Zeus to lead them and Apollonians to serve them.

An examination of the variety of co-operative organisations operating in the UK, which range from co-operatives of craftsmen, local community re-development schemes and welfare organisations to chemical manufacturing and motor-cycle makers, reveals that the successful ones are always *led* by some kind of charismatic energising figure. He tends to be an unusual Zeus in that his power seldom stems from ownership but from personality, ideas and initiatives – the kind of Zeus that Athenians and Dionysians can accept because his power justifies itself in action, so that he is continually re-authenticating himself in their eyes. Organisations of consent, in other words, have to be led – not managed. Indeed, if one wanted a criticism of our contemporary organised society, it is that it is currently *overmanaged and under-led*. The Zeus of the organisation of consent is therefore a critical feature, but he must be one of the gang, different only in his personality, his attitudes and the way he works, operating with power granted implicitly to him as leader, but depending always on his colleagues for their consent.

THE STEADY-STATE VILLAGE

The organisations of consent and contract still need an administrative steady-state: jobs which have to be so prescribed that individuality has to be squeezed out, where any problem-solving has been done at the design stage and is, it is hoped, no longer required – Apollo's section.

Goods and money have to be counted, products and services checked for quality, offices cleaned, computers fed, and machines emptied and filled again. Trains must still run on time and cannot be left to the individual entrepreneural instinct of the drivers. How are the steady-state sections of our organisations to be run (managed?) under this new cultural revolution?

Apollo, it must now be emphasised, does not disappear in this confrontation of the gods, he only retreats. Individualism and professionalism, with their Athenian or Dionysian attitudes, are widespread but they *mix* through the other cults and *overlay* them, they do not *displace* them. Just as Zeus, infected by Dionysus, is a more personal Zeus, so Apollo, when infected by Dionysus, becomes a human Apollo. Lots of people, in other words, whilst wanting individual recognition, still have the propensity for order, the liking for discipline and routine in work, and the tidiness of predictability. The new Apollo has a human face.

How is this achieved? Essentially by reducing the *size* of the Greek Temples of each steady-state so that those who work there have names, not just roles, and names that are known to the rest of the organisation, and where the duties attached to each role have meaning because everyone can see the end result and can understand how his role contributed to the outcome.

Small, in this context, is not so much beautiful as essential. Without the appropriate scale, Apollo loses his human face, our Dionysian instincts are denied and the old symptoms of the resistance to Apollo emerge. When Dionysus is denied, his claims and pressures dominate. Once placated, our other cultural instincts can come to the fore. Apollonians, treated as individuals, can devote themselves to predictability, Athenians, to planning, knowing that each is necessary to the other.

DROWNED IN APOLLO

James Robertson, an articulate advocate of a new social balance, has described his own personal experience of the British Civil Service.*

> *A young man in the Colonial Office of the 1950s, as the desk officer in charge of one of the colonial territories (or two small ones such as Mauritius and the Seychelles) still had a clear responsibility of his own. In the Cabinet Office in the early 1960s, he could still carry well-defined responsibility for useful work not far from the centre of the action. During that spell, I had heard about the 'soggy middle layer' as one of the personnel problems of the Civil Service, but it was only when I went to the Ministry of Defence in 1963 that I met it personally.*
>
> *It was a profound shock to discover after ten years of rewarding – indeed, exciting – work in Whitehall that so many of the stock criticisms of it were justified. There appeared to be literally thousands of people – real, live, individual people like oneself, many of them potentially able or once able – whose energies were being wasted on non-jobs (most of which would be done all over again by someone else and most of which would in any case make no difference whatsoever to anything of importance in the real world), whose capabilities and aspirations were being stunted, and who were gradually reconciling themselves to the prospect of pointless work until retirement.*

It is at this point that we need to change the model to reflect the changing face of Apollo in the organisations of consent. The *village*, with its villagers, must replace the Greek Temple as the centrepiece of the organisation. Villages are small and personal, their people have names, and characters and personalities. What more appropriate concept on which to base our institutions of the future than the ancient organic social

---

* In *The Reform of British Central Government*, London, Chatto & Windus & Charles Knight, 1971.

unit whose flexibility and strength sustained human society through millennia?

How big, then, might these villages be? It is hard to say, but let us at a guess give the organisational village a *maximum* of 500 working individuals. Above that number it is no longer possible to know everyone – anonymity sets in. It is clear that society has long ago outgrown the village as far as most of its inhabitants are concerned. And so have many organisations. But it is time to return to it, if we can. Psychologists speak of 'environmental disorientation', which can occur when distance or size or complexity gets too great, so that the individual withdraws from his environment or rebels against it. It is possible that aeroplanes or ships may become, or have become, so big that people no longer feel safe in them. It is known that some buildings, some conurbations, some institutions are simply so large that they are repugnant. 80 per cent of Britons in a recent poll said that they would prefer to live in a village or small town, rather than in a large city.

Sir Frederick Catherwood, then head of the British Institute of Management, said recently that the new challenge to management was to find a way of running our organisations with 'no more than 500 heads under one roof'. It was a call for the organisational village to replace the temples of Apollo.

THE RE-ORGANISATION OF WORK

The realignment of the managerial gods however cannot happen in isolation. We have just seen the implications for the size of any steady-state activity. The implications go further than that.

TOO BIG AT 65?

The Urban Church Project in Poplar, London, has been investigating the odd phenomenon that whatever the size of parish, the average core church congregation levelled out over time at 65. They also noted that the numbers who turned up for their annual meetings were of the order 55-65, and that the average staff of secondary schools had drawn back from 100 to between 60 and 70. They began to read and think.

It is widely held, they discovered, that the primary group saturates at 12, after which it is difficult to know everybody well. Within a group of 12 there are 66 possible relationships, and within a group of 66 there are 2,145 relationships, which is very close to the point where any further increase becomes meaningless, a community becomes a crowd with whom one cannot identify.

They began to find that if congregations grew over 65, they broke up into separate groups.

THE HARNESSING OF TECHNOLOGY

In the Apollonian era which is ending, man is the servant of technology. Men are hired to operate, service or often just to watch increasingly sophisticated equipment, working in an increasingly advanced technology. The equipment is often so expensive that man must march to its tune, adjust his working day to its, his habits to its, learn its language and be in many senses its servant.

The relationship must be reversed if the Dionysian urges of our new workforce are to be satisfied. Technology must once again become the servant of man. Ideology and preaching won't bring this about, of course. But economics will. The cost of providing servants for dominant technologies will, through the exercise of negative power and the hijack, outweigh the economics of scale which originally justified the creation of the technology.

Wherever the professional or craftsman attitude has been dominant – in photography, fashion, science, farming for instance – technology has been developed to *extend man's capacities*. The resulting equipment has remained essentially in the control of one man and his assistant. In Apollonian cultures, the technology, e.g. the computer or the assembly line, was developed to *do as much of the work as possible*, leaving man to service the machine and do those bits that the technology could not handle. Craftsmen (Dionysians) need tools, Apollonians need machines. The distinction seems semantic or philosophical – it is not. It is of crucial importance in the future design of the work of our organisations.

The design of technology to extend the capacities of one man or one man and his *small group* of colleagues calls for an advanced rather than a simplified technology. It is easier to design a series of specific machines with men to bring the work to them and to service them, than it is to design some all-purpose robot-like machine-tool for the individual craftsman machinist. It is easier to design a large chemical process plant than a small one. Only when the costs of staffing the large one become intolerable will there be *economic* incentives to design the smaller one. Only when it becomes prohibitively expensive to man an assembly line will we look for ways to automate the line completely and give it to one man to run, or find ways of doing without it.

Economic forces follow human forces as often as not. It's the lag that brings the pains. Wise men anticipate economics, others react. Which shall we choose?

FLEXIBILITY OF WORK

The organisations of consent and contract prefer that money is paid for work done rather than time spent. This allows the individual to control his own allocation of time and effort within overall deadlines. The attempts by Apollonian organisations to pay piece-rates have always foundered because they confused piece-rates with time spent. To couple the two, to determine norms of work for periods of time, must be self-defeating for it is seen as prescription, control, manipulation, with all the connected overtones disliked by people who might respond to the challenge of fees rather than wages. Any return to contract or piece-work must be uncoupled from time spent. There is no inherent reason in many industries why this should not be done. Even in such an Apollonian world as that of life-insurance, the salesmen are essentially on contract to be paid, by commission, for work delivered, leaving them free to allocate their own time.

Organisations of consent and contrast find it hard to insist that all work is done on their premises. The old tradition of out-work remains with artists, writers, designers, teachers, and is carried over to many consultants, research scientists, and many managers who find it easier and more productive to do some of their work at home or in a place remote from the main organisation.

Flexitime is but a small and partial step down these roads. Those organisations who have experimented gingerly with flexible working week arrangements (a set number of hours to be worked in flexible patterns agreed between the individual and his working group) have found no ill-effects, but the experiments still deal in minutes or hours rather than days or weeks.

The trend will need to go much farther to satisfy the Athenian and Dionysian needs of the new professionalism. There will have to be far more scope for *part-time work*. Individuals will work for more than one organisation *simultaneously*. Work will be done at home to be brought in at regular intervals, or communicated electronically to a central point.

Once again, economics will be the spur. For certain specific (professional) tasks it will be cheaper to use part-time rather than full-time employees, even after allowing for the extra co-ordinating time. The possibilities of more part-time or contract work will tap new sources of talent – including the under-employed housewife. The increasing cost of transport to work (reflected ultimately in wages) will make out-work more economically attractive to both individual and organisation. The increasing availability of real-time on-line communication links will make it both unnecessary and expensive to have people in one building in order to co-ordinate them. If people wish to be rewarded with discretionary time (university teachers traditionally have 20 per cent of their time for their own pursuits) instead of money, it may pay the organisation to accommodate them, instead of binding them full-time to the organisation with disproportionate amounts of money.

Existing Athenian organisations (consultancies, laboratories, universities) find that flexibility suits their work-flows, which are seldom copy or flow ones. Other work-flows will have to begin to adapt as Apollo retreats. We shall find ourselves investing in the *breakdown* of flow technologies such as assembly-lines, but the investment will be justified by economics not ideology, as the costs of manning those flow technologies become prohibitive.

SELF-CONTAINED UNITS

The specialisation of work will get reversed in the organisations of consent and contract. Specialisation involves the fragmentation of activities and the consequent need for more co-ordination, systematisation and centralisation. With Apollo in retreat, each unit will want increasingly to be given the means of solving its own problems instead of hitching on to some central procedure. Instead of a central maintenance function, each operating group will want its own maintenance man to give it more flexibility and self-control. The accounting and sales staff which have progressively been pulled back into central offices will begin to be pushed out again. Groups will increasingly be judged by results rather than by methods. To use the phrase of Norman Macrae of the *Economist*, organisations will be *re-competitioned*. That is to say, organisations will have more than one unit doing the same kind of work. Those who do it better will provide the models for the others, for competition of this sort sets standards more cheaply and more acceptably than any central set of rules and checks. Large combines of railways, mines, steel firms, hospitals and local government will increasingly be divided up again, and, whilst their *areas* of operation might be defined to prevent wasteful competition, they will increasingly be allowed the means to secure their own ends. Organisations will then have to continue to resist the urge to *impose* the means that succeed in one unit on to all the rest, or to think that a rationalisation of activities will bring the economies it seems to promise.

The truth is that the economies of scale do not follow a constant graph with economies steadily following scale. Logic and industrial engineering would have it so, but the resistance to Apollo means that after a spurt of economies, increased scale produces diseconomies and the graph flattens out, till eventually the cost per unit will actually rise as the cost of operating the *controlling* systems spiral. Unfortunately, this rise is today concealed by inflation and, in any case, the alternatives are by now lost in history and not comparable – so that, too often, no one notices.

An economist in the Hungarian government once explained to me that on principle, even in their small country, they liked to have at least *two* of every type of plant, even if this principle went against the apparent logic of economics. 'It is easier, and cheaper, to let them set standards for each other than for us to try to fix and monitor those standards from the centre'.

THE SUCCESSFUL CABINET MAKER

The cabinet maker had been very successful. He now had 110 people working for him and had just won a contract with a big chain of retail stores which would more than double his output for the next five years. He saw that he would have to give up his rather informal 'village' atmosphere and regroup his people into divisions and hierarchies. Whilst the consultants he had called in were working on the problem, a delegation of his workers came to him. 'We like it the way it is,' they said. 'We don't want this factory to grow any bigger. If you want to grow, why don't you start another factory for this new business?'

And so was the group philosophy born. No factory had more than 110 workers. A new factory opened every year, then every five or six months. 25 per cent growth was sustained overall. Each factory made its own line of products and ran itself, asking the man at the centre only for new capital.

But eventually he had 23 factories. How long could this go on? The pressures for rationalisation were getting stronger. His factories were beginning to compete with each other for business and cutting their margins (his margins) to beat each other. The demands for funds were getting progressively larger – he needed more control over cash inflows if he was to provide cash outflows. The economics of centralised purchasing of services such as accounting and advertising were becoming more and more obvious.

And he still wanted to grow. That was his thrill. The old problem was here again. What should he do? If he rationalised, he might ruin the whole spirit of the factories, offend his workers and feed opportunity to the unions, build up an unwieldy and unwanted central organisation. But could he resist his own need and the apparent logic of greater consistency and control?

In the end, he divided his empire. He no longer has his fingertips on each enterprise, only on three lieutenants. He has lost something, perhaps, but his organisation retains its vigour and its enterprise – and its inconsistency.

The self-contained unit philosophy will have to spread to the service units of organisations. Organisations will increasingly find it cheaper to contract out much of their central services, such as their management services, computer bureaux, training departments and consultancy divisions in engineering, finance, advertising, etcetera. The desire of top management to have all these activities under their own control conflicts with the needs of the service groups to be independent, and eventually conflicts with the intolerable overhead costs of maintaining them as a free good for the operating units. There is no reason why these service groups should not be *owned* by the central organisation but not controlled by it, except in terms of results. Organisations will then find themselves sprouting small entrepreneurs, giving to them freedom under an economic umbrella, ruling by selection and trust rather than procedures and control. Zeus will outrank Apollo.

ORGANISATIONAL FEDERALISM

As Apollo is pushed into retreat and into the 'village', the apparent organisational imperatives of increased size and greater consistency will tend to be ignored, and indeed reversed: workflows will be broken up, units made smaller and more independent, and employees be working on contract out of sight and hearing. It would, however, be sad to see all the economies of scale and consistency disappear before the march of professionalism. Small may be beautiful, and even efficient on its own, but a lot of small self-centred villages do not necessarily create a great nation. Organisations will rightly try to retain the advantages of co-ordination and central planning, of copy techniques and specialised inputs, wherever these can be compatible with the new cultural mix of management philosophies.

It would be logical, therefore, to extend the village concept into a form of *federalism*.

Federalism is not just a new word for centralisation. Colin Ward (of whom more anon) talks of 'topless federations' and points to one of the most successful federal operations in the world: the international postal service, whereby it is possible to post your letter in Germany and have it delivered in China. Where, one might ask, is the building of the International Postal Authority? It does not exist. Or who, to take another example, can point to the International Railway Building? It, too, does not exist, yet your ticket can carry you across Europe. Federations can be merely agreements for co-operation.

Yet most federations are more than this. Autonomous entities, usually states or countries, decide to cede certain of their rights to a central federal authority the better to serve their joint interest. Organisational federalism will probably come about in reverse, by devolution rather than by acts of union, but the net result will need to be the same, a separation of rights and powers between the centre and the 'villages'. The centre may retain the ancient rights of shareholders vis-a-vis the villages – that is, the right to a dividend, to the appointment of strategic figures, and to the provision of new strategic finance. There may also be grouped at the centre the ancillary services, operating as self-contained units with their own entrepreneurial freedom. No doubt, there too will be some 'federal laws' and a law-enforcing mechanism to ensure a degree of homogeneity amongst the villages: perhaps on some industrial relations matters, on accounting formulae, on quality procedures. But these would have to be negotiated to ensure that they did not infringe the independence of the villages, nor the requisite variety needed for the long-term survival of the federal organisation. Theoretically, the federal centre *serves* the state.

THE CONDITIONS OF FEDERALISM

Derek Sheane of ICI in London has spelt out some of the conditions for 'Industrial Federalism' by comparing the workings of successful federal countries (e.g. the USA or Switzerland) with those of more centralised systems such as the UK and France.

Federalism suceeds best when:
- *There is a common external threat;*
- *There is a 'web of interdependence', so that one state cannot dominate the rest, but each needs the others for some resources;*
- *There is diversity, whereby each state has separate needs and can look after its own internal affairs.*

Federalism works as long as:
- *There is a separation of powers;*
- *There is a clear definition of the role of these powers;*
- *There is an inverse relation between the amount of power you give those in authority, and their tenure of office;*
- *The individual is assumed to belong to multiple groups, with a variety of interests.*

Federal Chambers of Parliament are usually horseshoe

shaped and there is no 'leader of the opposition'. The simpler 'them and us' polarity has no place in federalism, because life is seen as too complex a business to be dealt with in one dimension.

Villages in a federation would tend to have freedom to control the means and to negotiate the ends. This is quite contrary to Apollonian logic, which calculates which means are necessary to its desired ends, and then controls those means. In a federation of villages, if one village prefers a three-day week with 12-hour days, and another a six-hour six-day week, both would have freedom to do it their way as long as output over a period was the same. For villages are private territory. Even the landlord cannot enter, except by permission or if there is evidence of abuse. As long as the rent is paid and the federal laws obeyed, independence in a federation is guaranteed.

To permit local idiosyncrasy appears, to an Apollonian, to be lending indulgence to inefficiency. This need not be so. Federalism, unlike corporatism, can exploit the productive spur of competition. In the corporate state, in which *functions* are co-ordinated, each function must co-operate for the whole to work – an invitation to hijack. Concessions to one branch must be matched by concessions to another, which is ruinous competition. Under federalism the system can be uncoupled. If one village does not co-operate, the whole is not ruined: there will be other villages who, in return for favours promised or anticipated, will move into the breach. It is a bargaining, not a conflict, situation.

Indeed, if organisations are to avoid the increasing costs of hijack, they will need to uncouple their corporations as quickly as they can; though unions who have got used to exploiting the hijack may be expected to resist the spread of federalism, for it must weaken their power.

The professional urges for an individual to leave *his* imprint on *his* work, to make a difference, personally, and to work at his own pace and discretion, can all be accommodated within a village – by judicious design of the work, because of the flexibility that is possible if all the factors are within one's control. When nothing can be altered without discussion with other units, nothing is altered. That way discretion disappears. Zeus organisations stay flexible if they remain independent and small. Gangs came before factories. Factories which are sheds for gangs are more tolerable than those factories which are sheds for machines.

GANGS IN THE FACTORY – ATHENIAN VILLAGES

In the early 1950s Standard manufactured the Ferguson tractor in Coventry under licence, as well as their own cars, using a gang system. An American Professor, Seymour Melman, has described the process.* 'In this firm . . . thousands of workers operated virtually without supervision as conventionally understood, and at high productivity: the highest wage in British industry was paid; high quality products were produced at acceptable prices in highly mechanised plants; the management conducted its affairs at unusually low costs; also, organised workers had a substantial role in production decision-making. In production, the management has been prepared to pay a high wage and to organise production via the gang system, which requires the management to deal with a grouped work force, rather than with single workers, or with small groups. . . . The operation of integrated plants employing 10,000 production workers did not require the elaborate and costly hallmark of business management.'

In the motor-car factory fifteen gangs ranged in size from fifty to five hundred people, and the tractor factory was organised as one huge gang.

'The gang system sets men's minds free from many worries and enables them to concentrate on the job. It provides a natural frame of security, it gives confidence, shares money equally, uses all degrees of skill without distinction and enables jobs to be allocated to the man or woman best suited to them,

* reported by Colin Ward in *Anarchy in Action*, Allen & Unwin, 1973.

*the allocation frequently being made by the workers them-
selves.'*

*Alas, Standard got swallowed up in British Leyland in
pursuit of market clout, and Apollo took over from Athena
in the factory.*

FEDERALISM IN ACTION

*In Britain's GEC 130 businesses are encouraged to retain their
own original identity. In industrial relations, for instance, the
central staff consists of only six people, for a concern employing over 170,000. Each business makes its own agreements.
Shop stewards, as well as managers, are jealous of their independence and encouraged to be so. Yet uniformity can be
desirable in some spheres. 175 pension arrangements were
replaced by one.*

*When GEC took over AEI, the central bureaucracy of
AEI was reduced from over 5,000 to under 500.*

*In April 1977, Tube Investments took to the television to
promote itself as a collection of independent businesses where
'we made it big by keeping it small'.*

Implications for the Task of Management

No doubt it will be called government, or direction, or anything
other than management, but both the centre and the villages
need to be 'run' in these organisations of consent and contract.

THE CENTRE

The centre will be dominated by planning, by the need to
prepare plans, reach agreement on plans, disseminate the plans
and co-ordinate the village efforts to implement the plans. The
centre's aim must be to emphasise the interdependence of the
villages, the common threat or purpose of the federation,
whilst recognising the individual needs of the different villages
(Derek Sheane's preconditions for federalism).

The resulting 'plan' is not the rational exercise beloved of corporate planners. It is the balance of forces, the 'possible compromise'. The expectations of the villages and the projects of the centre have both to be allowed for, and incorporated in the ultimate jigsaw.

The process therefore is one of bargaining, adaptation, persuasion and compromise. Vision and imagination are required, but so are sensitivity, the ability to understand other points of view, patience, tact, the skill to weld groups and fuse perceptions. It is a job meet for Athenians, often led by a Zeus with a dream, a mission or a vision.

Derek Sheane's mechanisms of federalism will be required to implement the plans. There must be a separation of powers. Those who execute policy must not be exactly the same as those who legislate policy, for this would be to give too much power to one group. In federal organisations it will be increasingly common to find the two-tier board of policy makers (elected or appointed by various constituencies, e.g. the shareholders, the employers, the consumers) sitting above the management team. This is the solution increasingly favoured by West Germany (a federal country) and, in principle, advocated by the minority group of industrial leaders in Britain's Bullock Report on industrial democracy. Power must be inversely related to tenure of office in a federal constitution, claims Sheane, and policy makers and senior managers will serve for defined terms (the fixed-term contract). Management then is a task for a time, not a career – quite proper to the organisations of consent and contract. There is a clear definition of roles and power. Good fences make good neighbours, and a clear understanding of 'boundaries' in work makes it easier to negotiate, plan and compromise because expectations become more explicit. Those organisations which depend on contract labour, as in the construction industry, are *very* specific about expectations of quantity, quality, elapsed time, payment due etc. – about the *ends* required, but not the *means*. Federal organisations based on villages of consent and contract will need to be equally specific about roles and responsibilities if they are to survive.

Finally, it will be accepted and recognised that an individual has a variety of interests and can belong to multiple groups. He may be both an accountant and a person with a passion for his region or for a product. He may be a devoted citizen of the organisation half the week, and a part-time priest the other half. No group, no organisation should feel able to claim the whole of a man, of his time, his energy and his interests. Nobody can claim a monopoly of other men's loyalty. Again, this federal principle of multiple interests fits neatly into the ideas of consent and contract and the notions of individual freedom.

It will then not be an easy place to manage, the centre of these mini-societies. The problems will be constantly changing, and so will the composition of the groups to deal with them. The balance of power and of priorities will shift according to the problem and the degree of interest of the various constituencies. Authority will wax and wane for each individual, depending as it will on expertise for the task in hand, access to information or to sources of power. Decisions will emerge rather than be made, and it will often be hard to discover where or how they start or finish. A sensitivity for the possible will be more important than an understanding of the ideal. Conflict will be endemic, but if it can be focused on problems and issues rather than on factions or groups of people, it will be managed productively. It is not a place where many would choose or be chosen to work for the whole of their career. People will tend to move in and out of the federal government, staying for perhaps five or ten years at most. Careers at the centre are out. Jobs and roles are in. For a qualified Athenian none of this is frightening or unusual. It all fits his needs for variety, flexibility and mobility, for the politics of persuasion and the art of compromise.

THE TRUNCATED PYRAMID

Dr Irving Borwick has described the organisation, ITT Europe, as a set of truncated pyramids *with a* multigon *sitting on top of a traditional set of hierarchical organisations. The multigon is made up of the product groups, business groups, functions and associated organisations, which all overlap and interact with each other and sit above and apart from the national ITT companies.*

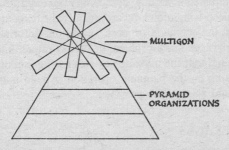

He points out that the nature of authority, influence, power and conflict changes when you move from pyramid to multigon. In the pyramid, authority depends on position in the hierarchy, influence stems from formal authority, decisions are made at prescribed levels, conflicts become established between departments. In the multigon, authority is derived from information and acknowledged expertise. Roles change frequently; decisions are managed rather than made, and emerge from groups rather than individuals; conflict is about problems or situations rather than between the departments.

All this, he points out, makes life very confusing if you are moving between pyramid and multigon, as many do. The multigon is a confusing, untidy political world to those from the pyramid.

The multigon seems very much akin to the federal centre I am proposing, even if the pyramids are not yet the villages. It is a world for Athenians not Apollonians.

But what about the Federal Bureaucracy? Will that not loom large? It should loom, but not large. There is need of an auditing function, an information-collecting mechanism, an accounting and financing operation, and an administrative support to the planning procedures. But they are there to inform not to control, to serve not to master.

Detailed assessment and appraisal systems should not be required, for the centre will not be responsible for the manning requirements of any community save itself. Financial controls need be minimal, recording only the outcomes not the details of the methods of each operation. Information will often be particular to a problem or project rather than routine. It is essential that the bureaucracy sees itself as subordinate to, and assisting in, the planning operation. Apollo must be subservient and as small as possible.

THE VILLAGES

Common purpose, informality, leadership, individuality, honesty, initiative. All good motherhood words. Words that indicate art rather than science. They are the materials of management in the village.

There are jobs to be done in the organisation village, and roles. But the place is too small for careers. To lead is not to manipulate, to bribe, cajole or threaten, with promises or fears of future happenings. Effort must come from the desire to play one's part in a common task, to be seen to be doing one's thing and doing it well. Dismissal or layoffs will be exceptional, promotions rare. It has to be management by consent and by inspiration. The villages are the heart of the organisations of consent.

There is a check-list for the would-be leaders of these villages – they need leaders not managers – which goes as follows:

1. *Recognise the Right to Disagree: in consent organisations John Stuart Mill's dictum that truth proceeds from argument is widely held. To be invited to disagree is everyone's privilege, but this does not imply that everyone has the right to take the decision. That right belongs to the one on whom the responsibility has been conferred*

by popular consent. Distinguish discussion from decision wherever possible.

2. *Control by Planning not by Checking*: it is legitimate to plan and to replan and to change plans. It is not legitimate to check what others are doing unless their specific agreement has been obtained. Information for planning is willingly vouchsafed, information for monitoring less willingly. The manager therefore has to work with a variety of planning cycles, and to be clearly seen to use past information as a base for future planning.

3. *Manage by Reciprocal Trust*: trust and control displace each other. If you are seen to control someone you are seen not to trust them. If you cannot control him you must trust him. Similarly he must trust you. Reciprocal trust is hard to establish and it is not self-maintaining. It is easier to trust those whom you have chosen than those you are landed with. Since firing will become impossible with tenure, hiring will become a vital decision in these organisations.

4. *Manage by Platoons*: individuals find it easier to identify with smaller groups. They also perceive themselves to have greater influence, the smaller their primary group. Trust is easier to create, the smaller the group. The concept of platoons (the ten-group in Antony Jay's phrase), has served the Army well and must be one of the buttresses in an organisation of consent. The platoon concept should be allowed to override other ways of organising work, which may look more rational but involve larger primary groups. Individuals may be individuals but they need a group to identify with. Everyone should therefore be a member of at least one platoon.

5. *Be Yourself*: organisations of consent are personal rather than impersonal. You cannot trust a façade. Openness and frankness and sincerity are valued. To act a role is to disappear as a person. Whatever your idiosyncracies or habits or values, let them be visible. Your own sense of identity and purpose gives identity and purpose to

your part of the organisation. It will be tolerant of un-
important differences, but it places great emphasis on the
concept of 'mission' or 'purpose'.

6. *Husband your Energy: leadership in these organisations*
   is exhausting. To treat individuals as individuals, to wel-
   come disagreement, to tolerate dissent, to listen more
   than talk, to be true to oneself as well as others – all these
   require a deal of energy. When energy fails we fall back
   on routines and general principles; we listen less and
   dictate more. Fatigue should not be a battle honour, it
   should be a crime. Protect what Toffler calls 'Stability
   Zones', the places of retreat, the times of withdrawal, and
   you will protect your colleagues.

7. *Think Conceptually: the ability to find patterns in things,*
   to connect the apparently unconnected, to make the words
   that shape the vision, this is what distinguishes the states-
   man from the politician.

8. *Emphasise the common task, purpose or output – not the*
   separate roles or functions. Tedium, unpleasant effort,
   even pain are acceptable in pursuit of a tangible outcome.
   A job is a job is a bore unless you can see how it matters
   to the end product. Roles detached from the end result
   are soulless. Means need to be attached to ends, and the
   end should be a common purpose signalled by a common
   language.

It is a check-list for Zeus, a Zeus with wisdom as well as
charisma. There will be Apollonians in the villages, looking
for security, predictability and tidiness. There will be Athenians, solving problems with their colleagues. There will be the
Dionysian craftsmen and professionals. All will be imbued
with the cult of professionalism. They need a Zeus to lead
them, to give them common purpose, recognise their interdependence and their differences.

In Conclusion

In these last three chapters we have argued that the tide of resistance to Apollo and bureaucratic corporatism cannot be halted. In an economy of plenty, individualism will flourish. To tamper with the organisations of Apollo through job redesign, or to soften the blow with talk of more years of life outside employment, will not make these corporate prisons any easier for the individualist. Apollo must retreat. We must find ways of designing and running organisations in which the other gods predominate and in which Apollo is encouraged to have a human and a smiling face. If bigness and consistency force an inhuman Apollo upon us, then bigness and consistency must be reduced.

Will it happen?

It is happening. In Britain three-quarters of the member firms of the Confederation of British Industries employ fewer than 200 people. In Germany the proportion is higher still. It is not in these organisations that the strikes and absenteeism occur. The British Donovan Commission on Industrial Relations in 1966 found that even in unionised small firms, only 25 per cent of the managers had ever experienced a strike, compared with 43 per cent in large plants.

In most countries the construction industry provides an interesting example of an existing federation of villages at work. It is a structure that has grown out of the nature of their work and their technology. Each job has to be treated differently – so that consistency must be left to the lowest common denominators. Sub-contracting is an accepted principle of the work. Groups of 'professionals' (artisans, experts or specialists) work together on site under the *leadership* of someone who, to be successful, has to be an accepted Zeus figure. The functions of the centre are perforce limited to obtaining new projects, selecting key staff, counting and collecting the money and providing a few advisory services. Attempts to rationalise the construction industry, make it more Apollonian and predictable through 'industrialised building' techniques, failed to have their expected impact. The nature of the work does not suit Apollo. The list of sub-contractors posted on a building site is the 'organigram' of an organisation of consent and contract.

Federations of villages and the accompanying managerial cultures were thrust upon the construction industry. Its companies were, in a sense, fortunate. Other industries and other organisations will have to follow by deliberate decision in place of instinctive reaction. We shall have to change our workflows, for we cannot wait for them to change us.

There is, however, a certain inevitability about all this. Large, non-federalised Apollonian systems are likely to self-destruct after a time if they do not change. But all will not then disappear. The work will remain, it is the bureaucracy surrounding it that will go. Phoenix-like, new villages will emerge from the ashes of the Greek temples. Society will go on, but after trauma and confusion. It would be pleasant to avoid them both by conscious thought and deliberate action.

In Germany, Scandinavia and France the trend towards larger organisations has slowed down and in some cases has reversed. In Britain size and consistency still seduce. Britain is thus being forced to confront the Apollonian dilemma more urgently and more dramatically than others. The developments of the next ten years will be watched with great interest by other countries. No doubt, with their puritan zeal, the British will publicise the traumas and not the successes, but there are bound to be some of both.

It is a conflict that has been long heralded by some, even if ignored by most. In 1951 Lord Radcliffe, the eminent British jurist, gave the annual series of BBC Reith Lectures. He said, 'The British have formed the habit of praising their institutions, which are sometimes inept, and of ignoring their character, which is sometimes superb. In the end they will be in danger of losing their character altogether and being left with their institutions – a result disastrous indeed.'

A journalist's report of one of Britain's multinationals shows an organisation well down the road to federalism, with the recognition of the need to balance autonomy with a common *image, of the dangers of self-perpetuating management and the benefits of villages.**

Small firms come in various sizes – very small, fairly small, middling small, not-so-small. At what point does a small firm disqualify itself by becoming too big? After all, that is what entrepreneurs starting up in a small firm aspire to and achieve.

Croda International is an interesting case in point. It started life in Goole, Yorkshire in 1925, with a staff of seven, a typical little local family firm, processing lanolin from sheep's wool. It still is something of a family firm, in the sense that its chairman today, Mr F. A. S. Wood, is the son of the first manager who was a nephew of the first chairman, and has spent his whole working life in the firm. By the time Freddie Wood became chairman in 1960 it was not-so-small, with profits of £134,000 When Croda went public in 1964 it had 350 employees. Now it is an international conglomerate with some 6,500 employees in 37 centres in Britain and 17 overseas, with pre-tax profits of £6,620,000.

Though Croda has been built up by mergers it has managed to retain some of the qualities of the small firm. You might say it has become a family of small firms. In the 37 centres there are more than 60 separate plants and offices. The company structure provides a large measure of autonomy for the plant managers and most of the plants are relatively small, typically in the range of 160 to 200 employees.

In that size of plant it is possible for everybody to know everybody else, and to have a good idea of what their bit of the company is about. The local management is expected to get on with it themselves and run their own show.

Most of the plants are in small to medium sized towns in the Midlands and the North. This too seems to make for contentment. Experience shows that country towns are good for industrial relations, so smallness pays off in that way too.

Another thing which makes for diversity is that Croda

* Harford Thomas in *The Guardian*, May 13, 1977.

products are neither standardised nor a rag-bag of random acquisitions as some conglomerates are. The company in its early days became highly specialised in the processing of lanolin for various purposes, including rust-proofing fluids, camouflage paint, insect repellent, and specialised lubricants.

As it began to expand after the war, it moved into soap and perfumery. Its first big merger, with United Premier Oil and Cake, took it into oil seeds and fatty acids. The merger with British Glue brought in gelatin and animal glues.

So there is consistency in all Croda's activities – they are based on natural oils, fats and waxes of one kind and another. Their mixed range of products whether soap, cooking oils, or adhesives, to mention only three, belong to the same broad area of industrial chemistry.

The advantage of the group organisation is that it can do some things in common for the individual plants. There is, for example, a central buying co-ordinator who can get materials on better terms than a single outfit could.

While the policy of devolution of authority to operation levels is fundamental, the company likes to present a coherent image. The board of directors, says Freddie Wood, is 'the central cheer-leading group'. Newly acquired companies 'get crodarised', with standard company packaging and advertising, and Wood and his colleagues try to put over the feeling and philosophy of the company.

Nevertheless, the individuality of the component parts seems to be the distinctive thing. Paradoxically, though, it is the concentrated area of Croda's interests which attracts the attention of the official watchdogs. In a climate of anti-merger feeling the takeover Panel, the Fair Trade Panel, and the Monopolies Commission are liable to be suspicious.

Is there a distinction to be made between the merger which obliterates identity and the kind of confederation of semi-autonomous operations which Croda comprises?

Freddie Wood is clear in his mind that the Croda style merger is in the public interest. One point he makes is too *many boards of directors are self-perpetuating private clubs, and sometimes not very good at the job either. The only practical way to shift the bad ones is by takeover.*

The result, he has found in his experience, is to uncover 'a fertile source of good managers at all levels'.

Croda has made good use of the management talent it has acquired. Ten out of the 15 directors have joined the board from companies acquired in the last ten years.

THE THIRD DILEMMA: INSTRUMENT OR COMMUNITY?

Demos Emerging

Organisations of consent and contract. Federations of Villages. Apollo in the service role to Athenian and Dionysian professionals, led by an accepted Zeus. Are these all the answers that we need to the ills of our organised society?

In the short term they will work. Or, putting it round the other way, it is likely that unless our organisations recognise the right managerial gods, and adopt their structures accordingly, they will find it hard to survive. In Britain some housing authorities have vowed to build no more blocks of high-rise homes. Similarly, the kinds of organisations symbolised by the organisational towers of our cities have reached the end of their era. If they do not change on their own initiative, change will be forced upon them by the changing societies in which they operate.

But the gods of management cannot help us in this third dilemma. The gods of Ancient Greece symbolised style of life, attitudes and attributes. They had nothing to say about the purpose of man or of life. Which is why, no doubt, they were eventually abandoned by their more sophisticated worshippers, who looked for a god who gave meaning and purpose to their lives. Similarly, the gods of management answer the question 'how should we organise?'. They do not help with the question 'why should we organise?' Yet the dilemma which is over the hill of our times arises precisely out of that question, the proper solved problem. In particular, the gods cannot help us with the crucial part of that dilemma, the proper role of the business or industrial organisations.

It is to this question that we turn in this final section of the book. The first two sections have assumed that the *purpose* of our organisations is clear, it is only their *methods* that are in doubt. I shall argue, however, in this third section that we are due for a major shift in our way of thinking about these things, a shift which will fundamentally alter the underlying relationships between individual, organisation and society and which may spell the end of the industrial society as we know it. This 'paradigm shift' as it is called will turn the work organisation from an *instrument* into a *community*.

The implications for society will be huge – but exciting. New futures with new goals will need to be created. Economic growth under the new conditions will no longer be the measure of all things. Indeed, new measures will be needed, that we may count new virtues. As with all revolutions in our thinking, be they in science as with Copernicus, or in politics, as with the creation of the American Republic, those who embrace the new way of thinking will thrive, those who resist it when it is established must wither. Organisations, however, are reactionary creatures. Like the frustrated chickens below, they find it hard to turn round, preferring to keep to their accustomed ways but to try harder. Yet for the new society to flourish not founder will need the regeneration of our organisations, particularly those of business and of industry, for more than ever will they be the building blocks of the re-organised society.

THE FRUSTRATED CHICKENS

One of the nicest studies of frustrated behaviour was done with chickens. Chickens are always easier to study than humans!

The chickens were placed along a line (A) and shown food (they were hungry) at point B. Then a wire fence (C) was placed in front of the food so that they could see but not touch the food. Faced with this frustrating obstacle, the chickens behaved in very predictable ways: some just went on pecking in vain through the bar, repeating their accustomed behaviour even though it was pointless; some got very cross and attacked each other; some gave up and went back to A; some, and eventually most, worked their way along the wire, still looking at the food, until they came to its end when they went round it.

Now the wire fence was changed, to look like this:

The chickens now had to turn their backs on the food in order to find a way round the end of the fence. None of the chickens could do this. To decide to move away from a goal as a first step to moving towards it involves too complicated an analysis for a chicken.

Can organisations do better than chickens?

In the new society which I foresee there will still be management and managers. The gods and the cultures which they represent will still be discernible and discerned. But there will be differences. I can see the organisations of the new society needing to be more sensitive, intuitive, creative and political. The science of rationality will yield place to the art of the possible. The gods will need to have a more feminine face; for they will be working as the agents of the *demos*, the people, the organisational community, however it will come to be defined, a fickle, irrational, sensitive mistress, instead of, as at present, the owners, however they be defined.

It would be nice, no doubt, for those who currently hold power in our organisations and societies, if things could remain as they are. Paradigm shifts are very uncomfortable for those currently in authority. It is hardly surprising that these revolutions in thinking are nearly always introduced by outsiders, by the young, by so-called deviants or revolutionaries. It is only normal that the managers of the old order should seek to placate or to hold back the forces of change in ways consistent with current philosophies. 'Social responsibility', 'industrial democracy', 'the mixed economy', 'corporatism' are current examples of remedies that are consistent with our existing philosophy of organisations, of business and of society. If I am right, these remedies will be mere placebos, pills to keep one quiet, for a time. Precisely because they belong to current paradigms, they will not work when the paradigm changes. They are, in fact, symptoms of a changing society, not cures.

Society under the new paradigm, as I see it, has a hopeful future, although the birth pangs may be painful for some. Demos is a benevolent master, for he is us. It could, and should, be a sharing and a caring society rather than a striving society, a society of personal service rather than of personal acquisition. There are challenges, of course. When economic prosperity is reduced from the principal goal to merely a means to other goals, it may get neglected. The society where scarcity has become a solved problem may rediscover the problem, unless we are careful. A value change of the magnitude envisaged in this section will not happen overnight, to all, simultaneously.

Those societies who change first, and last, may find the going rough and be pushed back into the older order. It is not enough for the work organisation to change – the organisation is but the mirror of a wider society where the institutions of politics, of education, of the family, must all change in parallel. Too many out of step and a march becomes a shambles.*

One thing seems certain. The task of management will be more important than ever, yet more difficult. In the new society the organisational community will increasingly become the cauldron in which the interests of the varying sections of society will be thrust. The new society will not automatically be a place of love and charity. There will still be sectional interests, groups who feel themselves discriminated against, individuals who want an undue share of power or privilege; there will still be consumers who feel cheated, workers unrewarded and skills unrecognised. The differences will be that money will no longer be the measure of all things but, more importantly, that these sectional viewpoints will be seen as legitimate, yet at the same time as issues which the community itself tends to solve. The organisational community will become a mini-state with its own political interest groups. The manager will be its Minister. It will not be an easy job, particularly within the conditions of direct democracy that will exist. It will not be a job that he will do for personal material reward, but a job done for the community and, no doubt, for the sense of satisfaction, even power, that that will bring him. In the new order any managers who were mercenaries must become missionaries: leaders with vision and political skill. It is a challenge worth meeting.

* James Robertson in his recent self-published book 'The Sane Alternative' (1978) refers to this kind of society as Sane, Humane and Ecological, the initial letters symbolising the feminine aspects of it. His arguments and reasoning have a lot in common with my own thinking in this speculative area of a changed society although we arrive at our conclusions from different starting points.

The Graveyard of Ideologies

Chapter 8

THE GODS THAT FAILED

We are in for a *paradigm shift*. The phrase comes from Kuhn's analysis of *The Structure of Scientific Revolutions*.* It applies equally well to social events. Kuhn argued that science has progressed by a series of revolutions, and not, as frequently supposed, by some orderly series of logical arguments and accumulating evidence. Each revolution introduced a whole new way of thinking. Things went on as before, but we now perceived them differently and so behaved differently. Copernicus' notion that the earth went round the sun rather than vice versa did nothing to change the motions of the planets, but it did profoundly affect the thoughts of men and the consequences of those thoughts. Kuhn uses the word 'paradigm' to represent the whole cluster of beliefs, values, theories and techniques shared by the members of a society or community. A significant change in such a paradigm is the prelude to a whole new set of efforts, and the new paradigm, when it is accepted, acts as a kind of framework giving direction and consistency to the new activities, and suppressing anything that does not fit the new approach.

It is only when the anomalies begin to pile up to a degree which cannot be ignored that conscious thought is given to new paradigms. These new paradigms come, not from the established order, but from 'new men', outsiders or youngsters uncontaminated by long exposure to existing ways of thinking. The arrival of the new paradigms is accompanied by a period of crisis as the old is replaced by the new – a revolution.

Kuhn applies his ideas to the history of science, but they

* *The Structure of Scientific Revolutions* by T. S. Kuhn, University of Chicago Press, 1962.

apply equally to other fields of thought. In economics Keynes produced a paradigm after the anomalies of the depression years, a paradigm which until recently fathered nearly all economic policy in the Western World. Arguably, economics now needs a new paradigm as the anomalies in the Keynesian and post-Keynesian systems begin to pile up.

Business, and the organisations of business, have been gripped by a variety of paradigms over the ages, as we shall see. Money and the creation of money have not always been fashionable, and the idea that organisations are desirable instruments for the creation of wealth is a comparative late-comer in the perspective of history. Nonetheless it is a philosophy that has served us well for more than 200 years. Perhaps its time is nearly up? If it is, then the changing paradigm of the organisations of business will have major effects on the wider society. We shall look in this chapter at some of the emerging flaws in the existing paradigm, before examining in the next chapter the likely and possible alternative.

CHANGING PARADIGMS
Social Attitudes to Business Through the Ages

The Ancient Greeks looked with disfavour upon businessmen. A merchant could not hold public office, own property or be an officer in the army. Commerce and business were thought demeaning pursuits for citizens, since trade added nothing to a product's worth and work performed for money was felt to be antithetical to the pursuit of goodness, truth and beauty. The accumulation of wealth through profit was seen as a sin and bad for society.

The Romans thought likewise. Businessmen were useful. They provided finance for wars, they operated many services, constructed roads and aqueducts, even collected the taxes, but could not hold public office or a military command. Although, as time went on, the Roman empire became an advanced commercial system, the personal standing of the businessman did not advance.

In the Middle Ages work was respectable as long as it was connected with the earth or the labour of one's hands. Trade, though necessary, was suspect, and thought to tempt people to value material wellbeing above spiritual value. To lend money at interest (usury) was regarded as a great sin. Later, as the Church itself began to benefit from economic growth, theological dogmas were redefined, particularly by St Thomas Aquinas. Trade, although neither good nor natural, was permissible if it helped maintain the country, while profit (and interest) was tolerated in moderation.

The Black Death, which reduced the European populations by one third in two years, started a change in attitude to economic activities. The Crusaders began a period of international venturing and the Protestant Reformation confirmed work in a new respectability: one could serve God, said Luther and Calvin, through one's work. Profit, provided it was reinvested and not hoarded, was acceptable, even encouraged.

The Puritans built on this in their insistence that one lived to work (for God), not worked to live. Wealth, provided it was not spent on oneself, was therefore a sign of attention to duty. The Protestant Ethic grew up, valuing hard work, condemning leisure, dignifying private property – what it envisaged, however, was not quite the hard-working peasant life that Luther had in mind when he started the Protestant movement.

The Industrial Revolution introduced the concepts of inanimate power to replace human and animal energy, and resulted in the growth of factories in place of the cottage industry system. Wealth now belonged to organisations (companies) and societies as well as to individuals, and was held to be desirable. The pursuit of self-interest in the accumulation of wealth was held to be justified if it led to an increase in the total wealth of the community.

The notion of 'efficiency' as measured by the creation of wealth spread to agriculture. Improved crop and breeding methods doubled the weight of English cattle in the eighteenth century: herds could be kept alive throughout the winter and wheat grown everywhere. Fresh beef and bread became universally available for the first time in England, providing visible and edible proof of the virtues of the new ideology of corporate wealth.

Adam Smith provided the philosophical rationale for the new capitalism. He based his theories on the notion of free market competition as the most efficient way of linking individual self-interest to national wealth. This idea effectively displaced age-old concepts of dictatorial control of the individual and his financial pursuits. It was a paradigm that proved an effective way of harnessing men's energies and talents for the creation of communal wealth and the virtual elimination of scarcity.

In the nineteenth century the corporation flourished in Europe and, particularly, in America. As an instrument for the collective accumulation of wealth through work, it proved far more effective than personal wealth; for it had undivided objectives, limited liability and a system of transferable ownership. Today the corporation is broadly seen to need to temper its objectives for the accumulation of wealth with responsibilities to its employees, customers and surrounding society. These responsibilities are, however, usually seen as constraints, no matter how legitimate, on its primary purpose of creating wealth.*

The Flaws in the Paradigm

The instrumental philosophy of the organisation is not working too well. What is good for the owners of General Motors is no longer demonstrably good for the country. Even the *enlightened* self-interest suggested by ideas of social responsibility do not guarantee happiness or even prosperity to the bulk of society. There are many signs that the free enterprise system based on competition between owners for the creation of wealth has outgrown its usefulness. There are those indeed

* This review is based on a summary by W. J. Cairns in 'The Social Function of Business' compiled for *Action* in April 1977.

who find remarkable parallels in our situation with Gibbon's description of the start of the collapse of the Roman Empire, and anticipate the end of an era.

THE DECLINE AND FALL OF ROME OR BRITAIN?

Gordon Rattray Taylor has summarised the symptoms of the end of the Roman 'paradigm'.* Without a new paradigm to succeed the one that failed, the pax Romana *collapsed into the Dark Ages. How many of these symptoms apply to Britain today? Rattray Taylor's list of symptoms includes:*

The break-up of small-scale farming leading to urbanisation and the formation of a 'mass society', with massive immigration as a further factor causing cultural disintegration;

The break-up of the empire and the development of an adverse trade balance;

The issue of doles and benefits to the urban masses and their growing preoccupation with conflict and violence;

The passing of power to the prime functional group, the army (in our day, to the trade unions), and their irresponsible use of this power;

The break-up of the aristocracy under middle-class expansion, followed by the destruction of the middle class in the interests of the lower classes;

A continuously escalating inflation, and ever heavier taxation to support the constant increase of army pay and of social services;

Decline of public safety as armed bands, drawn from the middle classes as well as the masses, seek to make a living outside society;

In place of lower classes modelling themselves on higher ones, the process is reversed and popular manners, dress, etc., are imitated;

Further concessions to the masses, all of whom are declared equal;

* In G. Rattray Taylor, *How to Avoid the Future,* New English Library, 1975.

Growth of superstition, beliefs in astrology and other occult systems and turning towards prospects of bliss in another world.

A reign of terror, in which spying, denunciation, torture and violence are employed – a wealth-tax is followed by confiscation of property outright;

Steady mounting of external threats: food supplies become unreliable because of irrigation failures, soil erosion and the desire of the third world to retain food for itself;

A decline from artistic and technical greatness;

Corruption and intrigue at unprecedented levels.

The detailed flaws in the paradigm have already begun to appear in the first two sections of this book. They are the first inklings of a paradigm change. It is time to pull them together – the five emerging problems of the instrumental paradigm.

1. THE FALSE LURE OF WEALTH

The instrumental paradigm makes the creation of wealth the paramount responsibility of the organisation. True, we must always remember, as R. H. Tawney reminded us in his great work *Religion and the Rise of Capitalism,** that 'industry, if it is not to be paralysed by recurrent revolts on the part of outraged human nature, must satisfy criteria which are not purely economic'. Social responsibility and the organisations of consent and contract will take care of that, so what then is wrong?

Well, it seems that wealth is necessary to solve scarcity – provided always that wealth is evenly distributed. It does not appear however to solve the problems of post-scarcity. For one thing, wealth is always comparative, some few are always going to be wealthier than the other many, even if the other many have a perfectly adequate standard of living. But those other many are not going to compare themselves with their less privileged brethren in the developing world and say 'how well off we are'. They will compare themselves with their,

* Penguin, 1938.

slightly, more affluent immediate neighbours and feel discontented. So then they work harder, don't they, to make up the difference? But that only makes others discontented. What's it all for? No surveys have ever been able to find a relationship between an increase in affluence in a community and any general feeling of increased happiness. This notion of wealth beyond the needs of scarcity brings us back into Professor Hirsch's notion of 'positional' or 'differential' goods, the ones that set you apart from your neighbours. If those are the goods which everyone is really working for – the minority goods – then the logical result must be a society where the majority always feel deprived. Wealth in other words *removes* deprivation in scarcity conditions (if well distributed), but *creates* deprivation in post-scarcity conditions. It is a recipe for an aggrieved society.

It is more than that, it is a recipe for a fantasy society. When most people are spending their disposable surplus (after taking care of their basic needs) on *symbolic* goods, goods that mark you out as different, then growth is effectively maintained by the growth of this part of the economy – what you might call the toy economy. Look at the shops in any capital of the affluent societies – they are full of symbolic goods. Who *needs* a Citizen Band radio in every vehicle, a wrist-watch television, or the pool in the dining-room which I encountered recently in a German house? Economic policies based on the growth of symbolic goods must be a recipe for a fantasy world, one dominated by managed fashion, advertising, built-in obsolescence and envy. Maybe we are not there yet. There are still enough distribution problems in our organised societies to ensure that the available wealth is not shared by all: until it is, more wealth must be created to spill over and relieve the remaining scarcity, or so it is argued. We are however, in all the organised societies, getting closer to the pocket-money economies beloved of some socialist politicians – the economies where all basic needs are provided by the state leaving earnings available for private indulgences, pocket-money extravagances. That is the ultimate post-scarcity society. If the creation of wealth remains its driving force, such a society will be, for the bulk of its people, a very frustrated society – because of the inevitably comparative nature of wealth.

But there are signs that people are beginning to see through that false lure of wealth. The movement away from symbolic goods, back to what people feel are the essentials of life, is growing. Of course in a 'welfare society' this movement is a protected one, for the essential services of roads, law and order, and often health and education, are provided by the wider society – from the wealth created by their organisations. But it is not only the 'back to the land' movement which rejects the lure of wealth. as the survey described below reveals.

THE DECLINE OF MATERIALISM?

Britons seem to be an unambitious lot as far as wealth is concerned.

Not for them, a recent survey revealed, the lust for wealth – they neither want nor expect a great deal more money.

The 'take it easy' approach was revealed in a national survey of 1,000 people conducted by the Opinion Research Centre and published in New Society.

It discloses that, despite record unemployment and cuts in living standards, the only revolution taking place is one of 'falling expectations'.

The British, says the survey, are a 'peculiar lot'. They are 'remarkably unambitious in a material sense and very few sincerely want to be rich.'

It adds that not only have people lowered their sights but many actually expect less *money than they did four years ago.*

In 1973 a survey by the Social Science Research Council discovered that 51 per cent of people would have been satisfied with an extra £10 a week.

Today, 61 per cent would be satisfied with the equivalent, about £17.

Asked how much extra cash was needed each week to live without worries, 17 per cent said none, 37 per cent said under £15, and only 10 per cent said more than £30.

Those questioned were asked to place themselves on a sliding scale representing their situation now, what it was five years ago, and where they expected to be in five years' time. Says the survey:

'In 1973, more than half expected to be in the top half of the scale in five years – today, only about a third expect to be there.

'In 1973, less than a third expected to stay at the bottom end – today nearly half expect to.

'The majority in Britain now only want to be just above the middle, rather than near the top.'

Asked if it was better to work as hard as they could for as much money as possible, or to work only as much as was needed for a pleasant life, 59 per cent chose the good life.

Political note: *Fewer people believe in an incomes policy – 39 per cent claim it is not helping to make Britain a fairer place to live in.*

Scottish note: *The 80 Scottish people questioned were unique – they were highly optimistic about the future.*

Common Market Note: *Most people gave Britain only three or four marks out of ten, compared with eight for West Germany.*

Do we care that we have fallen behind?

Only 15 per cent said they were 'very worried' – and nearly two-fifths said they were 'not at all worried.'

It is not only Britain that is beginning to find an empty promise in material prosperity. I asked a Swedish executive what he worked for, now that he had two homes, two cars, two televisions – two of everything it seemed. 'Time,' he said. 'And how do you want to use that time?' 'I suppose,' he replied thoughtfully, 'for some really satisfying work'. The wheel goes full circle.

2. THE COMPLEXITY OF WEALTH

The second flaw in the instrumental paradigm is the complexity that results if you put efficiency and the creation of wealth at the head of your priorities. This complexity creates new problems of its own, which society needs new resources to solve – resources for unnecessary problems.

Dr Schumacher, the apostle of Small is Beautiful and Intermediate Technology, argued that the upper limit for the average amount of capital investment per workplace should be the annual earnings of an able and significant worker, perhaps today around £5,000.

If the cost is significantly higher, the society in question is likely to run into serious troubles, such as an undue concentration of wealth and power among the privileged few; an increasing problem of drop-outs who cannot be integrated into society and constitute an ever-growing threat; structural unemployment; maldistribution of the population due to excessive urbanisation; and general frustration and alienation, with soaring crime rates, and so forth.

Concentration, specialisation and the over-investment that these entail, breed an inevitable complexity. Complexity in turn breeds a sense of powerlessness. We feel that events are beyond our control, with the kind of consequence that Dr Schumacher lists. Yet efficiency appears to demand concentration and specialisation, and few people have yet connected Schumacher's list of consequences with his premise. We continue to believe that there are separate remedies for alienation in society, for the maldistribution of population, and for structural unemployment. Indeed it is argued that these remedies need more wealth, therefore our organisations need to be *more* efficient – that is more concentrated and more specialised. Thus, if Schumacher is right, the problem feeds on itself as the solutions to complexity demand yet more complexity to pay for them.

The megalopolis is a very outward and visible sign of the complexity created by the search for wealth. Concentration and specialisation pulled people away from the countryside into the towns. For a long time, throughout the Middle Ages, the available technology limited the scale of these towns. A population of around 35,000 seemed both to be large enough to provide the range of skills needed, and small enough to be supported by food from the surrounding countryside. More specialisation, and the technology to transport and store foods from greater distances and for greater periods, allowed the towns to become cities. Today they are enormous and complex beyond belief. Any problem amid such complexity cannot be solved without more problems popping up in another part of the complexity. Roads provide the classic case: new roads to ease congestion in one place only pull more traffic into the town and create new congestions somewhere else. One man's solution becomes another man's law suit. Again, we find that more wealth is demanded to solve the problems created by the concentration and specialisation needed to create the wealth in the first place. Complexity feeds on itself in a process that has no ending.

But there are signs that the megalopolis has reached its peak, at least in the post-scarcity societies. In the Third World, where concentration and specialisation still appear to have benefits, the cities are still growing – and fast. In the West it is different. At present London is losing 100,000 people a year. New York, Chicago, Philadelphia and Cleveland are also losing population. Elaine Morgan, in a stimulating book* which records the history of urban civilisation, comments that those who are leaving the cities are mostly the middle-class adults aged between 25 and 35. As one of them said: 'The extra money I earned was going in psychiatry and double Martinis' – the costs of complexity. Elaine Morgan argues that as size and complexity increase, a city's need for flexibility rises but its ability to manoeuvre diminishes – too many sectional interests get involved, too many people with the power to hijack. The result: deadlock. She contributes a nice parable to illustrate the ultimate dilemma of increasing scale and complexity. There

* *Falling Apart*, Souvenir Press, 1976.

is now enough engineering skill and specialisation to build a building 400 stories tall. This could be an optimum use of expensive inter-city land. But the space requirements at the top to house all the machinery and equipment to service the higher stories would exceed the total space available. Similarly the cost of managing complexity can exceed its benefits. For many that has happened with our cities. If we counted the true costs it could be the same with many of our organisations.

One more example of the complexity of wealth: if one specialises and concentrates production, then there is needed a compensating wider area for distribution. Sustained growth demands wider and wider markets. Japanese car manufacturers cannot sustain their 20 per cent annual increase without continually expanding their overseas exports. That would be fine if no one else were making cars and the Japanese were buying their customers' steel in return: that after all was the basis of free trade – we will buy your cheap food so that we can make textiles cheaper for you to buy. But if everyone makes cars, then Japan's increase must be someone else's decrease unless they in turn find new markets. The complexity of this overlapping free trade is now alarming. No one dares to compute it, but the cost of the bureaucracy of the Common Market probably outweighs all the reductions in tariff barriers, if we take into account the delays and frustrations involved. Bureaucracy can be a greater deterrent to enterprise than taxation.

Yet growth demands ever wider markets. Can the trend continue, or will we realise that overlapping free trade (as distinct from counter-balancing free trade) is an invitation to the strong to rape the weak? Increasingly we see demands for protection from those about to be raped, even in the efficient industries of the United States. Growth, I believe, will have to become increasingly self-contained, with exports and imports negotiated on a bilateral basis, as with Soviet bloc countries. That will mean less growth. The unlimited creation of wealth will be blocked by the consequent complexity. The instrumental paradigm will be checked in full flight.

3. THE PARADOX OF PRODUCTIVITY

The third flaw in the paradigm is well known, but hides behind a conspiracy of silence. The instrumental tradition rests on the assumption that improved productivity is good. Of course it is, for the owners. But improved productivity inevitably means less labour for the same output. Only if output increases as fast as productivity improves, can there still be employment for the same number of people. It is therefore no accident that the most efficient (productive) nation, the USA, has the highest rate of unemployment among the industrialised societies.

The logic of efficiency has a good historical tradition. For centuries more investment linked to better management produced more goods at cheaper prices and more employment. But it was an equation which depended on constant growth to sustain it. It is generally accepted that a compound growth rate of something like 4 per cent is at present necessary to soak up the unemployment which would otherwise result from the improved efficiency. If Britain in the 1880s got even more efficient more quickly, for instance by massive re-investment of the expected oil revenue, then growth would have to exceed 4 per cent to sustain the present levels of employment.

Yet growth at that kind of constant rate is, as we are beginning to see, a hard star to follow. Even if we can conquer the problems of illusion and complexity, we are left with the very real problems of material resources. Too much has been written about this topic with too little real conclusion. It may well be that, if we hurry, we shall discover enough new raw materials and sources of energy to replace those which we consume at such a galloping rate today. But we shall have to hurry. In the meantime we can only expect those who own or control our diminishing resources to increase their prices and hoard their stocks. Growth will, at the very least, become much more expensive. To pursue it will start yet another vicious circle, as organisations seek to improve productivity even further to pay for the growth that will buy out the paradox. It is absurd economics, and before long people will realise it – long before the sun or the tides are harnessed to drive our cars and cook our food.

There is one alternative solution to the paradox of productivity – a reduced workforce. Disease, infant mortality, wars, have done this job for us before now. They are weapons which we shall, I hope, disdain to use again. A declining birth-rate may, in 20 years' time begin to have the same effect, although we should be in great danger if the birth-rate decline even began to approximate productivity increases over just one decade. Any other methods of reducing the workforce, even if they be called early retirement, longer schooling or shorter working weeks, are effectively arbitrary impositions of unemployment. They may be acceptable to some, but to many they raise the whole question of whether productivity is worth it: if all it means is food and shelter, but nothing to do except amuse oneself. This alternative was discussed in an earlier chapter, as an unrealistic way out of the Apollonian dilemma.

Productivity is becoming a boomerang. For a long time it benefited the owners and through them society as a whole. Until the pool of labour got too big for the outlets, productivity meant more work and more food and more goods for all. Now it *could* mean more food and more goods for all (if complexity were manageable), but it demonstrably does not mean more *work*. Productivity bargaining, as employers and unions in Britain began to discover, was a trap. Union peace was effectively bought by the promise of growth. If this turned out to be a false promise, the cost of the productivity bargain was either a reduced workforce (unacceptable to the unions) or an uneconomic labour cost (unacceptable to the owners). Society as a whole will discover the same problem if it continues to regard the organisation as the instrument of the owner.

Productivity is a boomerang when scarcity is a solved problem.

4. THE BONDAGE OF OWNERSHIP

The fourth flaw in the paradigm results from the tradition of ownership. It did not require Karl Marx to point out that nobody likes to be owned. Ownership is usually acceptable when applied to property, objects or animals, but not to people. The paradigm which views organisations as the instruments of their owners implies that the people who work in those organisations are also the instruments of those owners. It is a relationship which wise employers gloss over, indeed they would not think of themselves as owners in that context. But nothing can conceal the fact that people, employees, are costs on the profit and loss account in the same way that electricity, postage stamps and raw materials are. Materials, funnily enough, do a little better than people, since they get classified as assets or work in progress for part of their life. Shareholders are treated differently – they are beneficiaries, not costs.

Now costs are things that one minimises. However much the Chairman may pay tribute to the efforts of the workforce in his annual report, all employees know that, ultimately, fundamentally, they are a cost, part of the property of the organisation which it maintains and even cherishes, but only as long as they serve its purposes.

The instrumental ownership paradigm is so well entrenched in our society that it is not even mentioned. As on the plantations of America's deep south or the West Indies, the ownership of people is viewed as benevolent patronage, essential to the fabric of society.

The benevolent plantation owners found it hard to understand those who abused their system, calling it slavery and a violation of human rights. Modern organisations today find it equally hard to understand why people do not want to join their ranks, blaming the reluctance on prejudiced attitudes in the schools, a distaste for profit or a reluctance to work. When the young give as their reason a dislike of losing their freedom, they are not heard or understood. Such is the strength of the instrumental paradigm, with its view that the creation of wealth justifies all, or nearly all, else.

The rush to the professions, or to journalism, small enterprises, voluntary work, or teaching is, as much as anything, a reaction against the voluntary bondage implied by working as the instrument of an impersonal owner. Those who identify with the owners – the managerial class – may still be prepared to tolerate the earlier costs for the later rewards. Increasingly, however, managers in Britain, and elsewhere, are beginning to identify more with the owned than the owning. A union, after all, is still a form of protection against the owners. The rest of us will demand increasingly high compensation as the price of accepting what must be a demeaning relationship. And the power of the hijack will ensure that the servant gets his wages.

Those who cling to the traditional paradigm hope that the growing pool of surplus labour thrown up by improved productivity will reduce the monopoly power behind the hijack. Unfortunately for them, the specialisation of work which produces the productivity also means that a pool of labour is of little use unless it is filled with the special skills they need in each hijack situation. The increasing specialisation of work has seriously interfered with the free market in labour that used to be beloved of economists and politicians. Only in a few unskilled jobs does the theory still apply, and few jobs are now unskilled. The apparent pool of labour has turned into a scatter of specialist puddles in different parts of the country.

5. THE PITFALLS OF PROFIT

The instrumental paradigm depended on profit. That was the way in which owners got their reward for their energy, vision, risks and money. That profit could be re-invested in the enterprise, it could be transferred to other prospects (often via the stock exchange), and a proportion of it, theoretically, went to the state for redistribution by the politicians of the day. The lure of profit was supposed to pull money from decaying enterprises into successful ones, thus keeping society, and all of us, alive, well and thriving.

It no longer works quite like that, of course. For one thing it has always been true that profitability is not necessarily related to efficiency. There are often easier ways to make a profit, as I have already suggested, than by improvements to efficiency, particularly if there is not a totally free market – and totally free markets are probably an economist's dream. Profits often result from high prices, unchallenged for a time or a place because of the complexity, the ineptitude, the acquiescence or absence of proper competition. Great for the owners, lousy for the customers. Hence the increasing proliferation of anti-monopoly legislation, which is essentially anti-profit legislation, a recognition that profit by itself is a dangerous criterion in a wider society. Wise, profit-maximising businessmen progress through a series of limited monopolies, monopolies which they created by being first into an area, a market, or a technology. Whilst they are ahead of their competitors they can price above cost. Once the competition arises they must cost below price. That second way is much tougher, much less profitable.

Profit is, nevertheless, a useful way of comparing the value of outputs with the cost of processing the inputs. But if the value of those outputs is fixed artificially, then profit becomes an artefact. We have looked at the possibility that the outputs of an organisation are valued artificially *high*. It often happens that society wishes to value them artificially *low*. Railways, for instance, run at a loss in all countries. Since they are monopolies, it would be very easy to let them price their outputs above their costs, but this, it is universally judged, would be a licence to rape the travellers in the interests of the owners. Prices are fixed, by government, below any likely level of costs and the management is then required to work for a profit. Since this is clearly an artificial situation, management has to find other yardsticks for judging efficiency – quality, or the relationship of costs this year to last year, customer

satisfaction etc. Increasingly governments are finding it
necessary to regulate the prices of *all* significant outputs
(through Price Commissions of one sort or another), for it is
not just railways which need to have their prices regulated in
the public interest. The result is that profit becomes not a goal,
but an almost accidental residual. It is now a way of describing
the surplus available for the payment of dividends or for
re-investment – the scope available, in other words, for the
financial discretion of the management.

The advent of inflation has made everyone more aware of
how arbitrary is the definition of such 'available surplus'.
'Profit' never was an unambiguous term, but its nakedness is
now revealed for all to see. The Emperor is shown after all to
have no clothes. Indeed, so far removed is the present notion
and use of profit from its original intentions that it will not
be surprising if the term eventually ceases to be used. The
paradigm is out of date.

If profit did not guarantee efficiency, it at least ensured that
inefficiency was punished, or so it was thought. Inefficient
organisations die. This belief lay behind society's justification
for instrumental ownership. Whatever faults might lie concealed within the paradigm were redeemed by the ultimate
decay and death, through lack of profit, of organisations no
longer wanted. Increasingly however we find that old organisations do not die, they do not even fade away. The organisation remains even when its work is no longer required. New
work has to be found for the old organisation by investment
in a new technology, product or area, or by merging it with
new partners.

The growth of sit-ins in Britain when closure is threatened
is an overt declaration that organisations should have a life
that outlives any particular task. It is a principle that successive
governments in Britain have been forced to accept, in spite of
avowed intents to let 'lame ducks' die. The paradigm under
which failure to make a profit means organisational death no
longer works in practice.

Example or pattern

CHRYSLER UK LTD

In 1975 the British Government was faced with an important industrial strategy issue. Throughout 1975 the financial position of Chrysler deteriorated, until in November 1975 the parent corporation, the Chrysler Corporation of Detroit, advised the British Government that it wished to close down operations in Britain at the end of January 1976.

The British Government had just been presented by its 'Think-Tank' (The Central Policy Review Staff) with an analysis of the motor industry, suggesting that there was a considerable overall surplus capacity for the next five to ten years. The report also emphasised that the British car industry had lower productivity than its European counterparts.

The report was written within the traditional paradigm of economic efficiency and the implications were clear. The overcapacity must be reduced by the elimination of the least efficient. The Chrysler decision had to be taken against the undisputed facts of the CPRS study.

The agony of the Cabinet was public and obvious. In the end they agreed to subsidise Chrysler UK in order to keep the bulk of the organisation in existence, particularly the Linwood plant in Scotland where unemployment was already high.

It was actually an argument about paradigms, about the raison d'être of organisations, and the traditional paradigm lost. The wrong decision? Or a sign of new ways of thinking?

Social Darwinism, with its implications that self-interested organisations produce the optimum society, has in fact always been a myth. The law of the market-place never ruled unrestrained. Those who have pursued profit have always done so under a structure of rules and laws and moral principles, whilst the calculations of self-interest have never been used by the guardians of the market-place of self-interest. Indeed if any of the guardians is seen to be acting in his own interests, we are immediately outraged. They must never practice what they implicitly preach. Why so? Because a market society in which all buyers, sellers, workers, managers, corporations and consumers lied, tricked, stole and connived to promote their own profit would not work. The cult of profit is not and never was self-sustaining, it rests on deep feelings of a moral or religious nature which hold us back from indulging in pure selfishness.

The proliferation of laws and regulations in the market place, the growth of consumer associations, of government bodies concerned with Fair Trade, of crusaders for corporate responsibility, all indicate, perhaps, that the moral sanctions are no longer working as well as they might. The spread of the medicines may be a clue to the spread of the disease. A paradigm that cannot sustain itself by its own convictions is nearing the end of its life. Profitability, the cornerstone of the instrumental paradigm of the organisation, has lost much of its moral foundation as the rationality of self-interest has become glorified, as managers, and others, have become more mercenary and less missionary.

No one should blame them. Paradigms are powerful things, and when all the norms of society push us to adopt a self-seeking line of behaviour, that is where our energies are likely to be directed. Another paradigm – one which emphasised altruism rather than selfishness – might bring forth quite different behaviours. It is the unchecked dominance of the instrumental paradigm, and its corollary of private profit, that has led to its own imminent downfall.

The Death of the Paradigm

The flaws are there for all to see. They have been there for some time, but initially the problems with any paradigm are treated as inconvenient exceptions, unanticipated imitations. They will be dealt with in time, people say. A more enlightened use of leisure will nullify the paradox of productivity, and that same leisure will provide the scope for *all of us* to indulge our need for symbolic goods. The complexity of our cities and the bureaucracy of overlapping free trade areas will succumb in time to logic, rationality and that mysterious thing called management. Ownership is not a problem where management is enlightened – so enlighten more managers and let more of them loose on our cities.

Are the flaws inconvenient problems waiting to be solved, or are they, as I believe, indications that the instrumental paradigm has run its course?

Hirsch, in his book *The Social Limits to Growth*,* described bourgeois society as riding to prominence on the basis of three commitments. The first commitment was to a system of property rights, capitalism. The second commitment was to individual achievement expressed through a pyramid of incomes, inequality recognised by differentials. Finally there has always been a commitment to expand the degree of participation in democracy. This has always been an impossible trinity. 'Any two of these characteristics might be compatible,' says Hirsch, 'the three together were not'. That is, given unequal incomes, either democracy must lie dormant or capitalist principles must give way to a democratic political force.

For 200 years the impossible has, on the whole, been achieved. Democracy has, with minor exceptions, lain dormant in our organised societies. To some extent it has been bought off by material growth. The instrumental paradigm brought the evident conquest of scarcity and, as I have argued earlier only a tiny minority will prefer participation to potatoes when they are hungry. Then the principle of differentials offered individual hope to many. Although the statistics constantly show that only a few ever seem to benefit at the expense of the many, there are many who hope to count themselves among the few. Finally, for long the democracy was contained within the formal political conventions and did not exert its muscle within the work organisations – indeed was not organised so to do.

But today things are different. The increased vigour of the 'democratic imperative' has forced a continual erosion of differentials and a dilution of the principle of the pyramid,

* Routledge and Kegan Paul, 1977.

that principle which lies at the heart of the instrumental paradigm, while the concept of property rights is increasingly becoming irrelevant. Ownership is now more of a burden than an opportunity. It carries more responsibilities than it does rights, shackled as it has been by the commitment to democracy to the rights of the individual and the pressures for participation.

The democratic imperative is made manifest in the resistance to Apollo, the second dilemma of our organised society. The forces of individualism can be, I believe, harnessed by the organisations of consent and contract I have described, but the very spread of these organisations is a sign that the instrumental paradigm is no longer working as imagined. In practice few organisations today stick rigidly to the old paradigm. Those that do find that it lets them down.

We must begin therefore to face the hard truth that the gods of management have failed us. The precepts and principles which they stood for once, and which were outlined in the first part of this book, work within the old paradigm. Those who continue with the old religion under the new conditions will find their faith severely tested. Even the solutions that look so radical today (Women Directors, Co-Ownership Schemes, Employee Share arrangements) will be seen as mere changes in the rituals.

A new paradigm demands a new theism. New faiths for new horizons are now needed. Dionysus must be recognised, but if allowed to rule on his own he will herald a brand of undisciplined self-indulgence which will return us smartly to pre-scarcity conditions. Athena, Apollo and especially Zeus will remain as necessary components in the new scheme of things but Olympus, that home of the Gods, will no longer be omnipotent. As in Greece of old, the gods become servants of the new order, no longer masters of the old.

THE FLIGHT FROM A FAILING PARADIGM

Time *magazine, in its issue of 1 August 1977, chronicled the rush of European businesses to invest in the United States, as 'the last bulwark of capitalism'. Among the reasons given for the flight from Europe are:*

The cost of fringe benefits for the European worker. 60 per cent of a worker's salary has to be added on to his costs to cover all his entitlements.

The cost of holidays, sickness and absenteeism: 49 working days per year for the average Swede, much more in Italy.

A lower forecast growth rate for European countries – 2.75 per cent in 1978 compared with 5.25 per cent in the US.

The shifting political currents in Europe: in the Netherlands, for instance, where net profits have sunk to an average of 1 per cent on initial investments under the attack of high wages and high taxes.

For how long, one must ask, will the US be able to maintain the traditional paradigm?

I have drawn a picture of a dream that succeeded, but may now be failing. The instrumental paradigm produced wealth and conquered scarcity, but when that job was done the accompanying problems began to swamp the benefits. Gratitude is in order for past services, but gratitude pays no bills in the future. I have drawn a picture of society some two decades hence, if the paradigm stays the same. It is a society increasingly disillusioned, where a majority envies a minority and, cheated of growth, sees no hope of emulating them; a society full of symbolic goods, self-interest, profligacy and apathy. It will be a society hard if not impossible to manage, and one that perhaps few of us would choose to live in. People of course have been prophesying the end of society for generations. Marx thought it would happen within a generation, and 150 years later it still steams on. I am not prophesying doom however but forecasting change, for I believe that we can retain the benefits of efficiency and avoid many of our problems if we change the way we look at our organisations of work and their purpose in society.

The change, when it comes, will be a revolution in perspective rather than a revolution in violence. I see its seed in the organisations of consent and contract and in a new breed of emerging managers who see themselves more as people bequeathed with a trust than individuals committed to personal gain – missionaries more than mercenaries.

The demotion of the gods must not leave us without a faith. The new missionaries must bend the precepts of the gods to this new purpose. It is when that greater faith and purpose is lacking that the mercenary appears – the one who follows a chosen god because it suits himself.

Elaine Morgan captures the sick essence of the instrumental society in this piece from Falling Apart:

'It will surely seem (to our grandchildren) incredible that in our day it was profitable and seemed justifiable that people would take material out of the earth in South America, put it on trucks, drive it to the sea, load it on ships, transport it to the British Isles, unload it, package it with some style and imagination, advertise it, distribute it in vans to shops, retail it, and deliver it to blocks of flats and have it carried up a lift and laid in a corner in order that a British cat might excrete on it, and then it could be taken down again together with its discarded packaging and surrendered to the further energy-consuming processes of long-distance urban disposal.'

The Affluent Outworker

Chapter 9

THE RE-ORGANISED SOCIETY

The Chinese, I am told, use the same ideogram for 'danger' as for 'opportunity'. In the dilemmas of the current organised society there lies great opportunity if we wish to seize it. Efficiency and human dignity can be bedfellows, but preaching will not achieve it, nor pious aspirations, nor tough bargaining in wage negotiations, nor party political programmes. The marriage has to happen where the action is, in our organisations, through a re-organisation of work. It must be a re-organisation which allows a man, by himself or with a group, to see the result of his labours in a finished task, and to take pride or pleasure therein, as well as tangible and just reward. Yet it must also be a re-organisation that preserves the efficiency and the fruits of organised effort.

This is not a call for a return to rustic ways, to self-sufficiency, communes or folk-crafts. Such things must have their place in a re-organised society and will be a model for many, but they cannot be a universal recipe. To many people such ways are more of a threat than a promise. Do we have to throw away all the hard won comforts of the instrumental paradigm along with the bathwater of alienation? No, not if we are imaginative in our re-design of our organisations, using the new technologies thrown up by the instrumental paradigm in its heyday. We must use our old gods in new ways.

I have argued that the competitive wealth-creating world of that instrumental paradigm is coming to the end of its useful life. Although I can accept many of the starting premises of the two main contenders for the succession, contemporary Marxism and post-industrial corporatism, I cannot see them dealing with the dilemmas any better than the instrumental paradigm because both of them in fact continue to envisage an instrumental role for the work organisation.

It is because the work organisation now affects so many people that no change will matter much, unless it changes those organisations. To run away from them is no better, for I cannot envisage a society today which is not built upon formal organisations. The organised society in some form is here to stay. It just needs re-organising.

This chapter presents one vision of a possible society, a vision rooted in the design and management of the work organisation, an alternative paradigm for a re-organised society. It is not new in its conception, for its basic idea of *community* as the key to organisation has been around since Aristotle. Yet the idea has never fired a whole society except in fiction, because the pressures of efficiency combined with the needs of scarcity were too overwhelming. The time, however, is soon coming when the forces are working for the new paradigm rather than against it. Efficiency and human dignity can start to experiment with living together. Let it start in organisations and then spread. That way something might happen.

The gods, then, in the service of man? Yes, but let us call man 'demos' instead, not only to keep the Greek idiom but to emphasise that it is man in community with others that becomes pre-eminent. Managerial fashion cannot, in this new re-organised society, be a matter for personal choice or for external imposition but must be for the benefit of all those affected – the demos or the community.

ALTERNATIVE PARADIGMS

Others have glimpsed opportunity in the problems of modern society, opportunity to promote a whole range of alternative paradigms. Indeed the very multiplicity of alternatives is one more symptom of a failing paradigm. Here are just two of the more noticeable contenders:

MARXISM

All the major successful revolutions of the twentieth century have been inspired by Marx. Even Mussolini and Hitler sought their early justification in his thoughts. Misquoted and misunderstood though he often has been, this one man has given birth to a paradigm which has proved itself a most powerful enemy of traditional capitalism. In a way it is strange, because Marx is vague and confusing about the details of the ultimate socialist state which would result from the revolution of the proletariat.

Marx was above all a historian. History to him was always a sequence of class conflicts from which a new social order (paradigm) emerged. Capitalism and the rise of the bourgeoisie succeeded feudalism, but in its turn created the conflict between the owners of property and the workers, the proletariat. In the ultimately inevitable conflict the latter would win, and the notion of property and the state would disappear.

Because he sees it in terms of a class conflict, Marx has always been the bogey of the bourgeoisie. It can be argued, however, that much of what he wanted has come to pass. Private property still exists it is true, but in a much watered-down version, and greatly extended – particularly through pension funds – beyond the so-called property-owners' class. Listen to the detailed programme of the Communist Manifesto:

'The abolition of corporate property in land; adoption of a heavy progressive income tax; abolition of the right of inheritance; confiscation of the property of all emigrants and rebels; centralisation of credit in the state; centralisation of means of communication and transport in the state; extension of factories owned by the state; establishment of industrial armies, especially for agriculture; combination of agriculture with manufacturing industries; gradual abolition of distinction between town and country; free education for all children in state-operated schools; combination of education with industrial production.'

Marx himself might not have found much to quarrel with

*in much of Europe in the 1970s. Marx believed in centralis-
ation and specialisation, in factories and cities. The classless
society, to him, would enjoy all the benefits of efficiency. Work
is a moral stimulus, a right and a duty. Large-scale planning
means that money is no longer a source of power.*

*Modern Marxism still sees the present world in terms of a
class struggle. Those who would be deposed are right to fear
it. It is not clear however, with the revolution won, how the
revolutionaries would deal with the paradox of productivity,
the complexity of specialisation; nor what they would provide
for motivation in place of differentials or property. New
people, one suspects, but old problems.*

THE POST-INDUSTRIAL SOCIETY

*Daniel Bell is perhaps the best-known exponent of this
paradigm. He writes in* The Coming of Post-Industrial Society*
*that a post-industrial society is increasingly a communal society
wherein public mechanisms rather than the market become
the allocators of goods, and public choice rather than individual demand becomes the arbiter of services.*

*There are, he says, five dimensions of the post-industrial
society. First in the economic sector he sees a shift from a
manufacturing to a service economy; occupationally, there is
a new pre-eminence of the professional and technical class;
in government, the key principle of society becomes the 'cen-
trality of theoretical knowledge as the source of innovation
and policy'; there is technological forecasting, and decision-
making takes place by means of a new 'intellectual technology'. The 'new men' will be the scientists, the mathe-
maticians, the engineers and the economists. Whereas in the
industrial society business has been the 'focus of values and
the locus of power,' in the post-industrial society production
and business decisions will be subordinated to, or will derive
from, other forces in society; the crucial decisions regarding*

---

* D. Bell: *The Coming of Post-Industrial Society*, Heinemann, 1974.

*the growth of the economy and its balance will come from
government. Growth will be made subject to ecological
harmony, and some reduction in effluence may be planned to
check competition for resources.*

*Expressed in the idiom of this book, we can see in Bell's
forecast the rise to prominence of Dionysians (the professionals) and of Athenians (the problem-solvers). It is a recipe
for the meritocratic corporate state. What is unclear, however,
is the way in which these Athenians and Dionysians will work
together. How will the organisations work? Who will make
the key decisions and how will they be implemented? Can
Apollo and Zeus be eliminated just like that? The new priorities may be consistent with Athena and Dionysus and all they
stand for, but how will they be transmitted through to the
workaday world? Unless these managerial and organisational
questions are faced, the post-industrial society remains an
academic dream.*

FORCES OF CHANGE

The re-organised society of my vision will be helped on its way
by *three forces*, all of which can be glimpsed as seedlings in
today's situation. Give them twenty years and some encouragement and they could be in full flower. These forces are the
search for community, the *economics of quality* and the *revolution in communications*. Let me explain briefly what I mean
by each, before examining what that new society looks like.

THE SEARCH FOR COMMUNITY

There is nothing new here. St Benedict was praising the idea
of a community when he founded the first Benedictine monastery at Monte Cassino in the seventh century – a community
in which all were equal yet each was different, a community
where each man's individual effort contributed to some common task or mission, where work, leisure, and the good things
of life met in balance, where privacy and mutual aid were both

important. Sir Thomas More's *Utopia*, written whilst he watched Henry VIII of England create a very different society based on property and privilege, sought the same ideals.

In 1977 the Decentralist League of Vermont (see below) is in the best tradition of the great anarchist thinkers of the nineteenth century, men such as William Godwin in England, Pierre Joseph Proudhon in France, and Peter Kropotkin in Russia. It is a pity that anarchy has acquired an association with violence, with deliberate disorder and disruption, for the great anarchist writers were gentle revolutionaries preaching a world of small communities, based on mutual aid and 'free from imposed authority' (the true meaning of 'anarchy'). Listen, for instance, to Kropotkin in *Mutual Aid*:

> *To attribute, therefore, the industrial progress of our century to the war of each against all which it has proclaimed, is to reason like the man who, knowing not the causes of rain, attributes it to the victim he has immolated before his day idol. For industrial progress, as for every other conquest over nature, mutual aid and close intercourse certainly are, as they have been, much more advantageous than mutual struggle.*

THE DECENTRALIST LEAGUE OF VERMONT

In March 1977 a group of decentralists in the small state of Vermont, USA, issued a statement of principles as the first step in a campaign to move traditional political thinking away from Left-Right or Liberal-Conservative to Centralist-Decentralist. The organising group were all people active in Vermont politics, but drawn evenly from the traditional left and the traditional right.

Their statement of principles made the point that the trend toward centralisation in social, economic and political systems has given rise to a deep sense of powerlessness among the people, a growing alienation throughout society, the depersonalisation of vital services, excessive reliance on the techniques of management and control, and a loss of great traditions.

Their platform for action had ten points, some of which were
- *growth of local citizen alliances, which strengthen self-government and broader participation in economic and political decisions;*
- *widespread ownership of productive industry by Vermonters and employees;*
- *a decent level of income for all Vermonters, through their productive efforts whenever possible, or through compassionate help which enhances their dignity and self-respect;*
- *the reshaping of education to promote self-reliance, creativity and a unity of learning and work;*
- *a revival of craftsmanship in surroundings where workers can obtain personal satisfaction from their efforts;*
- *the use of technologies appropriate to local enterprise, and which increase our energy self-sufficiency.*

The search for community has always been closely linked with cries for federalism. Federalism looks for strength in diversity, distrusting any tendency to centralise, to put too much power in one place. Such ways of thinking never got far in Europe, whose states have always been centralist: even their revolutions sought to change the power at the centre, not to do away with that centre, and Germany had to have federalism thrust upon her at the end of the last war (in the misguided belief that a federal structure would weaken her!). This centralism carried over into our organisations, with the consequences which we have seen. It reflects, perhaps, the perennial (and futile?) concern of European thought with the search for the unifying principle, the one true system or starting premise. Pluralism, as it is called, never flourished in Europe in politics, religion or philosophy, in spite of such talented advocates as Burke, de Tocqueville and Weber. We live today with the consequences of this neglect, still imprisoned in the skyscraper towers of centralism – skyscrapers now so tall and complicated that there is no longer room at their top for the systems and services they need for their survival!

All the signs however indicate a revival of decentralist thoughts. Vermont is not the only boundary state to harbour federalist notions. In Britain, France, Spain – the major centralist countries – the boundary states are far more fervent than Vermont needs to be, located as it is in a federalist tradition. The creation of the Common Market has at least made the French and the British aware of the problems of centralism. Indeed the decentralist pressures which the Brussels Commission has provoked in response to its own centralist posture may yet be seen as its most lasting contribution to European history. What has been christened the 'New Tribalism' is breaking out all over. Even Cornwall has found a historical pretext for claiming a right to secede from the United Kingdom, whilst Corsica has made it unmistakably clear that it prefers the French to leave. Canada is facing the very real prospect of the secession of Quebec. In Switzerland the Jura is demanding independence. In all these cases it is hard to argue that independence would be *economically* beneficial. The reasons seem more deep-rooted than that – a need for a regional identity, a search for a territorial community, an expression of cultural uniqueness.

In a speech to the islanders of Barbados, Dr Schumacher praised the concept of 'islandness'. If London were divided up, he points out, into 'islands' or 'nations' of the same size as Barbados there would be over 30 such 'nations'.

Think of it: 30 nations like Iceland or Barbados, each with a parliament; a government: even a Central Bank and its own currency. Actually, Switzerland has an internal structure somewhat like that. With just over six million inhabitants it consists of 27 "cantons" averaging about a quarter of a million people each. Each canton has a government and a Kantonalbank. Small and very small countries can teach us many lessons. Quantitatively they amount to nothing at all, but they have a certain quality or personality of their own and thus they amount to something significant.'

Communities are not just small. They are different, the one

from the other, with each their own personality. More importantly, they are not owned by anyone nor do they own anyone. One *belongs* to a community as a member, and that community can in turn belong to a wider group by agreement. It is always by agreement, for contractual arrangements replace those dictated by authority, and the consent of the governed is a prerequisite of government. Communities, after all, exist primarily for their members and for future generations of members; as such they can outlive any task, survive any setback, outlast any product. Communities, unlike instruments, have a life of their own.

The underlying search for community in modern society is the first of the three major forces pushing towards a redesign of the work organisation. Organisations are the children of their parent environment, but children can influence their parents as well as be influenced by them. The pressure for community may appear in the organisations of work before they surface in the wider society. To think of organisations as communities rather than as instruments may appear as trivial semantics, but the implications go deep. We shall look at them shortly.

THE ECONOMICS OF QUALITY

The second force encouraging a rethink of the role and shape of the work organisation is the emerging notion of the economics of *quality*, as opposed to the economics of *quantity*. The ways in which we measure things influence hugely the ways in which we see things. Because accountants chose to put people on the profit and loss account instead of the balance sheet, we have for centuries viewed those people as the tools of the organisation. Football teams put their players on the balance sheets – as assets (or maybe liabilities). It makes a difference.

It is rather the same with economics. Orthodox economics is about the production and consumption of goods and services – quantity. Like those of accounting, many of its definitions are necessarily arbitrary. Economists have joked for years about the huge increase in GNP which would result if we each employed each other's wives as our housekeepers. This kind of arbitrariness should teach us not to take it all too seriously. Keynes after all advised mankind not to 'over-estimate the importance of the economic problem, or sacrifice to its supposed necessities other matters of greater and more permanent significance'.

Like many of Keynes' words of wisdom, this admonishment has got buried by the success of his techniques. In 1825 the Provost of Oriel warned against the establishment of a Pro-fessorship of Political Economy at Oxford. It was a science, he said, too 'prone to usurp the rest'. History seems to have heeded him, not Keynes.

For some time, however, we have been conscious of the omissions of economics. Note today the increasing talk of the so-called 'gift economy', covering things we do for love not money, and the increasing recognition that economics gives preference not only to the things which can be measured, but also to the short-term as opposed to the long. Social cost-benefit analysis, arbitrary though it is, is one attempt to bring the unquantified and the long-term into the calculations. There is, too, a growing feeling that the basic concept of economics ('everything has a price') is somehow demeaning and diminish-ing. How can you put monetary values, as we try to do, on the loss of a husband or the disfigurement of one's face? As Schumacher says 'it takes the sacredness out of life'. Today even the leading economists speak of the limitations of econ-omics. Professor Philips Brown, when President of the Royal Economic Society, spoke of 'the smallness of the contribution that the most conspicuous developments of economics . . . have made to the solution of the most pressing problems of our times'. Others have echoed him. Perhaps it is because econ-omics is essentially a study of means, not ends. Because of the pervasiveness of the science of economics, we have become obsessed with those means and given insufficient thought to the ends to which they lead.

But economics can change. The economics of quantity, of

measurable and priceable production and consumption, was the economics of scarcity, of Adam Smith and his concern with the Wealth of Nations. The post-scarcity economics will be different, because the assumptions about the 'ends' of the whole exercise will change. Perhaps they will be more like what Schumacher calls 'Buddhist Economics'. As Schumacher sees them, the differences between the new and the old economics goes something like this:

Traditional economics is mainly interested in the *creation of wealth*, whereas Buddhist Economics concerns itself with the process of living. Thus traditional economics regards consumption as the goal and the factors of production as the means. A man who consumes more is 'better off' than he who consumes less. A Buddhist economist would regard this as very irrational: to him the aim should be a maximum of wellbeing with a minimum of consumption.

Traditional economics sees labour as a cost to be minimised. Buddhist economics sees work as a way of developing and demonstrating human potential. Traditional economics invests in *machines*, Buddhist in *tools* which extend man's capacity but do not supplant him.

The traditional economics tends to take statistics showing an increase in the number of ton/miles per head of the population carried by a transport system as proof of economic progress; while to the Buddhist economist the same statistics would indicate a highly undesirable deterioration in the *pattern* of consumption, for those who achieve wellbeing with less resources ferried less expensively from less far away are likely to be living less complicated, 'better' lives than others.

Finally, traditional economics does not distinguish between renewable and non-renewable matter. It is all input, priced at its exchange value. Buddhist economists regard this as parasitical. Non-renewable goods must be treated with great care and reverence and replaced if possible, e.g. by planting trees.

The statistics and the measuring devices are often unchanged between the old and these new economics. They are the means, the methods. It is the ends that matter. Fewer and fewer people would today like to stand up publicly and proclaim that the principles of Buddhist economics are all wrong. Recognition of the new concepts is even becoming official. The Japanese have worked out a new index of Net National Welfare to replace GNP, which they use for their long-term planning. The Japanese suggestions involve the following changes:

GNP to be reclassified according to social goals. *At present GNP is simply a statement of who bought how much of what, but it doesn't tell you for what reason. Napalm production counts as an addition to GNP on exactly the same basis as food or medicine. Similarly money spent, for instance, as a result of a motor accident boosts the GNP even though it actually detracts from the qualitative side of society; and if more people spent more time growing their own food this would actually reduce GNP.*

Change from flow-economics to stock-economics. *Currently economic statements list what money has come in and what money has gone out. They are income and expenditure accounts. The Japanese would change these to asset accounts to record growth in stocks of assets: and by assets they mean not only goods but also trained people, doctors, teachers, architects. Assets would also include social capital, such as roads and parks; natural assets, such as clear air and water; cultural stock, such as pictures, theatre; and social institutional assets, such as a national health scheme.*

Non-monetary approach to a Welfare Index. *Many welfare items cannot easily be expressed in money terms. How, for instance, do you value physical wellbeing, or safety, or longer life? Could there be some other unit of measurement?*

Howard Wirtz, once the US Secretary for Labour, has called for a similar kind of index, claiming that people's energy, enthusiasm and wellbeing are our one unlimited resource.

The following account by James Seymour of his encounter with the new economics in India expresses better than I can how a redefinition of the 'ends' of economics changes the whole science. After reading this extract you will have some understanding of how the *economics of quality* could change the whole point and purpose of the work organisation.

CIVILISED SIMPLICITY*

As I travelled about India I received the impression more and more that the great issue in India is not the issue between capitalism and communism; but the issue between capitalism and communism, on the one hand, and the ancient Indian non-materialistic philosophy on the other. The first aim of both capitalism and communism is said by their adherents to be to end poverty. This can be done, it is thought, by creating more material wealth, or by distributing more fairly the material wealth which already exists. But the other kind of Indian – it would not be an over-simplification to call him the follower of Mahatma Gandhi – is not interested in ending poverty – at least, in what we in the west are apt to call poverty. He wants everyone to have enough to eat of course, enough and no more, but saving that he does not see anything wrong in what we in the west call poverty. In fact, he believes that poverty is desirable. He agrees with that other Asian who made the simile between a rich man and a laden camel . . .

He does not wish to mechanise agriculture. He points out that an acre of land ploughed by oxen, provided it is ploughed deeply enough, does not produce less food than an acre ploughed by a tractor – slightly more, in fact, because of the dung of the oxen. He freely admits that the acre can be ploughed in fewer man-hours if ploughed by a tractor, but, he says, what about all the hidden man-hours behind the tractor? The man-hours that were needed to make the tractor, and which are needed to maintain it, and to maintain the fantastic urban structure that makes tractors possible? Also, he does not see any advantage in saving man-hours in the village,

* from James Seymour, 'Three Ways for India', *Resurgence*, February 1977.

if all the result is that nine-tenths of the ploughmen are to be forced away from their homes, to go into the towns and, presumably, spend their lives producing more tractors. . . .

Of course,. your Gandhian does want to abolish hunger. It is his first aim. But he thinks that this can be done by improving farming and village life in other ways than by mechanisation. A man can walk all day behind a plough and a pair of oxen, and, if he is not in debt or in trouble, his mind will be at peace. And if he wishes to do so he can think and meditate. But no man can stand at a conveyor belt in a factory and meditate. Nor can he enjoy real peace of mind when he gets home. Then, the follower of Gandhi insists that whatever he uses shall have been made by a craftsman who enjoyed making it: not by somebody who made it in boredom, simply for commercial gain. 'Civilised simplicity' is an expression one constantly hears in India. The essential Indian does not look upon mechanical and electrical contrivances as manifestations of a high civilisation. He looks upon them as barbarous: signs of the west's immaturity.

I began to remember what was happening to my own country under the impact of modern commercialism and industrialism. I remembered watching the process of turning my green and pleasant land into one enormous and, to me, perfectly revolting garden suburb. I compared in my mind the old type of English countryman, with his dignity and integrity, his salty speech and earthy wisdom, with the new countryman – the shoddy, flashy suit, the smarmed hair, the de-tribalised, characterless language, the snatches of foreign song. I remembered the culture in which music is something which dribbles out of a loudspeaker when you turn on a tap, and in which art is an advertisement for hair-cream; where work means standing and watching a machine and leisure sitting watching somebody else play football. 'Work is prayer', say the followers of Gandhi.

In short, the impact which India made on me, against my strong resistance, was to make me lose confidence in what we call progress in the west – even in our best sort of progress. I

*now find myself constantly asking, as I heard so many Indians
ask, 'Progress – to what?' And of our famous efficiency,
'Efficiency – for what?' Industrial efficiency produces more
goods per man-hour. I have no doubt of it. But what do we
want with all these 'goods?'*

*I believe that nine-tenths of the product of our western
industry is not only useless but is harmful. It simply serves to
distract men's minds. It were better had it not been made.
Made, it were better if it were destroyed. Further, I believe
that if our civilisation goes on developing along the road of
commercialism and industrialism it will destroy itself, not by
war, but by destroying men's minds. The impact of India on
me has been to make me lose confidence in the present trend
of my own civilisation.*

THE REVOLUTION IN COMMUNICATIONS

In 1970 the price of oil was $1.80 per barrel. In that year the
US Cabinet's Task Force on oil stated that no substantial rise
in world oil market prices was to be expected in the coming
decade. Today it is over $12.00 and rising. That increase in
price, it is often argued, will call forth new ingenuity and new
sources of energy, although for the next twenty years or so
we may have some bridging problems. The real problem,
however, is not one of shortage, but of price and of the often
unnoticed split between the two forms of energy – stationary
and mobile. Stationary energy normally means electricity
developed from oil, coal or uranium in power stations. But
electricity does not drive aeroplanes, boats, or cars (if you
except milk-floats and its kindred). These need oil – the mobile
form of energy. If oil is increasingly reserved for cars and aeroplanes, there will probably be enough to last until we have
discovered how to use hydrogen in our cars without it blowing
up in our faces (it has a very low flash point), and how to use
nuclear fusion to make enough of the cheap electricity that is
needed to make the hydrogen out of water. Technological
forecasting is extremely hazardous, but all the problems could

not seemingly be solved in time to allow us to replace oil as a source of all mobile energy before at least 2020. In other words, for the next fifty years we are stuck with oil for physical transportation, and that oil will become continuously more expensive, at a rate that will be faster than any likely inflation.

Sources of stationary energy, however, will probably increase well before 1990. Solar heating, methane from sewage, vaporisation from the sea – there are various new sources which do not involve the controversial use of nuclear fuels. Electricity in the 1990-2020 period may well actually come down in price, until vast quantities become needed to manufacture hydrogen.

These are all, of course, guesses. The debate is endless, inconclusive and vastly technical. Gordon Rattray Taylor's book *How To Avoid The Future* provides one good overview for the scientifically inexpert, such as myself. One conclusion does seem clear from all the studies which I have seen – *it is going to cost increasingly more to move ourselves, and things, around.*

On the other hand it is going to get much easier, and perhaps cheaper, to move *information* around. The development of the computer, followed by miniaturisation, has allowed us to collect, handle and disseminate much more information, in more diverse forms, more quickly than ever before. To numbers have now been added speech and vision. The telephone we now all take for granted, but think again about its impact. The ability to communicate, in speech, directly with another person has allowed *human contact* to span space. On the one hand this means that the family can be extended across the land, keeping in spoken touch by the telephone. On the other hand it has reduced the role of, for instance, an ambassador by making it possible to give him real-time instructions and receive real-time information. To the telephone has now been added its visual counterpart. Tele-conferences are a real event, allowing meetings to take place with sight and sound communication even though the participants sit thousands of miles apart. Video-schools, where one centre can transmit video lessons to up to 30 different learning centres and receive comments back as they are made, are in production *now*. The radio is now readily accessible to the ordinary individual, through, for instance, citizen band radio systems, allowing one to talk to more than one person at once and at will.

The computer we all know about of course. Or do we? When we think of computers, we tend to think of the maxi-computer, controlling everything from one central base.

But the *mini-computers*, made possible by the introduction of micro-processors, which sit in missiles, aeroplanes, machine tools, designers' offices and rich men's yachts, constitute the real communications revolution, allowing decisions to be taken with speed and accuracy in locations far remote from the actual expertise. The navigator has only to feed in the variables, he does not have to possess the mathematical skill to relate the one with all the others in all possible combinations: that is all programmed in advance, and fed to him through his mini-computer where he sits.

Hitherto, this increased availability of information and greater ease in communicating it has been largely used to *centralise* everything. If all information, be it numerical, spoken or visual can so easily and quickly be transmitted to the centre why, it was argued, not group all your expertise at the centre and use the periphery as an information-collecting mechanism? Airline booking schemes are an example. The communications revolution allowed the decisions to be made in the centre, at which all current information is immediately available and to which all the booking desks can have immediate access. The system works, but it has turned the booking clerk into a human extension of the computer, translating the coded information on the video-screen in front of him into a spoken code comprehensible to the particular traveller. In time the costs of using a human to do this translation job will escalate so far that the computer terminal will do its own talking – in the appropriate language, of course. Another inconvenient human dumped into the leisure society.

But the whole operation can work the other way. Norman Macrae, of the *Economist*, challenged to find a way of making the airline ticket clerks' job more entrepreneurial, suggested that he be given the task of matching available capacity to individual customer demands at varying price levels. That sounds complicated! It would work like this: most travellers can adjust the time and date of their journey slightly if there is a price advantage in doing so. The airlines carry differing amounts of empty space at different times, although this information is not often predictable or quantifiable in advance. If the airlines were able to adjust their prices to match their space capacity, they could give the central computer rules for determining the marginal *cost* of each seat on each flight at any given minute. The job of the ticket clerk could then be to optimise the marginal profit (revenue above marginal cost) by presenting alternatives to the customer. You would need more ticket clerks of course, but the airline might make more profit in the end and the travellers get better value for their money. Why not? Everyone's satisfied. The communications revolution enables such complicated decisions to be taken by uncomplicated people on site and at speed. At present there are only IATA and, more importantly, the attitude of the organisations and their managers, to prevent it.

With this kind of computer revolution, Macrae suggests, more of us will be able to become *telecommuters*. Once the systems for modern telecommunications are in place, the cost of using them should not vary greatly with distance. 'People will move to areas with the domestic lifestyles (and local governments) they like, and telecommute to offices with the workstyles they want. Sensible people will want different lifestyles and sometimes different workstyles at different periods of their lives.' (*Economist*, 25 December 1976).

A DISPERSED ORGANISATION

Freelance International Ltd. was established in 1962 by one woman, Steve Shirley, and a capital of £6. Today it employs over 400 people and has a turnover of over £1 million. That success story may not be too unusual. What is unusual is that 394 of those 400 work at home.

Freelance International is in the computer software business, computer programming, in fact. It employs 350 freelance programmers, mostly women, who work at home for an average of 25 hours a week. 30 of them have terminals in their homes. There are only 26 full-time staff and only six of those work in the 'office'.

The management team are insistent that the group's primary motivation is not profit but finding expression for talent. They estimate that there are another 1,200 computer specialists in Britain who are home-bound for one reason or another, and whose talents and time are in principle available to the organisation.

Further details are given in a Guardian Report *by Peter Large of 9 September 1977.*

These computer specialists are the same kind of people as those described in part one of this book as Dionysians by inclination, Dionysians reluctantly confined within an organisation. Here their talents are still available to the organisation, but the way of organising them is now compatible with their personal lifestyles. Dionysian ways for Dionysian people.

Now, combine the possibilities of the cheaper and easier ways of communicating through the air with the increasingly expensive, unpleasant and time-consuming ways of moving around physically. What are some of the likely outcomes? Organisations will find that it no longer makes sense to pay people to spend time at the worksite when it is so difficult, expensive and often unnecessary to get there. They will pay them for work done rather than time attended (contract work). This will allow individuals to work where they want and how they want (fast or slow, for instance). The economies of scale will be retained by central, computerised co-ordination, whilst allowing individuals to become more individual or more entrepreneurial. Even the assembly line could become increasingly 'customised' if the computer control were sophisticated enough to allow room for individual modifications to be made to individual items. This already happens in our large car plants, but there is no reason why the technical facility should not be used to allow people to rent space, as it were, on an assembly line to produce their own versions of a standard product. In this way the line becomes a tool, not a machine, an extension of the individual rather than his master. Far-out dreaming? Not really, it's possible today if we want to do it.

Forget about the assembly lines of the factories and think about the clerks. Macrae must be right in predicting that the biggest revolution of work presently in prospect is that which is due in clerical operations. Even in 1970 in Britain 'clerks' accounted for 13 per cent of total employment (the third largest category after skilled manual and semi-skilled manual), and the number is probably growing. It will become even more ridiculous to pay for armies of clerical workers and typists to troop into our cities – an indirect organisational subsidy for public transport – when they could equally well telecommute, sending in their work rather than bodies. This would allow them to work at home, or more likely in locally placed group centres; small work communities where they would get the companionship so essential to clerical and routine work. Unilever, for instance, (as reported in the *Economist* of 3 July 1976) is experimenting with computer-assisted typing:

> *Typists are connected to a computer via individual keyboards, each with a video screen on which mistakes can be easily rectified (correction normally takes about 40 per cent of a typist's time). Standard letters, held in the computer's memory, need only the name and address to be attached. The typist handles no paper or carbon, printing (and filing) being done by the computer.*

Fine. Let the computer remove drudgery. But the typist can communicate with the computer from home in Weybridge just as well as from a desk in Unilever's office. And if the boss works out there as well – then why not? If the suburban trains run half-empty should we complain?

The New Organisation

These three forces, the search for comunity, the economics of quality and the revolution in communications, are all here today. They have each been widely written about and each, on its own, has been heralded as, in some way, the solution to society's dilemmas. Each on its own, it seems to me, would get us nowhere, but would instead be drowned out by the other pressures of the instrumental paradigm. The three together, however, will slowly force a change in the way we run our organisations. If we can welcome this change, adapt to it and build upon it, the new organisations will provide the new weave for a re-organised society which we might all enjoy living in, one in which efficiency does actually cohabit with human dignity.

What will this new organisation look like? It will be a *membership organisation*. It will be a *multi-purpose* organisation and a *dispersed* organisation. If I may once again revert to Ancient Greece, it will be a city-state organisation, a *citizen democracy* where *Demos*, the citizenry, is the ultimate source of power and of authority.

A MEMBERSHIP ORGANISATION

At present people are employed by organisations. In the new organisation individuals will *belong* to it, rather as one belongs to a village or to any other community. You cannot be *sacked* from your village (although life can be made fairly unpleasant for you by your neighbours), but you can leave, or choose not to join. You don't *retire* from a village, although you may contribute less and less in the way of energy, but not necessarily less wisdom. No one owns a village, not nowadays – the word 'ownership' is not appropriate and won't be to the new organisations. The village belongs to its inhabitants, perhaps, but also to the surrounding villages and the local market town, to the countryside, to a wider society and to all those who have dealings with it. It 'exists' and it dies only when it ceases to find a way of providing for its own wellbeing. Only the decision to cover it with a reservoir can actually kill it by external fiat.

It is in this concept of membership that the Dionysian urge in so many of us is recognised. Professionals (Dionysians) are not employed or owned by organisations, they *belong* to partnerships, associations or societies. The word 'organisation' is repugnant to many of them. Athenians, the semi-professionals, need the security of an organisation but resent its chains. For them too, the concepts of membership, of the demos paramount rather than management, of community rather than organisation, will all please.

Ownership therefore will become an inappropriate word in the new organisations, as it already is in the existing organisations of consent and contract. Take the theatre. Money is needed to mount new productions, but no one considers that the money-provider or 'angel', as he is supposedly called (it sounds so much nicer than 'shareholder'), owns the show or its performers. He has rights, of course, and is entitled to a fair return on his investment, with higher shares for higher risks. Similarly, nobody 'owns' a university even though, in England, the universities get all their funds from one source, the University Grants Committee, and in America the private universities get their resources from people who are well used to the shareholder role. The providers of finance can call some important tunes, but no one thinks of 'them' as owning 'us'.

In fact, it is not difficult to argue that this state of affairs already exists in industry and service organisations. After all, the public corporations are largely owned by institutions, insurance companies, pension funds and so on who see them only as investments. If they disapprove of the activities of one of their investments they will disinvest rather than try to exercise any of the power or authority of their ownership. Even in smaller privately owned organisations, ownership today seems to carry more responsibility than power, for the fact of ownership does not entitle the owner to act as he pleases with his human property.

If indeed this *is* the reality, then our rhetoric clearly needs to keep pace with it. If shareholders are recognised as only the providers of funds, no one can legitimately object to industrial democracy on the ground that it will interfere with the 'Board's responsibility to its shareholders'.

A change in the rhetoric from ownership to membership is long overdue. It will do much to remove the feeling of bondage. It will mean that the members of the organisation are seen as more than costs to be minimised, and it will force the organisation to find a consensus on its purposes from amongst all its members. Shareholders need not be frightened – they will still be free to invest and disinvest in their own interests, just as customers will be free to buy or not to buy. It is not shareholders, but managers claiming to act on their behalf, who put false weight on ownership.

A MULTI-PURPOSE ORGANISATION

The new membership organisations will be more clearly aware of the claims of all the various 'stakeholders', since the claims of the theoretical owners will no longer be paramount. These stakeholders are, of course, the same as they are at present: the members, the providers of finance, the clients or customers, the immediate community and the wider society.

There seems to be no reason why the interests of most of the different stakeholders cannot continue to be protected in the last resort by the existing mechanisms of the organised society as we know it today. Those who lend their money to an organisation are currently protected by the Companies Act and should continue to be so. The client or customer is ultimately protected by the mechanisms of the marketplace and by the laws on consumer protection.

The trouble comes of course with monopoly or oligopoly situations, and the temptations that these offer of customer exploitation. These new membership organisations may want to be just as selfish in their own ways as their predecessors, if allowed to be. In cases of established monopoly, as for instance in the state-owned concerns, there is a good case for giving the customer representation at the decision-making levels of the company. We cannot, however, pretend that this representation will prevail when outnumbered by other interests, unless those other interests wish to take heed. I suggest that the only practical way to ensure that customer requirements get due consideration is to locate the decision-making centres as close to the customer as possible. It is hard to ignore the customer when you talk with him each day – unless of course you have no power or authority to adjust things to his requirements. The discourtesy and disinterest which we have all encountered at the counters of government offices, or the reception desks of large concerns, is often a very natural adaptation by the people who sit at those counters and desks to the fact that there is little or nothing that they can do to change situations – they are there to pass information in or out. Fortunately, the dispersed nature of the new organisations will help to keep the customer or clients in the front of people's minds.

Representation within the organisation will help also to keep the interests of the immediate community in the sights of the decision-makers. Power and authority they cannot have much of, but they will at least be a visual and vocal reminder of some of the other purposes and responsibilities of the organisation. Ultimately however it must be a case of rules. Non-renewable resources need protection by a wider society, and the new organisations will have to be helped to be honourable in this respect as much as their forebears. The short-term drives out the long, no matter how decent our pretensions, and in these multi-purpose organisations the needs of next year can still obliterate our responsibilities to our grandchildren. Laws are the conscience of the good as well as the protectors of the weak. The re-organised society will have its full quota of laws. On the principle that good fences make good neighbours, freedom works best in well-defined situations.

The multi-purpose organisation will have one dominant purpose – its members. The other stakeholders have their interests which set the boundaries for the way the organisation can behave and for its activities. What these behaviours and activities should be will not be as obvious as at present, for it will no longer be beyond debate that incremental wealth, even if it all goes to all the members, is the key objective. Even today, in East Coast America, a survey of the Windham region in Connecticut, done as a basis for a new regional plan, revealed that what local residents wanted most in life was to enjoy nature, feel safe, and be left alone. They cared least about public transport, good restaurants, a more exciting environment and the chance to make more money. When the economics of quality is more widely accepted the criteria will become even more smudged.

Growth, however, must still be the over-riding purpose. It is, it must be, unrealistic to work to keep things the same. The advocates of 'no growth' do not mean 'no growth' – they mean 'no material growth' for they are talking within the instrumental paradigm and the economics of quantity. The economics of quality will allow us to debate and choose from a variety of growth opportunities, but growth there will be. Some may opt for more private time, some for achieving a more useful or more beautiful product, others for the best possible financial reward, others still for a beautiful setting even if it puts them at a disadvantage in terms of transport. All will be respectable objectives under the new rhetoric. The instrumental paradigm suggested that wealth brought freedom of choice. No longer. What few rich friends I have appear on the whole to have less choice of time, or friends or locality or lifestyle, than those who have no wealth to speak of. The freedom of wealth has proved a false dream, unless freedom consists in buying what material object takes your fancy. The economics of quality offers a far greater range of options for growth.

The new organisations must still survive materially. Villages must eat as well as look beautiful. The economics of quantity will always apply to the exchange functions. Profit, perhaps re-named 'operating surplus', will be not only desirable but necessary. It will be necessary, however, not sufficient, to use the logicians' distinction. A surplus will be a means to success, not success in itself, for success will mean 'improved well-being' and *that* covers a multitude of virtues. But there is more than one way to make a surplus. Surplus can be created equally well from high earnings, higher productivity or lower costs. Some may prefer a slower way of life with lower rewards to a hectic rat-race with money they have no time to spend. In a membership organisation, where such a consensus is obtained they could have it. And why not? The multi-purpose organisation is the road to a freer society.

Purposes may change from organisation to organisation, but each would be wise to agree within itself. The effective communities are those in which individuals differ in many respects but agree in one, their chosen values and priorities in life. Individuals will therefore choose their organisation more for its values than for its stock-market rating or its job opportunities. Salaries and earnings (not wages any more) will no longer be comparable between organisations, because those earnings will be only one ingredient in a whole cafeteria of options.

'Earnings uncompared?' the hardened union negotiator will cry – 'how is that possible?' It will be possible because the new *dispersed* organisations, based on contract and consent, will make it hard if not impossible for any union to arrange scales across industries, or even across individuals, although rates for work done may still be negotiable within firms. After all, freedom from those who negotiate on your behalf is as necessary as freedom from those you negotiate with. In a society of membership organisations, where scarcity is a solved problem, the role of unions must change. With no owners to negotiate against, this role may be one of protecting individuals from victimisation by the work community or of ensuring appropriate rights (of training, certification, and so on) for members of their craft or professions – for, remember, these will be the all-professional organisations envisaged in the organisations of consent and contract. The changing role of unions from wage-negotiating mechanisms to societies for the protection of the individual is already noticeable in some categories of society today. Managers, for instance, do not particularly want their salaries negotiated for them en bloc, but they do want their voices to be heard, their rights protected and their legal position clarified.

THE DISPERSED ORGANISATION

The new organisations will be more concerned to reward work done than hours attended. The revolution in communications will allow more people to do outwork in their own homes or localities, connected by electronic and telephonic means to a co-ordinating centre; to be *tele-commuters*. The search for community will encourage people to look for small groups of like-minded people to do part of the task of a larger whole, and economics, the changing economics of transport, will lend financial strength to their desires.

As physical transport gets more expensive it will no longer pay to make everything in one place and then distribute it around the continent. This used to be called 'rationalisation', and while the economies of scale were greater than the diseconomies of extra transport, it did make financial sense to close down small factories, depots and stores and conduct the whole operation out of one vast shed with huge lorries thundering forth with the finished product. But rationalisation will soon work the other way, as the *diseconomies* of scale (due to the hijack factor) get added to ever-increasing *diseconomies* of transport. Rationalisation will come to mean regional or local assembly and manufacture, with central co-ordination of planning, design and quantities (the things that can be transported through the ether).

But organisations will not only be forced to split up physically, they will also find it cheaper to split up organisationally, paying subsidiaries, or independents, for chunks of 'work done'. This type of 'toll manufacturing', where a very specific job is done by a small specialised firm for a wider range of end-users, is becoming more common because less expensive.

Vertical integration was convenient if it gave control and apparent flexibility. But vertical integration means big, and big has become too expensive, while high-cost transportation makes it further nonsense to do all your own sub-assembly work in Birmingham and ship it out to the regions, carrying with it your overheads as well as your petrol costs.

TOLL MANUFACTURE

Sir Frederick Catherwood was once a staunch supporter of the economies of scale. But his mind was changed, as he recounted to the Council of Engineering:

> Even the economies of scale in the American Aluminium industry with which I was so impressed were vulnerable to the small extrusion press giving a more local service, more neatly tailored to the precise needs of the customer. They took a very large section of this business away from the 'majors'. And while it was supposed that no smelter could make money under 10,000 tons a year, a foreign company came in with a smelter a fifth of the size. On closer analysis the only real economy of scale in the industry was the hot rolling mill. This had to have about ten per cent of the total national market to keep it going. But then someone started up a rolling mill to 'toll' roll other companies' metal, and though the mill required the same large output, the toll roller did nothing else and was in itself a tiny business employing very few people. When I was Director General of NEDO we tried to track down the elusive economies of scale and finally came to the conclusion that they had only existed in the mind.

To telecommuters and toll manufacturing must be added one more development – the *mobile factory*. The mobile factory is actually a highly versatile machine designed to produce the basic ingredients of common manufactured items. Take spectacles, for instance. Spectacles of various formulations are required everywhere in the world. Their production is quite an expensive process, requiring considerable expertise. Today, in the search for such expertise, the production centres are grouped close to major cities and they search for economies of scale to justify their continuing and increasing investment in professional human skills. But a machine can be designed to accept dial settings from the optician's prescription, and turn out the proper lenses – already mounted in a frame if desired. Such machines in fact existed in prototype back in the 1960s, and to put them into production today is not a serious design problem. The ice-cream machine, the photographic cubicle, the Xerox, the wire-nail machine, are just early examples of the mobile factory. Why has it not happened with spectacles? Well, there would be a lot of understandable resistance from existing manufacturers who would lose their businesses. A new marketing effort would be required to establish a new way of doing this traditional job, with a lot of scepticism and financial risk along the way. And for what? In Britain spectacles are a free (or almost-free) good to the end consumer, paid for by the National Health. Who then would benefit from the charge? Not the customer who would pay the same, nor the optician who would have more work for no more reward, nor the National Health Service who would have to carry the initial costs and trouble of a new distribution system. But it could happen, tomorrow, if we wanted it to.

Way back in 1962 Amber and Amber produced a list of basic products which were in widespread demand and could be manufactured locally through these mobile factory machines. Their list included:

Wire Hardware Products
Shingle Products
Concrete Products
Construction Board
Clay Products
Metal Tube and Pipe Fittings.

As they point out,* these machine factories could even be

* *Anatomy of Automation*, Prentice-Hall, 1962.

mounted on railcars so that they would be truly mobile. More likely is a local toll operation, using a machine for each area, rather like the equipment-hire businesses which have sprouted up all over the land in line with the increasing cost of new equipment.

Building on the ideas of 'toll manufacturing', the 'mobile factory' and 'equipment-hire', is the concept of the *community workshop*. So many of the finished goods we use are actually assembled from a whole range of components supplied from outside. There is no reason why we cannot do this for ourselves. The home-assembly kits are just a start down this route, but imagine a local workshop for hire with all the power-tools, machine-tools, gigs and presses that one might need for a whole range of operations, together with some expert help or advice. It is not only householders who could use this, but local entrepreneurs who would be encouraged to do local assembling for local retailers, undercutting the high overheads of the major, centralist, suppliers. Even motor cars, if you think about it, could be regionally assembled to a customer's specification, given the versatile robot-like machines already installed in Japan, Detroit and Coventry. Your car would not only be delivered by your local dealer, it would be *made* by him. This would be a much higher guarantee of reliability than any legal forms. Here lies the scope for many a local Zeus, currently bound down in Apollonian centralist organisations.

Norman Macrae (in that same Christmas piece in the *Economist* of 25 December 1976) also envisions a *recompetitioning of public utilities*. He suggests that only the state may be able to finance the enormous capital expenditure required by the high technology industries of power generation, transport, communications etc. But why, he asks, should these facilities not be leased out on a competitive regional basis to operators? His model is the commercial television system in Britain, where franchises are regional and come up for renewal on a periodic basis. He would even lease out the care and rehabilitation of the less hardened criminals, the maintenance of local law and order, as well as the more obvious candidates of housing and refuse collection. As the costs of centralisation soar, these 'dispersed' alternatives will seem increasingly attractive. They are already feasible, if we want them enough. Macrae's ideas are a charter for Zeus even within the heart of Apollo's empire – the public sector.

Given all these tendencies and options, the new organisations will be network organisations – the federal organisations of Chapter 7 – linking together a whole array of different organisation villages, providing from the centre the skills of co-ordination and design which can be communicated through the telephone, telex, or television; but leaving to the villages their separate tasks, rewarding them for work done, treating each village, or even each lone individual, as an entrepreneur.

NASA – A DISPERSED ORGANISATION

In the 1960s NASA and its work for Project Apollo provided a clear example of the dispersed organisation, it used a wide range of 'outside' resources, carefully co-ordinated by NASA.

As its peak NASA interacted with 20,000 different organisations. Two American academics, Sayles and Chandler, who studied NASA intensively for four years, reported:

Thousands of engineers, scientists, technicians and administrative personnel are employed in laboratory and field-development work, in basic research, in launching and tracking spacecraft, and in a whole host of support activities. While outsiders employed by the contractors may comprise 90 per cent of the workforce, a critical amount of designing, testing, planning and operating is conducted 'in-house' by NASA personnel. Further, NASA believes, with substantial justification, that outsiders cannot be successfully stimulated, managed or co-ordinated without a technologically sophisticated internal organisation.

A CITIZEN DEMOCRACY

In a membership community the members are in charge. Demos rules, OK? That does not mean that the whole day is spent in shop-floor meetings or village-hall debates. Far from it. The difference is that authority comes from the members and reverts to them. These are the organisations of consent. They are governed with the permission of those who are governed.

When the members of a community give authority to one of their members, they do two things – they define the boundaries of that authority very clearly, and they define the length of time that it is to last. In this way the community ensures that authority returns to itself, to the demos. Management therefore does not have tenure for life, or career (as is the assumption in today's corporations, where people talk of a 'career in management'), but holds office for a fixed period and is, in one way or another, elected to that office. It may be election at second or third remove: that is, the tricky problems of fitting talent to a role may well be delegated by the community to its elected leaders, so the demos will elect its leaders who will then appoint, for a term, its managers. In practice therefore we will find something not far off the two-tier structure presently found in Germany, the Netherlands and advocated in parts of British society, where the 'Board' is elected and in turn appoints the 'Management Committee'. This structure will allow for outside interests (the consumer, the community, society in general) to be represented at the Board level in order to reflect the multi-purpose nature of the new organisation.

But the citizens of the organisation villages will not delegate all authority to their elected or appointed representatives. Key decisions they will keep for themselves. This is where the village-hall debates can be expected. Key decisions will mainly centre around the disposal of the surplus at the end of each financial year. In the conditions of citizen democracy, this critical issue will not be left to the discretion of the Board, although it will be expected of those on the Board that they clarify the available options. Of this surplus some will automatically go to the State, as at present, by way of tax; some will be required for re-investment; some will be available for price reductions or product improvement; and some for distribution to the community. It is the exact proportions which will require the decisions of the whole community. No doubt some communities will make the wrong decision, sacrificing the future to the present. That shall be their privilege. Others have done so before them, with less justification, for it was neither their surplus nor their future. I, however, am confident that communities do not often commit suicide. Given accurate information, jam tomorrow will be at least as desirable as jam today – if it is *your* jam.

We have spoken of the community as if it all worked in one shed or one yard or one group of buildings. Often this will be so. But the community can be as dispersed as the larger organisation of which it forms a part. Out-workers, part-timers, professional stringers, can all be attached to the community in their different ways. All will be part-time citizens entitled to some say as well as some vote. Many will be citizens of more than one community. Community should never mean prison. The villages of yesteryear were prisons for many, places to escape from into the cities of opportunity, anonymity and freedom. The organisational villages must respect choice, individual differences and privacy. They must be partnerships of consenting adults if they are to work. Well governed and managed, they can be the cornerstone of a re-organised society.

TOMORROW TODAY:
MANAGING A CITIZEN DEMOCRACY BUSINESS

The Computer Management Group was a £4 million British company in the computer services business when in 1976 the Industrial Participation Association published an analysis of its management style. In that year it grew by 50 per cent.

There are three joint managing directors (the three young men who founded the company), and below them only two levels of management. An associate director will have no office of his own, no secretary, no parking space. Any decision he makes may be questioned by his troops and can be reversed. He himself can be openly removed from his position. Alongside the schedule of meetings on the bulletin board, is another notice that someone 'has stepped down from the position of associate director in this branch, and is now working as a customer account supervisor. He will be succeeded by . . .' This has happened, says Nancy Foy reporting on the company in The Times *of 13 September 1976, more than a dozen times since CMG started in 1964, and most of the ex-managers are still there. 'You have to be a glutton for punishment to be a manager at CMG,' said a competitor; but CMG has no problems in finding its managers – all from within.*

There are some firm principles:

- *deputies are not allowed: there are clear boundary definitions for each role and within that boundary you can have one, two or three people, but no assistants or levels;*
- *rational argument and consensus apply when decisions are made; no one can expect to get his own way all the time, but at the same time there is an implicit veto – if any of the group has a major objection the place does not go ahead;*
- *no secrets are allowed, and a crowded schedule of meetings (minutes available to all) is arranged to ensure a flow of information both ways;*
- *salary and pay scales are kept in the top quarter of the industry, and then topped up (hopefully) with a profit-sharing scheme usually equivalent to about 10 per cent of salary; employees are also encouraged to buy shares (over half have);*

Employee turnover is around 15 per cent, but the number of long service veterans is high. 'This isn't a very comfortable place,' said Bryan Mitts, Managing Director, 'you either like it or dislike it a lot. Many people have psychological needs that we don't meet – a father figure, for example'.

An organisation of consent works well if you see yourself as an Athenian or Dionysian (or the occasional Zeus). It's lonely for Apollonians.

The smaller membership communities, the villages, will often, I have suggested, be linked together in larger networks or federations. Even if ICI is devolved, if British Rail is regionalised again, if social welfare is recompetitioned and much of the infrastructure of government contracted out, there will still be a need in each for a central secretariat, co-ordinating, planning, designing. This will be the federal centre, the headquarter, a tower no longer, more the centre of a web.

Democratic principles will have to apply here too. The making and direction of policy will be the responsibility of elected representatives – elected by the constituent communities or other stakeholders. In the case of state enterprises the central government would be entitled to its own representatives at the policy level. In some cases the federal centre could be truly topless – policy being decided by temporary groups meeting periodically (like IATA in air travel, or the International Postal Conference). Appointed by the elected policy-making group will be the secretariat, the federal civil service, the federal *management*. They will be the career officers, Apollonians and Athenians in their ways and inclinations, subject ultimately to the demos of their organisation, but with the kind of influence granted by expertise and information. These will be the 'career managers' of the future, the federal secretariats of the larger organisations.

The re-organised society will be crucially dependent on these federal managers, for they will be largely responsible for achieving the efficiency side of the dignity/efficiency marriage. They will need protection and security, for in the new society those in the federal centre will be the real homeless ones in organisational terms. If a class union is justified in the re-organisation society, it will be for these meritocrats of federalism. In any euphoria over the membership communities of the dispersed organisation, those who serve in the centre must not be forgotten. There is a real danger that local Dionysian indulgences result in inefficiency for the greater community. In adapting our organisations to meet the very real needs of Dionysian and Athenian personalities, we must not forget that the co-ordinating systems of Apollo, and the attention to detail and procedure for which he stands, have to be retained. It will ultimately be the responsibility of a Zeus, acting in the name of the demos, to ensure that all the good of Apollo does not disappear with the bad and the intolerable.

Ring Out the Old, Ring in the New

Chapter 10

AND CONSEQUENTLY . . .

It will be a quiet revolution, if we are wise: a merger of the gods and of demos, not a takeover.

The economics of quantity may merge gradually into the new rhetoric of the economics of quality. It only needs a few national governments, the OECD and the IMF to start using indices of Net National Welfare to put traditional economics in its proper place – as the necessary but not sufficient condition of national success. We have seen the rhetoric of international finance change, as reference to Special Drawing Rights gradually replaced talk of gold, sterling or dollar balances, and as floating exchange rates replaced the previously sacrosanct fixed parities. We have seen a changing rhetoric emerge in British politics, as minority governments became the rule of the day and parliamentary defeat for government measures became almost commonplace, making government by compromise and negotiation a new reality. The unthinkable can become thinkable. Rhetorics do change, sometimes suddenly, more often slowly, unnoticed, almost surreptitiously.

The great centralised corporations do not have to wait for bankruptcy to pull them tumbling down, the crumbling skyscrapers of the organised society. The notions of federalism, of network organisations and intermediate technology are around, and are talked of in boardrooms today. It only needs an opinion-leader such as ICI in Britain, IBM or Ford internationally, to announce that it has voluntarily federalised, dispersed and democratised its organisation with only good effects, for the bandwaggon to start. It won't happen tomorrow. We are today in the grip of the instrumental paradigm with its wealth-creating priorities – but there is time enough. The full force of the third dilemma is still a decade or two away.

The organisations of consent and contract, with the different management styles which they require, will happen sooner. They are the response, after all, to the second dilemma. Indeed it is their example, as it becomes fashionable, which will encourage the leaders in the organised society to think more seriously about membership organisations, telecommuters, contract workers, and re-competitioning.

Laws too must help. Laws usually tend to ratify the status quo. They are enacted *after* society has endorsed new practices with the rod of social approval. But laws can act in advance of public opinion, educating the common weal, moving with the reforming minority of the times. The laws on censorship, homosexuality and abortion in Britain in the 1960s were cases in point, although, almost by definition, these laws had many opponents. Revisions in Company Law, substituting the rhetoric of membership for that of ownership, asserting the rights of the different stakeholders, and defining the elective nature of management, would advance the timing of the quiet revolution by many years. Some of this legal prodding may occur, but not all of it. The instrumental paradigm is too deeply enmeshed in our legal tradition. Ownership is still sacrosanct.

No, if we want the quiet revolution to be both quiet and in time, the managers of the next decades must take the lead: quiet revolutionaries, missionaries of a new order, tempering efficiency with human dignity. If I must predict, the changes will come first in the newer, more experimental, more professional type of firms (like the one quoted on p. 283). It is in these firms that Dionysus and Athena are more readily acknowledged. New paradigms come from the outside.

What sort of world will it be? Are there wider implications for the political and economic structure of society, for agriculture, for the balance between town and country, for social life, for education, for religion, and of course for the new managers? I believe that there are. On the assumption therefore that the reorganised society comes peacefully into being in due course, with the new paradigm of the membership organisation at its base, I want to speculate, very briefly and sketchily about those implications. This is fortune-telling with a vengeance, wishful thinking even. Speculation invites counter speculations and there are many other alternatives to the ones I shall list. But missionaries, like leaders, are concerned to create self-fulfilling prophecies. Here are mine.

POLITICAL STRUCTURES

The search for community and the communications revolution will lead to increasing pressures for local self-government. Recently a resident of Manchester, in Britain, complained that the national Press was no longer national. It was largely written and edited as well as printed in London, and whereas in the past many a Mancunian travelled frequently to London and understood Londoners' ways even if he did not always like them, the escalating cost of travel had put a barrier between the two cities. The national Press was no longer national. We needed, he said, a federal Press system. Federalism will not be confined to Manchester, or to the nationalist fringes of the Bretons, the Basques, the Scots and the Welsh. It will break out all over. Schumacher's vision of a nation of a hundred islands will be a reality (duly watered-down of course by the forces of compromise).

Political parties will then assume a more regional character, coming together in occasional national alliances. Coalition governments will be as common in Britain as they have been in Scandinavia or Italy or, in effect, in America. A larger proportion of taxation will be regionally assessed and collected, to be spent on the enlarged regional responsibilities for educational policy, welfare and social services. Defence and Financial Planning would remain the well guarded prerogatives of a federal centre.

Pluralism may then at last shake off its mantle of class.

Society has been seen by many as a melting pot of different interests, 'pluralist'. These interests balance themselves out over time, we hope, by constant jiggle and joggle, by argument, negotiation and compromise. The conflicts in society, particularly the mechanics of industrial relations in our organisations, have then been seen as the necessary signs of pluralism working itself out. Pluralism, it is held, is good, is democratic, is better than any imposed 'unitary' view of the organisation or of society. Therefore conflict is good, or at least necessary. This is all very fine. Few today can deny that there are many different interest groups, each entitled to some sort of say. Pluralism is much more respectable than it was when Edmund Burke was hammering the same theme in an England where the ruling classes assumed that their, unitary, viewpoint should prevail.

But pluralism as it worked out, particularly in Britain, tended to become a clash between classes, both at work and in a wider society, because in a centralist system the differences have to be marked out *vertically*. If you've got only one pole to measure things on, then all those measurements willy-nilly end up in one vertical scale. In Britain it was always the relative power of class. More poles more scales, different poles different scales. Decentralist systems permit more types of competition, so that pluralism can work itself out in more than one arena. That is why centralist states end up with two-party systems, federal states with multi-party systems. Britain, judging from the growth in nationalist parties, is well on the way to federalism, but is still in the grip of her *converging hierarchies*, with power tending to go all in one direction.

Devolution, combined with the more eclectic nature of the economics of quality (there are more ways than one to success), will widen the arena for pluralism in Britain so that people can dispute the differing virtues of differing regions, ways of life, definitions of success, forms of education or brands of religion without always ending up with a problem of class. Let pluralism be unconfined, let the hierarchies diverge.

Economic Structure

Under the present instrumental paradigm, capital is a plentiful resource and labour a high-cost troublesome expense. The inclination is therefore to go to capital-intensive industries and to minimise the number of people wherever possible. Service industries with their high labour requirement are particularly unpopular.

Under the new paradigm, priorities will change. Once people cease to be interested only in the maximum reward for the minimum work, and are interested in the work itself, then people become the plentiful resource. They already are so, in fact, but we don't look at them that way, in spite of the zooming unemployment figures.

The re-organised societies will therefore do well to move towards those industries where the mark-up due to skilled labour input is high, and to import from the third world (of the oil-rich capital-rich labour-poor countries) the products of capital-intensive industries (oil, chemicals, steel, popular cars), and from the fourth and developing world the low-cost labour-intensive products, raw materials, commodities, shoes, toys.

The post-scarcity societies will therefore tend to become skill-oriented economies. The financial services of the City of London are skill-oriented businesses. So are consulting, design work, education, specialist ship-building, sports car manufacture, aero-engine design and manufacture. Switzerland is a good example of an economy largely based around professional skills (until watch manufacturing became capital-intensive and mass-production).

Many have advocated that Britain, like other Western nations, should be a 'service economy', because the high value added to the 'raw material' in service industries alone can justify the high costs of labour, and still employ relatively large numbers of people. Those macro-economic arguments will still apply in the re-organised society – we must still export to import – but added to them are the organisational pressures which result in the organisations of consent and contract. These are the organisations of skilled men. The cost and trouble of managing them is justified only if they are 'high value-added' businesses, the 'personal-skill organisations'.

Re-tooling with highly versatile robots to extend man's capacity, can turn machine-based manufacturing into personal-skill businesses. Quality hi-fi equipment, up-market boats, planes and cars, high fashion fabrics and furniture, can all be turned into craftsman products, one-off items with a high added value. In this way room can be found for Dionysians in what has been Apollo's domain.

This is where state finance can help to re-structure industry. Capital-intensive industries should be allowed to go to our capital-rich fourth world, using the personal design skills of the new 'fifth world', plus any technological and marketing know-how. New capital must then be pumped into all possible outlets for personal-skill businesses. It is folly, for instance, for Britain to cut back on her educational sector and to compound that folly by limiting the intake of overseas students. She should, according to the logic of the new paradigm, charge them full costs (subsidising the indigent where need be), and expand her facilities to meet all available demand. Why *not* be the Athens of the modern world if people want it, it pays, and we can provide it!

A personal skill society under the new paradigm is likely to have slightly less total work for rather more people. Because of the increased added value, a lower total output will reward more people. If furthermore not all those people are interested in getting the greatest amount of reward for the smallest amount of work (because of the new paradigm of community), then there will be even more to go round more people. Unemployment, in other words, should be reduced and could be eliminated (apart from seasonal and specialist pockets perhaps), if a wise re-investment policy were followed.

If re-investment policy is not wise, the attempts to run mass-production organisations as federations of consent and contract will bankrupt them. Re-investment will then be inevitable, if traumatic.

Agriculture

The rising cost of transport will, in agriculture as in industry, work against the economics of *specialised operations*. We may expect to see much more regional self-sufficiency. The same applies on a national scale. There will be economic pressures for Britain to become self-sufficient. Imported foods will become increasingly expensive. Beef should become a luxury item as we gradually move over to an 'Italian diet' of veal, pork, chicken, pasta, bread and vegetables. Our present diet was fixed in the days when the Corn Laws were repealed to allow cheap food in from abroad, which in turn permitted low wages for the workers to man our factories. The situation has changed and so will our diet. At present for instance, we import 75 million tons of grain per year. We feed 89 million tons to our cattle to get 400,000 tons of beef. If we eliminated the beef herd we would actually become net exporters of grain – our major current food import. There would still be cattle, but cattle living on grass and often killed young as veal. Without the necessity to support beef herds, more land would be available for dairy products, sugar beet and vegetables – large quantities of each of which are currently imported and getting more expensive each day.

Not only will our diets be changed, but so will the structure of farming. Currently capital intensive and specialised, it will become management intensive. Each corner of each field will need individual attention, as the greater variety of crops required by each region demand their own special nutrients and forms of care. There will have to be a return to the land. At present only 2.9 per cent of the labour force in Britain works on the land, compared with 11.5 per cent in France and 24.9 per cent in Ireland (still largely an agrarian nation). (Of course, to those figures must be added all the support labour force making the machines, chemicals and so on for the specialised capital-intensive agriculture of the British.) Perhaps the British figure will begin to look more like the French one.

The workers themselves will be highly skilled, using a

variety of multi-purpose machines and drawing on a range of technical support services in the local region. Toll or contract farming for very specialist operations will also increase (it already exists of course), but on a local basis. Farms may well decrease in size. Large acreages with small workforces are manageable only if one or two crops are grown. With more varied cultivation and more pressures for regional self-sufficiency, the large units will need to be subdivided if management is to remain close to the problems.

Skilled workers will demand high wages and deserve them. They will also need training and re-training, housing, schools and the support services that have progressively been run down in the rural areas. Our food will not be cheap if it is to pay for all these things. All the more justification for careful field-by-field intensive farming adjusted to the needs of the region.

Farming, therefore, which has been the prerogative of Zeus (with the occasional Apollonian complex), will shift to Athena – small groups adapting to local requirements.

Town and Country

The return to the land, the dispersed organisation and the continuing search for community will increase the drift away from the towns which already exists. For a short time the drift may actually be held back by the increased costs of the country. This may sound strange, but the new rush to the provinces will force up the price of houses, and will put more pressures on schools and public utilities. They in turn will finance their expansion by increased taxes. In the meantime, house prices will fall in the cities, allowing work and living to return to the inner city, and taking some of the pressure off the inner-city housing authorities. As the towns of the organised society begin to get dismantled there will be opportunity and room to create more recreational space in the inner city (as long as it isn't given up to parking lots).

In short, the re-organised society should, with price-induced hiccups, begin to redress the balance between town and country, making both more habitable by a wider range of people. No longer will all artistic and cultural talent flee to the centre in pursuit of patrons and audiences. There will be enough of both in the regions. Already it happens: as theatres close in London, new ones open in the provinces. The new National Theatre in London, fine though it may be, was accused by many of being counter to the devolutionary mood of the times. So it may have been.

Back in the 1930s, Sir George Stapledon, the eminent agricultural scientist, had a similar vision. He said that the aim was

'nothing less than gradually and methodically to rehumanise millions of inherently innocent, simple and lovable members of the race. To plan simply for "welfare" will get us nowhere; to plan to rehumanise ourselves will truly open the gates to happiness and prosperity.'

Stapledon, revered though he was by many agriculturists, was dreaming and preaching. Dreams and Sermons will not bring about the re-organised society. Michael Allaby, who quotes Stapledon in his book *Inventing Tomorrow*,* believes that agriculture and the need to feed ourselves will restore the town and country balance. I argue that even that will not be enough, it is the inevitable restructuring of our organisations which will do the trick.

The village for living in (as well as that for working in) may thrive again. Those 80 per cent of Britons who dream of a village life may be able to realise their dream. But it is the provincial towns and the regional capitals which may see the real renascence, as law courts, administration, stock exchanges all move their physical presence out to the regions, linked as and when necessary (e.g. the stock exchange) by television and computer.

The Apollonian tide which threatens to engulf our cities will recede. Under the influence of Apollo the life of the average citizen in a city has begun to be a melange of specialisations. For every problem you call a different number on the

* Hodder and Stoughton, 1976.

telephone. Even if you are competent to solve your own problems, fix your own plumbing, mend your own wall, the complexity of city life requires that you call in the licensed specialist. Ivan Illich calls this new powerlessness of the average citizen 'modernised poverty'. It is Apollo's threat to the individual.

The move to smaller towns and villages will allow us to discover the power of community – the demos – which will, we must hope, restore to us some control over our own daily lives, letting the individualist and problem-solving parts of ourselves (Dionysus and Athena) re-emerge. Community permits a re-alignment of the gods.

Social Life

The reorganised society is not a Marxist or a Communist Society. Although the ownership of organisations disappears from the rhetoric, private property, private savings and private wealth are desirable things – up to a limit. The limit is approached when the private property in fact becomes ownership of an organisation. A gardener and someone to clean one's house (by contractual arrangement) is hardly an organisation. Nor is a yacht or even a private aeroplane, even if serviced by people under contract. If someone wants the protection of the Companies Act for his property (i.e. by making his farm a Company), he may find that the principle of 'membership' makes this impossible. If he treats it as his private garden, all right, but then he has none of the protection of limited liability. *Organisations* will no longer be *property*.

We may also expect to see taxation on excessive private wealth receive social approval, whilst taxation on individual earnings is transferred to the organisation, where it is both easier to collect and less demotivating. Indirect taxation on a local basis will replace central direct taxation, in order to give more regional discretion in financial matters. But within these broad constraints, individual differences in earnings and wealth will be tolerated more easily than they are at present because they will not, under the new paradigm, be seen as so important, so totally definitive of success.

Dirty jobs, for instance, will still exist. Even the most versatile of machines will not collect garbage unaided, clean the sewers, drive the buses, guard the streets, wash the hospital floors. Small communities will not make up for all the monotony of some work. We may expect to see high rates paid for these jobs, so that *some* people can earn their economic needs in a short, and not very pleasant, time and have more time left over for activities in the gift economy. It may, in fact, become socially respectable to be a part-time dustman, while the night-shift hospital cleaner may often turn out to be an artist in disguise.

The increased diversity of jobs allowed by the new paradigm, the increased availability of contract work, of intermittent education (to be discussed below) and telecommuting, will all allow a much more diversified form of home life. The Monday-to-Friday grind, relieved by a family excursion in the school holidays or by weekend gardening, can be abandoned if one chooses, without loss of earnings or fear of losing one's position. Flexibility of living is built into the organisations of consent and contract and the new paradigm. Intermittent education and telecommuting will make it easier for women to work whilst children are young, and easier to reskill themselves if they wish to return to full-time work later on. Indeed the flexibility of work should do much to remove the disparity between the sexes, bringing more women into management. Athena, after all, was a woman.

Retirement may then cease to be a word in common use. People may not talk of 'retiring' but of 'scaling down their commitments', adjusting their contribution over time. Each community may be expected to make its own decisions on the adjusted roles and work loads of its senior citizens, although there will be some overall minima decreed by the state and there will be unions around to see fair play. No longer however will it make sense to try to get the most money out of the community at the earliest opportunity for the least amount of contribution. There will be enough younger citizens there to put their countervailing point of view, for your pension is always someone else's expense.

It sounds self-indulgent. It is, but it will only work if the self-indulgence is disciplined by consideration for others. Laws, I have already argued, are a necessary feature of the new society. (All future scenarios always provide boons for lawyers), for the law will set boundaries between interest groups and arbitrate the conflicts. But the law will have to be reinforced by a strong public morality, to make people aware that the other side of freedom's coin is self-discipline and a respect for the necessary freedom of others. The new society will only survive if it is a caring society, in which individuals take personal responsibility for the needs of others. The 'state' or 'the community' is no longer some impersonal social service mechanism. It is us. The demos, not Dionysus, must be paramount. Education and Religion will have a crucial role in spreading this new morality.

The regionalisation of life will help. The extended family may return as people seek their friends among those nearest to them, rather than among those theoretically dearest but distant. As more work, and schooling, takes place within the home community, relationships should be closer. The old will tend to remain in the community, rather than be exported to some distant and specialised institution ('Quite obscene,' said a Middle Eastern visitor to me, 'the way your society treats its old, exporting them to die') – cost again will be the crucial factor, reinforced by the new morality in which self-interest is tempered by community.

Education

Education has always had three functions, which have too often been mixed up in one curriculum. The first function is to equip the young person with the essential knowledge and skills for survival in his society; the second to nurture in him the values and behaviours desired by society (call it conditioning if you will, but no education is neutral); and a third is to provide the young adult with the special skills and knowledge which he will need to earn his living.

It has been a characteristic of Anglo-Saxon education to believe that all these three functions can take place within one institution – a school – and that they can all be dealt with and finished with in the first two decades of one's life. I, and many others, believe these two assumptions to be mistaken. My hope is that in the reorganised society, formal education will become more dispersed, in line with other features of society, and more intermittent.

The survival skills can be taught in a conventional school, but they could also be taught at home, given some technical assistance from television, radio and learning kits. Survival kits for the reorganised society must include reading, writing and numeracy. Numeracy needs to be more widely defined than conventional arithmetic, I would suggest, for the ability to handle, compare and communicate numerical information, including the use of computers, will be essential in the network world of the future. This is an ability easier to give to young children than to aged adults. But the survival kit for the future must also include some rather more ill-defined skills such as self-reliance, learning to learn, relating to others, living with change. Although some schools deliberately attempt to 'teach' these skills, they are hard to acquire in a school, any school, which has to be a world where self-reliance is guided, change is controlled, and the 'others' are people very like oneself. It is hard in a school to learn how to relate to adults who are not in authority over one, hard to grasp the concept of interdependence except on the sports field, hard to realise that people can have very different perspectives and priorities when all around you in school these are roughly identical. These skills are the stuff of life as it is lived, not life as it can be taught. They can only be learnt by living. If we delegate them to schools, we deceive ourselves.

The 'social orientation' or socialising function of education again does not have to take place in schools. Families, local communities, kinship groups are more effective. But schools provide a powerful way of doing it, a trapped population in a controlled environment. Over the ages, any group in society who wanted to ensure that its young grew up with certain values have made sure that it had its own schools to reinforce those values. The assumption by the state in many countries of the control of schools and their curricula has frustrated this impulse and caused deep frustration in those traditional groups (today it is the professional middle class in Britain who feel that their educational rights have been usurped by the state). Although schools are theoretically unnecessary, they are so convenient that they are bound to continue in the re-organised society. It is therefore *crucial* that the teachers reinforce the new paradigm of community pluralism, choice and caring, rather than the old one of self-interest. The education and selection of tomorrow's teachers will be a key to the continuing success of the new paradigm.

The third function of formal education – the provision of technical or professional skills for work – can again be done in schools, colleges and universities. It can also be done via apprenticeship schemes, as in medicine, law, accounting, architecture, and farming – or, more usually, in combinations of college and apprenticeship. I would expect to see a gradual freeing up of the qualification processes for work, allowing for a more modular approach, with many modules accepted for more than one qualification.

How might all this happen? I would like to see a wider commitment to the idea of intermittent education. Intermittent education means that one can opt in and out of formal education or school with more freedom than at present. For many young people the business of living had much better begin at 14 than at 16, provided that they are not thereby deprived of technical education later in life. The current hierarchical nature of education, where one qualification is piled on top of another, means that those who opt out early can seldom get back in again. A system of vouchers, entitling one to so many years' free education at a time of one's choice (compare the educational credits described in Chapter 7), and the self-instruction via schools of the air, should free the school system to allow people to reeducate and redirect their lives at intervals. Fourteen-year-olds at work may seem an unwanted intrusion on organisations, but where the work community was more closely linked to the home community this apprenticeship period could more readily be viewed by the work community as their educational responsibility – a sort of national service at work.

The teacher selection and education problem would be partially solved if there were more to and fro between education and work. In this way one would be sure that the values of the school reflected the values of the work community. Perhaps the managers of a reorganised society ought also to be its part-time teachers? A more dispersed, modular and intermittent pattern to education would make these more flexible arrangements more likely. In the instrumental paradigm, where specialisation is the key to efficiency, we have also specialised our education and divorced it too much from the world it is intended to serve. Many teachers, most teachers, have never worked anywhere except in their schools. It is a worrying thought. In the reorganised society education must be more clearly wedded to the communities of work.

In education too we may then predict the end of the Apollonian reign. Vast schools, conglomerates of specialisations, will be built no more and some may indeed be dismantled. Education will return, in many of its aspects, to the demos, to family or community. The skills of Dionysus or Athena (craft, professional or problem-solving) will be learnt in the ways of these gods – by apprenticeship and experience, in small groups, through problems not routines.

THE TRIDENT TRUST

The Trident Trust is an existing British experiment linking the worlds of work and of school. Its success must point the way to the future.

The Trident Trust is an educational charity registered with the Department of Education and Science. It was conceived in 1970. Its purpose is to provide young people between the ages of 15 and 16 with personal experience during the school term which would help to develop their maturity and, at the same time, to persuade employers and society at large to value skills, experience and personal qualities not measurable by examination results.

By the end of 1974 there were Trident operations in eight areas of Britain. 3000 work opportunities were on offer from hundreds of employers. Several thousand young men and women had been through the scheme. All the evidence received has been positive, reporting increased self-confidence, greater awareness of life and of the world, more interests in both study and work, more considerate behaviour, and a new ability to relate to people. As one parent said 'You learn more by practical experience than talk in a classroom.'

Details are available from The Trident Trust, Albany Buildings, 39 Victoria Street, London SW1.

Religion

Stephen Verney, Bishop of Repton, was recently talking with a group of British clergy about their mission. 'Do you recall,' he asked them, 'what command was it that was given by Jesus to his first disciples as he faced death at the hands of the established order?' 'To preach repentance', they replied after some thought. 'Correct,' said Bishop Verney, 'but the original Greek word is more revealing, it is *metanoia* which is better translated as "a new consciousness". That,' he added, 'is still the task for today.'

I have called it a new 'paradigm'. 'Metanoia' is perhaps a better word, with a more illustrious pedigree. The reorganised society will need a new sense of purpose, a new consciousness, a new alignment of priorities, if the economics of quantity is going to be kept in its place and if 'wellbeing' is to be defined in more than material terms. The pluralism of the new society must be bonded together by a new morality as well as by new laws. The morality distributed by the schools and practised in the organisations must be forged somewhere.

Ivan Illich, that turbulent priest who has abandoned organised religion in his pursuit of a radical humanism, has called for a new 'conviviality'. 'I consider conviviality to be individual freedom realised in personal interdependence, and, as such, an intrinsic ethical value. I believe that, in any society, as conviviality is reduced below a certain level, no amount of industrial productivity can effectively satisfy the needs it creates among society's members'.* It is a cry for a new paradigm, a new religion.

Others have looked back to the European Middle Ages for their new idea. Here was a society which was conceived of as a *communitas communitatum*, a community of communities. Whether that community happened to be monastery, guild, university, knighthood, manor, fief or patriarchal family, it was the individual's duty to serve his community. Society was conceived by medieval philosophers as a great chain ranging from God at the top to the simplest organism at the bottom. God, and his instrument the Church, held all together. Everything was done for the glory of God. Science was undertaken for the greater understanding of God's works, art was the glorification of God. Fairing and Sharing were the orders of the day. 'To each according to his need, from each according to his contribution' would be a more accurate description of the medieval ideal than of modern Communism. Growth was irrelevant and did not happen.

The community of communities of the Middle Ages is too imprisoning a model for the reorganised society as I see it. The glorification of God was too often an excuse for dominance by the priesthood. Hierarchy was good in the Middle Ages where man knew his place, but it will be temporary and elective in the reorganised society. Yet the notion of one all-

* *Tools for Conviviality*, Calder and Boyars, 1973.

governing purpose, continually articulated in society, is a common theme to this book, to Illich and to St Augustine, the saint of medievalism.

Where will this new morality, this new religion come from? It could of course come from the established churches. A group at a consultation on 'The Price of Progess' organised by the World Council of Churches in 1973 produced what Michael Allaby, one of its members, called 'the new theological paradigm':

 a) *We must recover a lost sense of wonder, sensuality, spontaneity and wildness;*

 b) *We must recover our ability to celebrate within constraints; we must accept freedom as the recognition of necessity;*

 c) *We must recover an ascetic sense, an ability to sacrifice; we must find new ways in which the Church may die for the life of the world, for God theologically and ecologically, only as life is lost is life found.'*

Fine stuff. I do not however see it happening through the traditional offices of the traditional churches. The priests last led society's thoughts when they last led society – in the Middle Ages. History convinces me that the new morality must be articulated and practised by the new leaders of society – among them the leaders of the work organisations. The new paradigm needs to be expressed at work and in the home, in art, music and literature, as well as in church. No doubt there will be a continuing role for places of contemplation, research and writing, the seminaries and monasteries of the reorganised society, but I cannot help but think that if the new morality (which is a deeply Christian one as well as deeply Buddhist and Muslim) is to flourish, then the established Churches must die in their present guise in order to live again in the new communities of the reorganised society. As that study group said – 'the Church must die for the life of the world'.

Managers

Let me end where I began, with the managers.

Who will they be, how can they best be prepared for their role, who will thank them or reward them under the new authority of the Demos? Let me distinguish, as I did earlier, between leaders and managers. The leaders will be those elected to fixed-term policy-making positions in the smaller membership organisations or in the federal centres. The managers will be the executives appointed by them.

Neither leaders nor managers will have role-security. That is, they cannot be *guaranteed* permanence in that role subject to good behaviour and performance. It is likely of course that a good administration secretariat, particularly in the federal centres, will outlast several changes in leadership. But their continuance in office will depend on their acknowledged expertise, their earned credits, not on any statutory obligation. Management, and leadership, in other words is likely to be the most precarious of the occupations in the organised society.

Given the *temporary nature* of the managerial role, managers would be well advised to have another string to their bow. Professionals like to be managed by their fellows, craftsmen by craftsmen, although they prefer them to be better managers than they are craftsmen. A 'managerial career' will be much more a rarity than it is at present, and the managerial class will no longer be identifiable as such.

It seems then to be asking a lot for anyone to take on this temporary, inglorious, insecure role. Why should men do it, particularly when they are subject to democratic control, in effect the servants of the Demos?

I imagine that there will have to be some temporary inducements, to compensate for less professional experience and for the arduous nature of the job. More money, perhaps, for some, or a promised sabbatical on full earnings at the end of the term of office for reskilling. Ultimately however men will do these jobs because they are more interesting to them than the job of craftsman, consultant, expert or whatever. Management may be regarded as a chore by the professionals in the organisation of consent, but to some it has always been a fascinating challenge.

Politicians are not usually influenced by the prospect of personal gain: power, or the feeling that you can make things the way you want them to be, is more often the lure. Ministers must be missionaries if they want to do their job, though not all might agree with their cause. Managers, too, though they may have been mercenary in the past – in the belief, perhaps, that the pursuit of their self-interest profited society – will find mercenary motivations ill-rewarded in the reorganised society. They will need to be missionaries to do the job at all.

How does one prepare a missionary? There are technical and professional skills which they may learn. The managers, as distinct from the leaders, will be Apollonian and Athenian in their ways. They will require specialist knowledge, training in procedures, professional qualifications in some cases – much as at present. Business schools, organisational training centres, professional certificates, will continue, although perhaps on a diminished scale. Certainly their courses will not be regarded as guarantees of a secure career.

And some things no school or course can teach them. Missionaries must find their driving beliefs within themselves. Many of them will, for a time, find themselves among the elected leaders of their organisation. There they will have to add to their training those qualities which are born or developed but seldom taught: the capacity to articulate a vision, to deal perceptively with one's fellow men, to influence by character, example and wisdom rather than by precept, to have the courage to compromise as well as the courage not to compromise – all those qualities of greatness down the ages, Zeus par excellence.

Such men will be the real architects of the new society, if it is to exist. Men who work for personal ideals or delight rather than for personal gain. God send us many such.

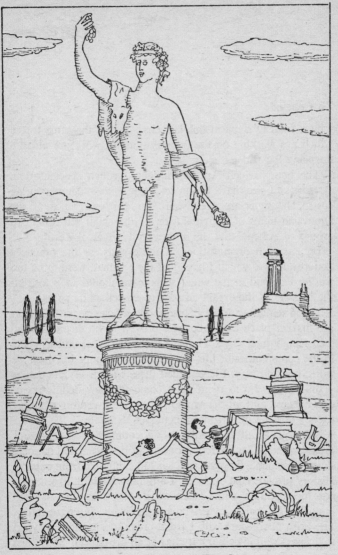

Dionysius Turned Zeus?

To Conclude

I have tried to show in this last chapter that the same forces which are working on the organisations of work are also influencing the wider society.

The boons which Apollo brought, through specialisation, systems and size, have begun to produce their countervailing costs. The signs are everywhere for a re-emergence of the Dionysian urges of individualism, of the small self-contained groups of Athena, and the intuitive initiatives of Zeus.

But, as with organisations, if these gods, or the practices and attitudes to which I have lent their names, were to be too readily indulged in the wider society we should soon lose all the benefits of the organised society as well as its pains.

The disciplining force of economic efficiency measured in the market place has, I believe, proved to be distorting and increasingly ineffective. The new discipline must find its roots in the communities of life, the places and groups in which we work, live and play. I have called these collectively the demos – the people. From them must come the new definitions of effectiveness and efficiency, not from some central planning agency nor the impersonal dictates of the state.

Many will call this reliance on community a fallacious dream, a recipe for anarchy, communal hedonism and national chaos. Discipline, they will say, has to be imposed from outside. History provides the evidence. I am more hopeful. Freedom is not incompatible with discipline if that discipline is self-imposed. The past provides its lessons for the future to refute. The prize of freedom will, I trust, prove too precious to yield to license. Man in community has often proved self-disciplined when given the chance.

If leadership is the art of creating self-fulfilling prophecies, then now is the opportunity for the leaders of tomorrow – to choose the right blend of gods to serve the demos, man in community.

FURTHER READING

The principal references are listed in the text and cited in the Index. I am listing here a few suggestions for further reading for anyone who wants to pursue these matters. They are authors and books which I personally have found interesting and useful.

The First Dilemma: Slack, the Thermometer of Incompetence
The theory and practice of organisational efficiency has been studied and tested endlessly. I commend particularly.

SCHEIN E. H. *Organizational Psychology.* Prentice-Hall, 1965
A good introduction to the psychological factors at work in organisations. Short, compact and readable.

DRUCKER P. F. *Management.* Harper, 1976
A compendious overview of current management thinking, written with the good sense and pragmatic wisdom for which Drucker is well-known.

HANDY C. *Understanding Organizations.* Penguin, 1976
My own attempt to summarise the existing state of the different arts in this field, the book in which the first rudimentary theory of cultural propriety is suggested.

MACCOBY M. *The Gamesman.* Secker & Warburg, 1978
A good research-based study of the different executive styles in U.S. companies.

The Second Dilemma: The Rise of Individualism
SHEANE D. *Beyond Bureaucracy.* Management Research, 1976
A stimulating essay written by a man concerned to preserve what is best in the large industrial concern.

HIGGIN G. *Scarcity, Abundance and Depletion*
An inaugural address given at Loughborough University of Technology in 1975.

WARD C. *Anarchy in Action.* Allen & Unwin, 1973
A stimulating introduction to the proper theory of Anarchy directed at working institutions.

HIRSCH F. *Social Limits to Growth.* Routledge & Kegan Paul, 1976
A difficult but important book which puts the Apollonian dilemma in a grander societal context and in an historical tradition.

The Third Dilemma: Instrument or Community?
RATTRAY TAYLOR G. *How to Avoid the Future.* Secker & Warburg, 1975
A good general introduction to all the Doomsday theories. Useful to set beside Hirsch's *Social Limits to Growth.*

ROBERTSON J. *The Sane Alternative.* Robertson, 1978
A well-argued plea for a new approach to the problems of the post-industrial society.

SCHUMACHER E. F. *Small is Beautiful.* Blond & Briggs, 1973
This well known book is essential reading for anyone interested in positive possibilities.

MACRAE N. *The Coming Entrepreneurial Revolution. The Economist,* London December 25th, 1976
A long article with a lot of provocative thoughts about new ways of running things.

INDEX